P9-EKR-434

Beyond Habitat

Moshe Safdie

Beyond Habitat

Edited by John Kettle

 The M.I.T. Press, Cambridge, Massachusetts, and London, England

Copyright © by Moshe Safdie, 1970
Published simultaneously in Canada by Tundra Books of Montreal
and in the United States of America by The M.I.T. Press, Cambridge, Massachusetts.

ISBN-O-262-19083-4
Library of Congress Catalogue Card Number: 76-130455
Printed in Canada

The production of this book took place in Montreal.

Design was by Rolf Harder, Design Collaborative.

Photographs appearing in this book were taken by the following:
Jerry Spearman of Media Extensions, N.Y.C.; The Montreal Star-Canada Wide; Keith Oliver; Kero;
Official Expo photographers; Moshe Safdie.

Text was computer set in 10 on 12 point Helvetica by Fast Photo Typesetters of Canada and
the printout made on a Fototronic Model 1200. Films for the album of photographs were prepared by
Klaus Unterberger. Printing was done by the Offset presses of Pierre Des Marais, Inc.
Binding was done in the Des Marais plant.

The Enver Azizi cartoon was translated from the Spanish by William Weiss.

The following are quoted with permission from sources stated:
Buckminster Fuller: Nine Chains to the Moon, published by the Southern Illinois University Press
Hermann Hesse: Siddharta, translated by Hilda Rosner, © 1951 by New Directions Publishing Corp.
Piet Hein: Grooks, published by The M.I.T. Press, Cambridge, Massachusetts
Desmond Morris: The Naked Ape, published by Jonathan Cape Ltd. London, England
Lao Tzu: Te Ching, published by Penguin Books, Ltd. London, England
D'Arcy Thompson: On Growth and Form, published by the Cambridge University Press, London, England.

First printing October 1970
Second printing March 1971

For Nina

Foreword

This book is actually one half of a dialogue – my half of discussions with John Kettle that started when we met in 1961, long before the book was taped, – and continue on. The tapes we made were transcribed, the transcriptions edited and considered; sometimes I have re-written and added to them. At times the observations are of a kind one confides only to a friend; I have let them stand because I have learned that ideas and process cannot be separated, that they must become one if we are to bridge the gap between concept and reality, in the environment as elsewhere.

It was after a lecture I gave at M.I.T. while Habitat was still under construction that Michael Connolly, editor-in-chief of The M.I.T. Press planted the seed for this book by urging me to write it. It might have ended being another academic architectural statement if it were not for my Canadian publisher, May Cutler of Tundra Books, who from the outset insisted that the communication of ideas concerning the environment must not be limited to the involved professionals, that if the contemporary city is to change, these ideas must be communicable to everyone.

M.S.

Contents

Introduction

I had never lived in a house before. Habitat was the first.

It was what I always imagined living in a house could be, and yet it wasn't a house as we know it. There were things happening around us all the time. We lived in a way we could have lived only in a big house in a fancy suburb; and yet we did things we could have done only in an apartment on, say, Sherbrooke Street in downtown Montreal, or Fifth Avenue in New York. We had both.

The wonderful thing about living in Habitat during Expo 67 was that it was exactly the way I envisaged it to be – a community, almost rural in nature, *in the city.* People were around you in great numbers; not only those who lived there, but all those who were visiting Expo. There were shops, and there were movie theaters, and there were exhibits and parks and fountains, and there were ships docked in front with people coming to visit the city, and there were all the elements that make a good city.

And yet with all those millions of people, when you closed the door, you were in your own house. You had privacy; you really were alone. You looked out at the view and you were not aware of the crowds of people surrounding you even though they were there by the millions. You had a feeling of seclusion, of quiet. Never in all the months I lived there did I hear a neighbor through the walls or the floors. We would wake up in the morning and open the sliding doors and we would have breakfast in the garden. Our children would open the front door, get on their tricycles and ride down the pedestrian street to the playground, meet other kids and become friends with them, continue playing half the day there and throughout the structure outside our house. We had a dog and we could take him for a long walk right outside our door.

These things, I suppose, would have been possible if we had been living on a quiet residential street in a suburb such as Westmount, with our own house and garden. We could have gone out and had breakfast in the garden and so on.

There was nothing unique about it except that we happened to be *on the tenth floor, in an environment that had ten times the density of Westmount.*

But in Westmount, if you wanted to go and see a film or go to a library, or even if you wanted to go to work, you would either have to get in your car or get on a bus or subway. In Habitat during Expo you went down ten floors and you were together with fifty thousand people. You could see the best movies, go on to a visiting ship docked close to the building and join the party, eat in any of dozens of good restaurants.

That mixture of being in the busiest, most crowded urban meeting place and, at the same time, a hundred feet away, going through a door and being alone in your house, was an incredible experience. This sense of seclusion was achieved by the fact that the houses were free in space: they all opened in three or four directions. From some windows you saw the city, from others the river or Expo. You had morning sun in some rooms, sun in the evening in other rooms, and you felt the sun going round you all day.

Everything about it gave me the feeling of *house* and yet it gave me all the other things I had always wanted in a house but never found in the isolation of the anonymous suburb.

A portfolio of photographs

1
Working on thesis at McGill University, 1960

2
One of the models of the thesis
"A three dimensional modular building system"

1

2

15

3
My sketch for the Expo master plan as it was
finished on December 6th, 1963

3

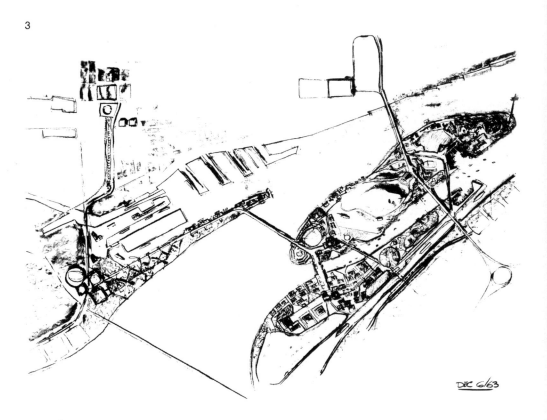

DEC 6/63

4
The original Habitat design as seen from the
St. Lawrence River. The inclined rhomboidal
planes of terraced houses are contained by the
A-frames under which are the public facilities,
shops, the art gallery, the school and offices

5
The original Habitat design looking towards the
river as presented with the feasibility study. In
the foreground is the hotel, with the terraced
houses, and the inclined A-frames containing
the stairs and elevators spanning MacKay Pier

4

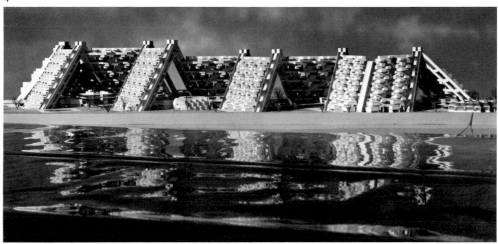

5

6
The press conference announcing the construction contract of Habitat to Anglin-Norcross. At
the table left to right are Leonard Franceschini,
president of Francon; Jim Thompson, project
manager for Anglin-Norcross; Ed Churchill, installations director of Expo; Robert Shaw, deputy
commissioner general of Expo; John Eric
Harrington, then president of Anglin-Norcross
(standing); David Fitzgerald, project manager for
Francon; Edouard Fiset, chief architect of Expo;
Moshe Safdie; Tony Peters, project architect
for Expo; Fred Laurendeau, deputy director of
procurement and contracts for Expo

6

7
A quieter moment in the office in
Place Ville-Marie, with Dave Rinehart standing
beside me and landscape consultants Doug
Harper and John Lantzius on the right in the
photo

8
Nina christens the first box of Habitat;
Pierre Dupuy, Expo's commissioner general
presiding

7

8

9
The basic system of Habitat was a single
repetitive module forming a variety of house
types of different plans and sizes

10
This cross section of Habitat, phase 1, as
constructed, shows the pedestrian and mechanical streets, the terraced grouping of the
modules, the roof gardens and the parking and
plaza levels

9

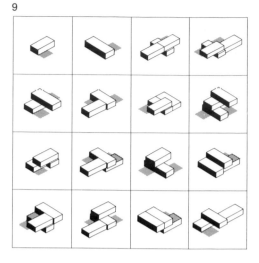

10

Pedestrian Street
/Galerie pour piétons

Mechanical Space
Gaine de mécanique

Pedestrian Street
Galerie pour piétons

Mechanical Space
Gaine de mécanique

Pedestrian Plaza Level
Niveau de la plaza

Storage Cubicle
Cellule d'entreposage

Parking Level
Niveau de stationnement

M   6
FT   20

11
The reinforcing cage ready to be transported into the mold

12
Concrete has been poured and the concrete box is being removed from the plant to the assembly line

13
The pre-fabricated fiberglass bathroom is being placed into the finished module on the assembly line

14
The finished module with all components installed is being transported to the crane for erection

11

12

13

14

15
Towards the completion of the working
drawings, the office and a few of the consultants
took a few minutes off to pose for this photo

16
The celebration in honor of the casting of the
last box

17
The Canadian and Anglin-Norcross flags were
hoisted into place at the topping off ceremonies
of Habitat

15

16

17

18
The crane lifts the 70-ton module into place

18

19
An aerial view of Habitat under construction
during the winter of '66 '67 shows its location
on MacKay Pier with Montreal, the frozen
St. Lawrence River and Expo in the background.
This photo was taken when the last modules
were being placed by the crane

19

20,21,22
A few samples of the cartoon fun that Habitat evoked

The following two pages show Habitat lived in

23
Terraced houses and gardens

24
The continuous public spaces sheltered by the houses and streets cantilevering over

25
Looking out from a house towards the garden

26
Inside a fiberglass bathroom

27
My favorite photo of Habitat: a young lady watering her Habitat garden. Taken by Kero of Montreal

20

Drawing by Porges ©1967
The New Yorker Magazine, Inc.

21

Daigneault in The Montreal Star

22

Ting in the London Free Press

23

24

25

26

27

28
Aerial view showing the grouping of the units and the roof terraces, the pedestrian streets and the elevator cores

29
A pedestrian street overlooking the St. Lawrence River

28

30

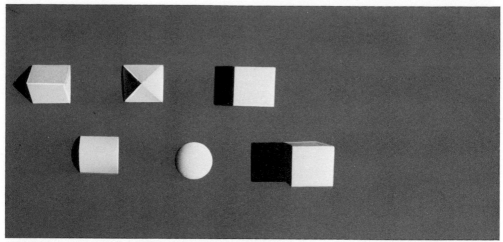

31

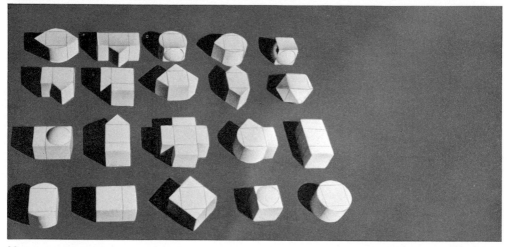

32

30,31,32
The 6-module component system presented at
the Aspen design conference in 1968

33
The first post-Habitat design. It was done for
the Public Housing Authority of Washington, D.C.
for a site in the suburb of Anacostia

33

34
A view of the East River Drive with the first New York Habitat design. Based on the octahedron module, it was to span the highway, north of Gracie Mansion

35
The final Habitat New York design for a site on the East River between Wall Street and the Fulton Fish Market, with the proposed stock exchange downriver. Housing units are suspended from catenary cables supported by three towers. Shops, hotels, offices and the marina penetrate the structure below

36
A section through the final design for Habitat New York showing the service towers with the catenary cables from which housing units are suspended

35

36

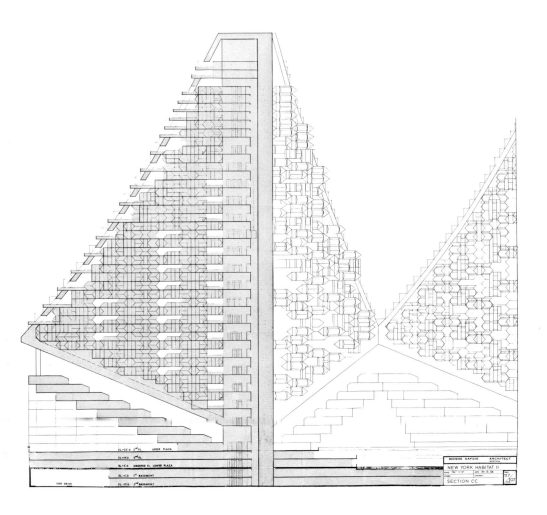

37
The San Francisco State College Union.
Below a view from the campus green showing
the inclined walls forming stairs on the building
surface. Dark texture on the other inclined walls
represents planting covering and penetrating
the structure

Three views of the San Francisco State College
Union

38
The basic system showing a repetitive
element forming large, medium and small rooms
for different functions

39
Walking up the walls

40
Interior view of the main dining room

37

38

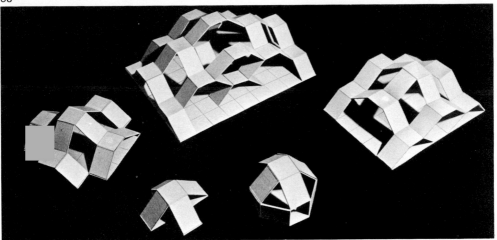

39

40

41,42,43
A sampling of the literature of the San Francisco
State press when the design was turned
down by trustees of the California state colleges

41

The Daily Gater

Volume 100, Number 17   San Francisco State College   Monday, Oct. 14, 1968

Colossal petition drive

Art students support Union

A colossal petition drive to blitz the Board of Trustees into accepting Moshe Safdie's unique College Union concept will begin today, boosted by an outraged band of art students.

The artists—infuriated by a Trustees committee rejection of the Union for its "incompatibility" with SF State's other buildings — sculpted a model that the Trustees would accept.

"It's built of square blocks and topped by a capitalist symbol that the Trustees should love—a Nazi footlocker," one of the designers said with a sneer.

The new Union proposal is located in the Art Department sculpture yard.

"It's great. I'm constantly surprised by how much support Moshe's design plan has here," said AS Vice President Albert Duro, the spearhead of the petition push.

Duro and the o t h e r hard core Union backers will set up a table in front of the Commons between 10 a.m. and 2

p.m. everyday until the Trustees gather again Wednesday of next week. They will collect signatures and conduct other "agitation and propa-

ganda work" in this location, Duro said.

Instructors will also circulate the petition in their classes, he added.

The 11 story high U n i o n would be located on the present site of the Commons and huts. If the Trustees okay the project next week, ground will

be broken "a r o u n d May Day," Duro said. The key first phase will be finished about 1½ years after it is started.

Construction of the f i r s t phase will require destruction of the huts and the C o f f e e Shops entire seating area, at minimum. The AS and the SF State Foundation are still trying to figure out what to do when this occurs.

A recent recommendation by Safdie's San Francisco associates and the chancellor's staff architects would move the Union 30 feet north, taking out most of the R e d w o o d Room for the first phase.

"The Trustees felt that the Union would be visibly too close to the Library unless it was moved. But remember, the Union would slope away from the L i b r a r y," said Franklin Sheehan, the Administration's man in charge of the College Union.

The 30-foot move is only a recommendation, not a final decision, S h e e h a n emphasized.

Art students designed a "compatible" College Union for the Trustees

42

The Daily Gater

Volume 100, Number 18   San Francisco State College   Tuesday, Oct. 15, 1968

Union petition drive grows

by Alan Korsfeld

The updated plans for the proposed College Union will be presented js SF State students and faculty by AS Vice President Al Duro, Director of Campus Planning Franklin Sheehan, and two associate architects of designer Moshe Safdie tomorrow at 8 p.m. in Mary Ward Hall.

The presentation coincides with a mammoth petition drive here to show campus support of the Safdie project to the Board of Trustees, who will be sitting in judgment next week.

A committee for the Board earlier dismissed the plan as "incompatible" with the other campus edifices, but the Board agreed to reconsider the plan at its next meeting at Fresno State, October 23 and 24.

Duro, who is also acting chairman of the College Union Council (CUC) which has coordinated the lengthy planning of the Union, will present the petitions to the Board at that meeting.

"We hope to get at least five or six thousand, and maybe more," he said.

"Support for our petition campaign is excellent," Duro said. He also expects support from the Fresno State Chapter of Students for a Democratic Society (SDS).

The $5 million Phase One of nthe project will then be completed by Fall, 1970, according to Duro.

AS reserve funds will cov-

er $200,000 of the initial cost, supplemented by $1,100,000 from the Foundation, he added.

"The rest of the costs will be made up with student fees," he said, which may be levied at up to $20 a year per student.

In the elections of Spring, 1966, students agreed to pay between $10 and $20 in fees a year.

Included in the Phase One plans is the 11-story building which will feature a banquet-ballroom seating 750, a duplication center, offices for the AS, the Foundation, and other organizations, a bookstore, a library, lounges, a hostel, a crafts center, student shops, and a dining room that holds 1.5 times as many students as the Commons.

The 11th story will be reserved for use as a "meditation room," Duro announced.

A recreation center and a

500 - seat auditorium will be built during Phase II.

Construction, which will be supervised either by Safdie himself or a representative of his firm, will be completed by the simultaneous construction of several other buildings on campus.

The huts and the Redwood Room of the Commons will be

removed to construct the controversial structure, but the Bookstore will remain intact.

During construction of the Union, however, a seven-story addition to the library will be going'on, as will:

• The Life Science Building;

• T h e Physical Science Building;

• The Administration addition;

• The Humanities Building;

• The new residence hall;

• The new residence dining room.

As Sheehan described the upcoming campus predicament, "the number of jackhammers around here will exceed the number of students."

Students sign Union petition at CUC table in front of the Commons.   —photo by H. L. Smith

REVOLUTION

© 1969 BY REVOLUTION
PUBLISHED TWICE MONTHLY

MARCH 15, 1969
SAN DIEGO, CALIFORNIA

VOLUME 1, NUMBER 2
20¢

BLACK ARTS STUDENT UNION QUEST P. 3

GARW STATE

DISCO

BOOKS

Robert Miles Parker P. 6 — ACTIVIST ARTIST

AN INTERVIEW with MORE SNYDER P. 4

SF STATE REVOLUTION PART II PAGE 12

44
Habitat Puerto Rico shown here on the first site
of the San Patricio hill in Hato Rey, San Juan

More varied views of Habitat Puerto Rico

45
A section through the mountain showing the
clusters spanning the service drives. The split
level module provides for both internal and
external circulation by virtue of its shape

46
Pedestrian streets running parallel to the
mountain with other walkways connecting
them up-hill. Each cluster shelters the parking
areas underneath

47
A view of a typical cluster showing the window
arrangements and the terraces overlooking the
city

44

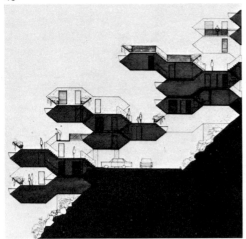

Enver Azizi in Margaro

41

49,50
Tropaco, the St. Thomas, Virgin Island resort.
It will be manufactured in the Puerto Rico
Habitat factory and assembled on its site, a
peninsula jutting into the Caribbean Sea

49

50

51
Habitat Israel, 1,500 dwelling units covering the
Manchat hillside in Jerusalem, was commissioned by the Government of Israel in the spring
of 1969

The following three pages show:

52
A typical cluster containing 19 dwellings

53
A diagram showing how the dome window and
shutter adjust to each season and time of day;
an open roof garden, a shaded terrace or a
greenhouse

54
A cluster with the driveway and covered parking,
pedestrian street, private terraces and
the rotating dome window

55
An overall view of the Jerusalem hillside
showing the roads spiraling upwards, bridged
by the clusters of houses

51

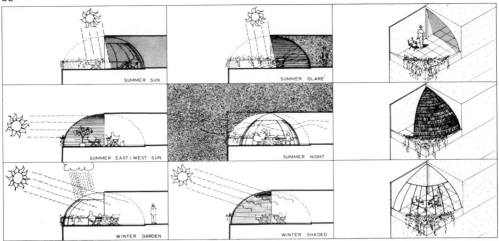

SUMMER SUN

SUMMER GLARE

SUMMER EAST / WEST SUN

SUMMER NIGHT

WINTER GARDEN

WINTER SHADED

1   Haifa

You say the word "house" and it means so many different things to different people. One person sees it on an open road in the countryside; another sees a village. One thinks of a farm; another of a cliff dwelling in the urban landscape. Environment is culture and culture is archetypal; it grows from deep within you, embodies long-lived feelings towards shelter, family, community and self. To me the word "house" calls up images peculiar to my early environment.

It was a unique time when I was growing up in Israel. It was Israel in the making. Those were the days when the immigrants were coming in. The British were trying to stop them. There was the war of 1948. I was ten then.

I clearly remember the 14th of May, 1948. We were off school, about thirty of us boys and girls aged ten, and we rushed down to Haifa's city hall square. Loudspeakers were strung on the trees and light poles. There were so many people we could not move. All of a sudden, there was silence and over the speaker came the voice of David Ben Gurion: "We members of the National Council . . . by virtue of the natural and historic right of the Jewish people and by resolution of the General Assembly of the United Nations hereby proclaim the establishment of a Jewish state in Palestine to be called Israel."

It seemed everybody around was crying. At that moment the word "family" meant everybody around us. The word "community" had such a special reality that for many years after I was reluctant to use it. It had a kind of reverence that bears no mention.

In those days people did not lock their doors because there were no thieves. Tel Aviv had no prostitutes; it has today, because it's a "normal" place, but then it was a collection of people who had come there for special reasons through a very selective process. There was an air of being part of something unique.

We all were active in our youth groups, each with its specific political allegiance. Starting at the age of ten, boys and girls met twice a week, organized hikes into the country and spent the summers in kibbutz work camps. We would work half-days and, in exchange, the kibbutz gave us food and lodging and the use of their recreation facilities. We did everything with the kibbutz members, ate in their dining room, washed in their showers, worked in their fields. We worked hard. This life made us independent; in one sense it detached us from our families; it made us dependent on that bigger family, those fifty boys and girls with whom we spent our whole waking life.

This detachment from our parents, this kind of independence, meant that from a young age we had an unusual relationship with them, the kind of relationship between equals that made possible communication as between friends. Many of the children of the kibbutz – for whom this relationship is even more pronounced than for us, the children of the city – expressed this symbolically by calling their parents by their first names. Authority was clearly not a thing to be gotten by decree or by virtue of happening to be mother or father, but rather by the assertion of one's personality and convictions. The greater family was to become a permanent fact. When I returned to Israel in 1967, after fifteen years of absence, a good part of those fifty friends came to Haifa where we once again met. They came with their husbands and their wives and we sat and talked until late. We had all developed in different ways and in different directions; some of us had little in common. But we still felt linked to each other the way only members of a family feel.

At the age of twelve, we went on a five-day hike into the mountains of Galilee. We would march twenty to twenty-five kilometers a day, sleep in crusaders' forts and in deserted ruins of temples. Our group leaders were only sixteen and they were the oldest. Thinking as a father now, I can't imagine my daughter, when she is twelve, going with fifty other people her age into the country, with three people of sixteen to lead them.

Our ideal as children was that when we were eighteen, we would leave home and, after the army, start our own kibbutz. Four out of five in my generation belonged to such youth groups and had the same idea. All my social thinking was in terms of that kind of life. In the end, maybe one in five did it, maybe not even that. But it was our social dream.

We were in very close contact with nature. Haifa, my home town, which is a high-density city by North American standards, is a hill overlooking a harbor. The whole city has roads that follow the contours up the hill. These are connected by steps everywhere, so we spent our lives walking up and down stairs rather than driving.

Haifa as a city had a lot to do with my feelings about environment. Even though I lived in an apartment, like most apartment buildings there, it was so arranged as to give each dwelling its own private entrance on the hill. I had fifty chickens and two goats, and I had two beehives – a little farm in the middle of the city. As in other Mediterranean cities, the line between rural and urban is softer than in North America. There is more interpenetration. Yet, at the same time, it's an *urban* environment, not a suburban environment. It's dense, compact, mixed – probably a little denser than Habitat. Except for the old part of the city which was stone built by the Arabs, Haifa was basically Bauhaus architecture, i.e. it was built during the thirties and forties by Europeans who were part of the modern movement. It's probably one of the few places with a stylistically consistent architecture of the "international style," circa 1930.

In high school I drew cars and houses, as any kid does. I loved mathematics and chemistry and I probably would have enjoyed specializing in either. I could not have become a painter, but I could have become a mathematician. I even thought about architecture as a career but I could not reconcile being an architect with being a kibbutz member, and so I decided I would study agricultural engineering. I was also very interested in – in fact, obsessed with – animals.

The beehives took a lot of my energy. Bees are fascinating creatures. You get a wax base on a frame which is put into the hive and the bees build a very regular pattern of hexagonal cells upon it. No machine has ever been able to match their accuracy in making the actual honeycomb. If you make it by machine the bees won't use it. Some of the cells have white spots in them because there is a bee developing; some have liquid in them, the sugar syrup; some are sealed with very dark wax because they are filled with honey; some of them are bigger because they are nourishing a potential queen. The male cells, too, are bigger than the female cells.

If you try to combine two beehives by putting one on top of the other, the bees kill each other because of the foreign scent. You have to separate them with a piece of newspaper. They immediately start attacking the newspaper, trying to go through it to kill each other, but it takes them about half a day to do it because they don't have the tools to cut paper, and, by the time they get through, the foreign scent has mingled with their own and they don't know who is who anymore.

Bees have such a sense of location that if you move your beehive two feet away, at night they will all come back to the spot where the beehive was and stay there and freeze to death. You have to move hives and bees a long way, five miles or more. When they emerge they find such a foreign environment that they re-establish their sense of location and learn to come back to that spot. This means that if you want to move your beehive two feet, you must first move if five miles away, leave it there for two or three days, and then move it back to the new spot. Otherwise, you'll lose all your bees.

I would, without doubt, have become an agricultural engineer if political events had not intervened. Half the heavy industry in Israel is owned co-operatively by the trade unions. It's not state controlled; it's not state owned; it's trade-union controlled and owned. More than half the people in the country are members of the Histadrut, the trade union federation. Like most independent businessmen my parents were not Histadrut members. Naturally, I was, like all my friends, "socialist" all the way. This gave rise to many discussions between father and me, and between many of my friends and their parents. I believed in the kibbutz as the only way, and in the co-operative movement.

I still believe that socialism in its co-operative form in Israel is the highest social development reached anywhere in our century. In my home town for example, the bus company was owned by the bus drivers. To join it, you had to have enough money to buy half a bus. You bought half a bus and you became your own boss. This is not bureaucratic socialism; it's a much more humane interpretation of Marxism. I think the kibbutz is an open-ended, civilized interpretation, respectful of man in contrast with the Russian misinterpretation. The kibbutz members actually live by the rule, "from each according to his abilities, to each according to his needs." There is no private property, only communal property. Everything is owned by the community, not the state, and that is a big difference.

In 1953, the Israeli government, in response to an economic and currency crisis, restricted imports, and that finished my father's business, which was importing textiles. It was terrible for him; he seemed to take it in a very personal way. He considered the government acts to be an infringement on what he felt to be basic private enterprise, and he refused to work in the flourishing black market. For a while he became politically active, working for the right-of-center party supporting the perpetuation of free enterprise. He also tried other business ventures but they appeared to be unworkable in the climate of the time. Slowly he ate up his capital and, in discouragement, decided to leave Israel.

I didn't want to leave Israel at all. I was very unhappy about it. But it was impractical for me to stay on alone at the age of fifteen. I left, declaring that I would be back by year's end, that as soon as I finished high school I would return. After a short trip through Europe we immigrated to Canada and settled in Montreal. I was still very unhappy and wanted to go back. For the first few months I spent half my time writing letters to my friends.

But I also found myself becoming more and more interested in architecture, in cities. It happened slowly. The kibbutz gradually became less immediate. By the time I finished high school, a year after I reached Canada, architecture was the one thing I wanted to study. I had no relatives who were architects, I had never met an architect, I had no contact with architecture. I was interested in designing buildings and cities, and that was it.

I met considerable opposition at home. My decision was disrupting an age-old tradition of middle-eastern Jewish families. For generations the elder son would join his father, learn his trade or business and then, with the years, take over and perpetuate the family business. My father expected, almost took it for granted, that I would join him just as my many cousins had joined their fathers. It was a blow that took some time for him to get over. For me, architecture was clearly the only thing I could do, and so I persisted and insisted. I went to work at a hardware store selling tools to earn my university fees. My parents had been wealthy in Israel, but now in Canada, it was a real struggle for them.

In the fall of 1955 I registered in architecture at McGill University. I had very few friends; for the first time in my life I started studying seriously. At McGill I did very well academically. It was surprising; I used to look down on anybody who did well academically. I still have suspicions . . .

I am not a born draftsman. I work in a sketch book with a pen. I developed my thesis in three sketch books, which traced the whole evolution of a building system from the first ideas to the final presentation. I don't think of them as beautiful drawings. I use drawings to think out basic problems. I use models to work out spatial relationships and three-dimensional systems. My buildings are so complex three-dimensionally that I can't conceive them on paper. I can't design that way.

Douglas Shadbolt came to teach at McGill. He began talking to us about the problems of mass production and about industrializing the building industry. I was impressed; a basic political conviction in me resonated. In Shadbolt's class we had to design a public housing project for Vancouver. The program was real, the actual program for a Central Mortgage and Housing Corporation project that was underway, and we were working with CMHC people as our critics. Looking back, I realize this was an important moment for me. Here was a typical public housing project – two apartment slabs with one-and two-bedroom units and efficiencies, plus row houses at the bottom with three or four bedrooms. I just couldn't get down to doing it.

I was very confused. The more I thought about the separation between slab and row houses, the less sense it made. It ought to be one thing, I thought. I kept drawing and making models of buildings that built up, pyramid-like, from row house to high-rise, and I made cardboard models of houses independent of each other that were not cells in the major slab structure. Shadbolt would come around and talk about costs and areas and other realities, and in the end I came up with an unresolved model of terraced units piled one on top of the other, set back in some way. But though I couldn't solve my problem, I felt the fallacy of the currently acceptable formula.

That summer CMHC initiated a scholarship; a group of students, one from every school of architecture in Canada, was to travel around North America looking at housing. I was top of the class academically and got on the tour. We looked at suburbia all over the United States; we looked at public housing; we visited forty-storey towers in Chicago and Philadelphia, luxury housing in San Francisco and Toronto; we had appointments with Edmund Bacon, and Mies van der Rohe, and Harry Weese, all kinds of architects, planners and administrators, and housing authorities. We met five or six people and looked at five or six projects a day. We were constantly on the go – a fantastic experience.

When we came back we each had to write a report. I found two things going on in the United States and Canada: high-rise apartment construction, which seemed not to work for families, and suburbia, which also seemed not to work, though it offered amenities that people generally preferred when they had a choice.

I found suburbia wasteful of land. It lacked privacy and it depressed me. The highway systems couldn't cope with it. Low density development was choking the city. I came to the conclusion that one couldn't re-house all the families living in slums in Chicago, in single-family housing – it wouldn't work because of the sheer numbers of people and areas of land you would need to do it.

Yet high-rise didn't work either. We saw it in the most dramatic form: kids clinging to wire mesh balcony railings on the thirtieth floor, corridors and balconies with cages over them and kids running up and down, people complaining about the horrible life. For the first time I experienced the life of a newly-built slum. It made you feel compassion for the people; it made you hate those buildings.

In retrospect, I had set out on this trip with preconceived ideas, feeling suburbia was bad – after all, the Mediterranean cities were my background. But my conclusion was new: I felt we had to find new forms of housing that would re-create, in a high-density environment, the relationships and the amenities of the house and the village. I remember coming back to Ottawa and saying so in our formal presentation; and I remember Humphrey Carver, then on the CMHC Advisory Committee, replying that it couldn't be done, that families belong on the ground, they belong in low-density. At that point I said, "Well, I'm going to try and do it." I decided to abandon my plan to do a parliament building in Jerusalem for my thesis and instead do a housing system.

This decision posed some problems because one did a "building," not housing, and not a system, for a thesis. I didn't want to do a building; I wanted to do a system that could be applied to any site. I didn't want to tie it to one particular site. That was very unorthodox because students were supposed to choose museums, theaters, synagogues, churches and libraries for their theses. Eventually I got reluctant permission.

Everybody looked very skeptically at the whole thing while I was developing it in the sixth year. But then Jane Drew came from England to visit the school and after her lecture she went around looking at the sixth-year projects. She stopped by my desk and said, "That's fantastic. There's nothing I can tell you; you know what you're doing. I wish you the best of luck." There was a changed attitude after that. It became something that students and teachers were interested in. I called my thesis "A Three-Dimensional Modular Building System": *three dimensional* because it dealt with the three-dimensional organization of a continuous urban structure; *modular* because it was a construction system based on the use of the repetitive three dimensional modules; and *system* because it was a system capable of application to various sites and conditions.

It had all the ingredients that were eventually to make up Habitat. There were boxlike space cells manufactured in the factory. The modules were combined in many different permutations to make up the variety of house types. Each house was an entity in itself, recognizable in space. The modules were grouped in spiral formations stepping back from each other, each roof forming a roof garden for another dwelling. I had developed three possible systems each with its own geometry and structural system, and I then made a model showing what a community of five thousand people would be like.

When I submitted my thesis, it got the highest mark at McGill and the gold medal, but when it was submitted for the national Pilkington scholarships it didn't get mentioned at all. One was supposed to do buildings and this, they felt, was not a building. At any rate, with the gold medal came a travelling scholarship which made it possible for Nina and me to make a long trip.

By that time Nina and I were married and had our first child. Nina Nusynowicz and I both came to Canada in 1954, and met shortly after. Nina was born in Poland and spent all the war years there before going to Israel in 1946. We met at a party of Israeli expatriates. She had finished high school and, shortly after we met, had started working for the Bell Telephone Company as a secretary. We knew each other for four years before we were married. Nina kept on working until I graduated from McGill; in fact, we lived on her income during those first years while I was still studying. In 1961, while I was doing my thesis, our daughter Taal was born.

People often ask me if Nina is an architect and I say, "No, but she almost is." She has no architectural training but I feel that because she was totally involved throughout my own education as an architect, came to many of the lectures and helped in the work, she is almost an architect. She is certainly an incredibly lucid critic.

After McGill I went to work for the van Ginkels, Sandy and Blanche, in Montreal.

Sandy van Ginkel has been very important in my development. I first saw him in a lecture he gave at McGill when I was in fifth year. (He had taught there previously.) In his lecture he talked about many of the experiments in Europe, about his work with Aldo van Eyck his partner in Holland, about CIAM (Congrès International d'Architecture Moderne). When thesis time arrived in sixth year Doug Shadbolt, as my teacher, was my immediate critic, but I asked permission to have van Ginkel as a critic as well. Even though he was no longer teaching at the school, he agreed to do it. Once a week I would go to him with my sketch book and we would talk and discuss the sketches. He was an inspiring critic. It was through him that I became familiar with European thought, and with the ideas of CIAM and the people around it.

It is difficult for me to talk of Sandy without seeing him in action with his red hair, his red moustache, wearing his woolly Harris tweed jacket, and colorful silk ties. He has a persistent penetrating stare in his blue eyes; when he talks, particularly about architecture, the words come out like eruptions in a fencing match, waiting for a chance and charging again, yet it all comes out with a gentleness inherent in his slight Dutch accent. He knows what's good, he really recognizes a high quality environment; he is also therefore, an excellent critic. But he is more than that because he draws ideas out of you almost as if he sees them in there and must bring them out. Later at Expo 67, installations director Ed Churchill said of him, "He's the best recognizer of talent I've ever known." Sandy is also temperamental and moody, and working with him you come to expect the occasional burst of anger rooted in frustration. In contrast Blanche, his wife, is cool and calm, reserved and withdrawn, a highly articulate woman. When I worked for Sandy we would sometimes sit after hours, late at night, with him telling me of his experiences with van Eyck, or his trip to the Sahara, or the CIAM meetings. I felt much devotion and loyalty to him.

It was he who sent my thesis to the Dutch magazine *Forum,* a mouthpiece of the post-CIAM group, known as Team 10. Soon after, the entire thesis, drawings, photos and text were published. I worked at the van Ginkels' for a year, day and night. It was an inspiring year because from the problem of a housing system, I was turned to the problem of a whole town. Instead of thinking at the construction level, I had to think of growth patterns, patterns of change, movement, transportation – all the things I didn't think about when I did the building system. It was a wonderful switch. Sandy had a commission to design the master plan for a town of one hundred thousand in Ontario, known as Meadowvale. I developed the Meadowvale master plan in a sketch book, just as I did the thesis, point by point, sketch by sketch, until the plan emerged. Each evening at the end of a day's work I would sit with Sandy and review it. Sandy would talk about the plan, would react and respond to the proposal, would make suggestions and give directions. It was a natural extension of the way we had sat and discussed my thesis the year before.

Meadowvale has never been built, but in the planning stage there were two generating ideas. One was that the city had to grow from an initial small development to a large urban center. This had to take place in the context of North American economics where basically, density is directly related to land value. Therefore, we had to design a city that would be fairly low density to begin with and, as it grew in size and land values rose, would be able to accommodate higher densities without destroying the initial low density development. Now this is a totally different situation from, say, Russia where the central government can decide that the optimum final density is fifty or a hundred units to the acre and therefore from the outset develop at that density. North America is different. Planning is not by decree; the development in a sense is more organic. When there are few people and much open space, people tend to spread. As the community grows and there are more and more people, everybody wants to be nearer the center of things. Thus, the need for higher density.

The problem, of course, is that in the rigid static plan, say the typical gridiron, it is impossible to achieve high density except by replacing earlier built low density areas. Thus, instead of a natural evolution in which development of increased density is added to earlier construction, we have to destroy one development to create another. The problem then is to develop a plan form in which increased density evolves naturally without the destruction of what has been built in the earlier stage.

The plan for Meadowvale is based on a spine with sectors along it, each of which begins at low density and, as the pressure builds, follows a spiral to increase in density. Yet at each cycle of the city's life there is a choice of low, medium, or high density living areas. As the spine of public and commercial functions grows, so do the cells along it. Each cell is made of rings increasing in density toward the center.

We worked on the plan for a year and by the time it was completed I decided I wanted to go and work for Louis Kahn.

3   Philadelphia

Kahn was the only architect on the continent I wanted to work for at that moment.

I had seen his Richards laboratory building in Philadelphia on the CMHC trip, and it impressed me very much. It was the beginning of a way of looking at a building as a system and not as an individual, finite thing. It was not a fixed composition; it could grow. Kahn has since moved the other way. His recent buildings are becoming more and more finite; they are becoming compositions. But for me his work then was the stimulus for seeing environment as a continuum. Kahn never used the word *system*. He talked of *order*. I had also admired his project for an office tower in Philadelphia, a three-dimensional space matrix; it too was to become the generator of ideas. I felt Kahn was also one of the great teachers of architecture of our time, probably a greater teacher than Le Corbusier.

I wrote. I didn't get an answer, so I picked up the phone. Kahn was about to go into hospital for a cataract operation but he said, ''All right, you can come in Saturday.'' I drove down and took my sketches, my thesis. He gets many applications from all over the place, but most of the people in his office at that time were his former students from Yale or from the University of Pennsylvania. He made an exception and hired me.

But first, Nina and I went on a two-month trip with the travelling scholarship money. We wanted to see the American continent; we preferred to travel America rather than make the traditional European tour.

We bought an old car, which continually broke down. We drove along the flat plains of the prairies and down the rocky California coast to San Francisco and Los Angeles. We revisited many of the places I had seen on the CMHC travelling scholarship. Then came the real treat. We went inland. After the hardness of the American city, after the glassiness and squareness and massiveness of Chicago and Lakeshore Drive, after the long grey car rivers of Los Angeles, the Grand Canyon was soft and brown and richly textured, more of the scale of a city than any city I have known, more of an urban reality than the unreal scale of the inorganic man-made places. And as if growing from this great Canyon City – made in the image of the ridges and plant life in the rocks – were the Indian pueblos. These cliff dwellings built in the rocks, and the adobe clusters on the hill-tops and in the plains were, more than anything else I had seen, the expression of people living together harmoniously in nature and true to nature, building an architecture of unquestionable morphological truth in the context of the native material and the climate and the landscape.

Then south to Mexico and to the causeways and pyramids of the ornate yet rigid Mayan and Aztec cities. It was the little villages surrounding these great cities (houses with whitewashed stone walls, with curved ends and thatched roofs leading to enclosed walled courts in the rear) that reminded us the pyramids were temples and they too had been surrounded with a living city built in the tradition of the pueblo of the north. We were overwhelmed with Taxco, a town sitting on a hill with walkways and stairs interconnecting it and a unity that seems to have been achieved by cobblestones, whitewash, and planter-boxes all like lace-work on the steep hills. We came back through the south, Alabama, Mississippi. I took thousands of photographs. I don't really sketch that much when I travel. I get impatient. Now, I have also stopped taking photographs when we travel because I found that I started framing everything as a photograph and it disturbed me.

The pueblos and Taxco were immediately more meaningful to me than any work of an individual architect. I can't think of very many buildings that have moved me as the little hill town of Taxco did. I find that I have shut off to many contemporary buildings, although there have been the grand exceptions: the breathless feeling I had entering the great space of Frank Lloyd Wright's Johnson's Wax building, or approaching ''Fallingwater'' through the woods, or a few years later walking through Le Corbusier's buildings in Chandigarh.

We returned to Philadelphia just when Lou Kahn came back from his operation. He was working on a closed competition for a planetarium at Berkeley. It was a week before the deadline. Anne Tyng, who has been with him for twenty years, was working on it and I began helping out. She went home after an argument and for the next week I found myself working day and night with Kahn. I would stand next to him while he was sketching away, talking of the scheme. I found it difficult to believe I was actually there working. When the project was completed he put me to work on a synagogue he was doing. Later on, when the Institute of Management College in Ahmedabad, India came in, he put me on that.

Kahn has a thin, very scarred face as a result of severe burns he had as a child. His longish, silvery-white hair is always hanging loosely. He is a short man yet very solidly built. Nina used to say jokingly that he looks like a Jewish tailor. After his operation he had enormous lenses in his glasses that enlarged his eyes. He speaks softly, in a semi-whisper. He is a born preacher, a poet. His lectures are a dialogue between himself and his poems; he inspires you by personifying and giving life to walls and windows and spaces and light and he then makes them talk to each other so that you can never again ignore them. He is my image of the archetypal Socratic teacher. There is a prophet-like quality to him that seduces everybody around him.

Kahn was born in Estonia but went to the United States when he was very young and grew up in Philadelphia. It is said that his family was fairly poor, and it took him many years to get work as an architect, so he spent those years theorizing and thinking and talking and teaching. Then, at the age of fifty, he became a world-famous architect. Now he has more work than he can handle. I think it is remarkable that Kahn, trained in the Beaux-Arts tradition, has become the generator of thoughts that are the polar opposite of that tradition.

It was 1962 and the planning of the New York World's Fair was well underway. One day I decided that this would be the place to build my thesis. I clipped it from the pages of *Forum,* made a specific sketch showing how to build half-a-dozen houses as a pavilion, and sent it to the Portland Cement Institute in Chicago with a long letter explaining that this could be built for a limited cost as a great exhibit. They never acknowledged receipt of it.

I met a number of people in that office who became friends, but Dave Rinehart and Anne Tyng, each in a special way, became particularly close and important in terms of the evolution of my ideas. Anne, had worked with Kahn for many years, and was very interested in geometry. Dave had just returned to Kahn's office, where he had worked earlier, when I arrived. He is a few years older than me. Dave's interest in architecture is almost the opposite of Anne's. She approaches the environment from the atoms, molecules and crystals that make it up and the systems that structure them; he approaches it from the image of the whole.

Dave is an American, a midwesterner of German origin. He studied art in Chicago, then went to Philadelphia to study architecture under Kahn. Dave's architectural heritage is rooted in America and Frank Lloyd Wright. In many ways Dave thinks of himself as an uncompromised and true American. His views of the individual and of nature and urbanity are rooted in Jefferson and Wright. He often expresses a resentment of the pseudo-European tradition of the east coast schools of architecture and planning, and their refusal to accept American values for what they are. He's a very sensitive man. He draws beautifully. It is difficult to talk of someone who is a very close friend, almost an alter ego. I always feel his judgments and values to be those of a complete architect, values I have always trusted.

Many fundamental differences between Dave's approach to the environment and mine became apparent during our discussions, differences coming from our respective cultures. Dave thought of the environment in terms of the individual; I thought of it in terms of groups of individuals. In his spare time Dave would design houses, I would design communities or groups of houses. As Dave put it one day: "You always think of numbers, I think first of the singular."

An international competition for a master plan for the center of Tel Aviv was announced. Kahn was on the jury and, as his employees, none of us could enter. But Anne, Dave and I decided that the problem was an interesting one and we would get together and work out a solution as an intellectual exercise, even though we couldn't submit it. We met several times a week and talked about the center itself, and transportation and its relationship with the rest of the country, and produced sketches. It was an intense involvement and there was a great deal of tension because each of us had strong ideas about how things should be. As a result, the three of us were never able to agree on a solution. One evening the whole situation exploded. I went my way and developed a solution, and I think they did the same.

The Arab city of Jaffa and the Jewish city of Tel Aviv became a single city after 1948. The no-man's land in between became the geographic center of the new city and consequently the natural place for a city center. Part of the scheme was to consider ways to allow the city to extend into the sea by reclaiming land. There were three fundamental problems. The first was the relationship of the new center to Tel Aviv and areas beyond. How do people get there? Why do they come there? Who lives there? Where do they go from there? The second was how to plan for growth and at the same time create some kind of validity to the city structure at each stage, so that it was not just an incomplete part of a whole to be completed in a hundred years. The third problem was how to relate the city to the sea in that particular climate – a question which most cities by the sea ignore.

In the case of Tel Aviv, when we considered the nature of the center, with its theaters and newspaper publishing offices and shops and other facilities, in addition to residential and office development, it became obvious we were not dealing with the center of Tel Aviv at all, but with the center of Israel. If you're planning a center that is going to have a life of fifty or a hundred years, you must consider people's ever increasing mobility. They would come from Haifa, Jerusalem, or the Negev to Tel Aviv to see a play or visit a certain agency. If Israel, a thin, three-hundred-mile-long area, had a transportation network that moved at an average speed of three hundred miles an hour, then the whole country would become a single urban region. The area we were working on was at the center of this linear development.

From that basic idea of an expanded city things started falling into place. Israel was planning many new towns, in the Negev and the north. They were being scattered, half randomly all over the place, linked by a road system, sometimes also by a railway. But, if we came to the conclusion that Israel was one city and that one city was served by an extremely efficient spinal transportation system, then every new city as it was being considered would have to be part of it. The alignment of the transportation had to be based on potential industrial development, topography, climate, security, agriculture, and so on. Basically, it was a regional plan of Israel conceived as a single city, that had to be designed. That totally changed our approach to the center of Tel Aviv.

Interestingly enough, the length of Israel is much the same as the distance between New York and Washington, or Toronto and Montreal, so that in fact there is a whole country that is a prototype regional city, with a city population of three million people.

That year I also started to work on a theoretical plan for a new city to resettle the Arab refugees.

This was to be a model city, a model community, and the site I chose, a hypothetical site, was around the Pyramids at Giza, outside Cairo. The political idea was that the refugees, who are in camps and who have compensation money coming to them, would be encouraged to move to a site that appeared to have economic potential. A number of industries would be established there, including building industries. The refugees, many of whom are now idle, would first be given training so that they would actually build their own city, using sophisticated mass-production methods. The compensation funds, instead of being distributed in small pieces and just burned up by each individual, would form the capital base for setting up the industries; labor, which represents half the cost of building the city, would be supplied by them. They would co-operatively or individually own the whole city as their form of compensation indeed its value would multiply because their own labor had gone into it.

This could be a prototype of what could be done in many underdeveloped countries, a process of urbanization in which the population could move to a new place and physically build their own environment, letting the industries continue as part of their economic life.

My thoughts on transportation, three-dimensional planning, and growth patterns were all part of the solution. This was a community that had few assets, especially few cars, so it had to be a city that could work without depending on them. I designed the framework for a city for about a quarter of a million people which you could move through without reliance on a personal vehicle, just public transportation, without ever having to walk more than one thousand feet. Out of that came what I nicknamed "The Giza Plan," a whole series of transportation systems moving at different speeds in continuous motion. Later that became the basis of a proposed demonstration system at Expo 67 and the first Expo plan was entirely based on this idea of inter-linked transportation systems.

Quite apart from the political ideas behind it, the refugee city became a kind of vehicle for constantly developing and expressing my image of the utopian city.

The first proposal consisted of a series of inclined sloping transparent membranes, thirty to forty storeys in the air. The membranes were made up of houses, each an entity in itself, with gardens and public parks penetrating them. The membranes formed a kind of continuous shelter, like the leaves in a forest, under which was a continuous concentrated meeting place – the shops, the recreational facilities, and offices – the sun penetrating it, right through the membranes. The parks and the open countryside and the city continuously interpenetrated. At any given place you were within reach of the parks.

There was complete mobility; you could move anywhere. You got onto a slow-moving ferris-wheel-like vehicle to reach pedestrian streets up in the air. In certain areas, it would speed up and running parallel to it, having decelerated to that speed, would be a train. Then in motion, without stopping, without ever waiting, you could get from one system to the other. The train would accelerate again, and in another section it would run parallel to another system running even faster. Just as the wheels in a gear system are all constantly turning but at different speeds, so here there was to be constant and continuous mobility in the ever flowing arteries.

Halfway through my year with Kahn, I started to question what he was doing. It would be different if I had to go and work for him today. I'd say, "It's his office, let him do what he wants." I would be much more tolerant. But my own ego needed much more assertion at that time. It takes a special kind of security to accept being subservient.

I constantly criticized what he was doing; I challenged ideas and concepts; I made counter-proposals. Kahn would make some sketches and I would independently develop my own schemes. I would constantly try to assert my proposals which I intensely felt had validity, but he would just look at them, nod his head slightly, cover my drawings with a fresh piece of sketch paper, and reassert his design. Later, when I had my own office, I came to know what that sad nod was all about.

Kahn was designing the Ahmedabad College residences in India. He wanted the houses to form a V, pointing into the prevailing wind. I felt we should group the houses as an inclined hillside, creating all the public spaces in the shade under them and making the whole thing a draft tunnel so that it would catch all the prevailing wind and force it through. The meeting rooms and classrooms, which he put into separate free-standing structures, I put right under the residences. He would nod: "This is good. But try that." He just went on with his own scheme. I got into the habit of working at night on my own plans and during the day in the office on his. The college was completed. I have seen it built now. I feel deeply I was right, although it's a beautiful thing – beautiful, artful, but for the time and place irrelevant.

Something had to give. At one point I wanted to go to India to supervise the college construction. Kahn wanted me to go too, and then he changed his mind. That was the breaking point. I felt I had to leave. I didn't want to stay in the office. Working on his building was not satisfying any more. I had learned what I had to learn and had become restless. I suppose the restlessness was rooted in vanity, but also in impatience – an urge to come closer to the realization of my ideas.

Then, out of the clear blue sky, Sandy van Ginkel showed up in Philadelphia. Montreal had just been chosen as the site of the 1967 major international exhibition. Claude Robillard, head of Montreal's city planning department, was being made director of planning, van Ginkel was to be the deputy responsible for physical planning. Would I come and work with them on the master plan?

I told Sandy I had some conditions: I should be able to take some time off to work on the housing system; I should be able to develop it within Expo; I needed ten thousand dollars a year to live on. He wrote back accepting. We packed up with two weeks' notice and went back to Montreal. That was August 1963.

4   Expo 67

I went to Expo 67 partly because I was very interested in working on a real plan on a large scale, but mostly because of the possibility of a housing exhibit. I felt I would have the opportunity to realize it in some way there.

At first I worked on the exhibition master plan, which was still in a state of flux. A year and a half earlier I had done some work in van Ginkel's office on a preliminary master plan, in anticipation of the exhibition. It was a combination of three sites, all of them in the city, and in that early plan I had designed a housing exhibit as the central feature of one of the three sites. It included MacKay Pier – where Habitat was eventually built.

The work on the Expo master plan was for me the next evolutionary stage of ideas that began with Meadowvale, continued with theoretical work in Philadelphia on the master plan for Tel Aviv, and the refugee city of Giza.

But the Expo 67 master plan was specific; it wasn't just theoretical. There were four main areas of concern. One, there was the location of the exhibition itself and the relation of each part to the others. Two, relating very closely to the first, there was the exhibition's transportation system, within the site and in relationship to the city. Three, there was the problem of urban design. (How do you relate buildings designed by different people? Were you or were you not going to have national pavilions? What was the place of the theme pavilion within the whole exhibition?). Four, there were the details of making the thing work on the site.

There had been considerable excitement over the decision to have an exhibition in Montreal in celebration of Canada's one hundredth birthday. Groups were formed to discuss what kind of exhibition it should be. This culminated in a conference at Montebello, Quebec, where men and women from various parts of Canada, a kind of task force of the intelligentsia, came together and tried to establish guide lines for the exhibition. Among other things, they decided to avoid the symbolic vertical structure that had become a cliché of world fairs, and they felt that nations should exhibit together according to certain themes and that national pavilions should either be eliminated or played down. There was vibration in the air. This was to be a very special exhibition.

Sandy van Ginkel had put together a group of about eight architects and planners. We were all in our twenties or early thirties; we all had in the past worked either with him or with colleagues of his. There were Jerry Miller and Adèle Naudé who had just come out of Harvard, Steve Staples who had more of a planning background than any of us, Tony Peters who was then in Sandy's office, and several others.

When I came back to Montreal in August 1963 there was a great deal of discussion about the actual location. By that time, Guy Beaudet, the harbor manager, had suggested building islands in the St. Lawrence river between the island of Montreal and the South Shore, and Mayor Jean Drapeau had agreed. They had decided to build Ile Notre Dame and to extend Ile Ste. Hélène north and south. But they had not decided whether there would be any exhibition on the mainland itself. Our first effort was to extend the exhibition back to MacKay Pier and so assure the long range benefits of the exhibition to the city as a whole. There was a great deal of controversy and it took a number of weeks before the extension was agreed upon.

There still remained the big question of what was to go where. Opinions were flying in the air. For example: Commissioner General, Pierre Dupuy, I believe favored – at least it was expressed in one particular plan – the "noble nations" (that is, Canada, the U.S., Britain and France) being on Ile Ste. Hélène and the "others" on Ile Notre Dame. The planning group felt that the amusement park should not penetrate the exhibition, it should be off by itself. It kept longer hours and it was a permanent installation. We felt that the Canadian pavilion, the pavilion of the host country, should not be at the entrance, it should be at the end of the circulation path. In the same way, more or less as if we were designing a shopping center, we said the U.S. and Russian pavilions ought to be at opposite ends of the circulation pattern, like two big department stores, with all the small pavilions in between like small shops.

For a long time we continued to hope that the theme pavilions would form the major spine of activity, straddling the transportation stops, with fingers radiating out to other pavilions. A plan was drawn in detail on that basis. For the sake of the city's future on the waterfront and for the sake of Habitat, I suggested that all the permanent buildings (the administration building, the stadium, the broadcasting center, anything that could remain permanently) should be placed on MacKay pier as the beginning of a future community. Eventually, after considerable discussion, this was agreed, and at that point MacKay Pier became part of the exhibition proper. From our point of view, this was essential if the city was to establish a beach-head of development on the river front for the future.

I felt transportation in the exhibition should go beyond the problem of just getting people around – it should be part of the exhibition, it should be an exhibit in itself of how a city could function, and we had a miniature city to deal with. There were four different areas, all of which had attractions that people wanted to see. This created a tremendous volume of traffic between the four points. In the end, we built a train that had five stops and ran as a shuttle service. In the planning stages, however, I proposed a system that was based on two assumptions: first, that the mobility of the individual was the most important thing in an exhibition – the more mobile he was, the more he could see; and second, that the exhibition ought to be experienced by movement at a variety of speeds. Some things should be seen moving at thirty miles an hour, some when you were strolling at two miles an hour. Yet, they ought not to be considered as separate systems, but as part of one overall system.

I proposed a miniature model of a three-part urban transportation system based on the Giza plan: the "C" system, moving through and around single buildings at two and one half to five miles an hour; the "B" system, a number of loops each serving an area at five to ten miles an hour; and the "A" system, moving at ten to thirty miles an hour and linking the city and the islands. You could call them moving sidewalks, horizontal elevators, and trains – all accelerating and decelerating but none ever coming to a stop. You could transfer from one system to the other in motion, you could constantly move through all parts of the exhibition without ever coming to a stop, you had total mobility.

I managed to arouse considerable interest for the proposal in the Expo management and it became apparent that the only way to assess its feasibility was to discuss it with the leading manufacturers of transportation and control systems on the continent. We were authorized to do so. Joe Kates, who was then the prime transportation consultant to Expo, Jerry Miller, and I were to go and visit the major transportation corporations, particularly American Machine and Foundry in Connecticut, Westinghouse Transportation and Research Division in Pittsburgh, and Stevens Adamson Moving Sidewalk Division near Chicago.

Our most interesting meeting was with Westinghouse. They were very excited by the idea and felt they could build it in the time available. They thought the approximate cost would be forty-five to fifty million dollars for the total system, including the computers that would run it. They wanted a contract to make a more comprehensive feasibility study.

We returned from the trip enthusiastic and encouraged. Westinghouse wanted fifty thousand dollars for the feasibility study and we tried to get it authorized. But, at that point we were confronted with one of the problems of an exhibition undertaken with public funds. One could not just give a contract, even for a feasibility study, to one company – there had to be public bids. Expo management insisted the public bids be for any transportation system that could handle the anticipated volume of visitors. It would be up to the bidders to determine the nature of the system. Needless to say, that ruled the whole thing out.

I felt it could have been one of the great attractions of Expo. There would be buildings, and exhibits within the buildings, but the actual structure and arrangement of the whole exhibition would have been the main exhibit. It tied in with the idea of Habitat – that you build an exhibit that is a living community.

As a last resort, I proposed a compromise system. We would have separate "A", "B" and "C" systems, but the stops would be combined and the systems synchronized so that when "A" train came to a stop, so "B" system would simultaneously come to a stop in the same station. People would then get off one system and on to the other without having to wait. Even this modest improvement would double the average speed of the individual in the exhibition. This also proved too demanding for the cumbersome procedures of government contracting. Bids on the "A" system were to be called immediately, as it would be part of the Expo budget, but the "B" and "C" systems, if they were to exist, would be concessions. In the end, the "A" system survived as the Expo Express and the Minirail was installed as a secondary system.

We had proposed that the system should be totally free. That was accepted for Expo Express and worked very well. It became clear seeing it in action that this was the way the city should function, with public transportation as a service you don't pay for except as a taxpayer.

As the theme pavilions shrank (they became Canadian rather than international) the spine dwindled and the site became more and more a collection of miscellaneous buildings. What could be done to give the whole thing unity? We were of course fortunate in having a magnificent site. Building the islands in the St. Lawrence River was the responsibility of the City of Montreal as part of the Tri-Government Agreement (i.e. an agreement between the City of Montreal, the Province of Quebec, and the federal government of Canada). The City had dug enormous holes in the islands, quarrying rock needed to build the dikes to extend the area. These holes were a hundred and fifty feet deep and the City was increasingly concerned about how to get enough fill for them. It was at that point that I suggested – an idea born out of desperation – filling them with water. There would be series of, not so much canals as *spines* of water with the buildings on either side, connecting the lakes formed in the holes. Water would become the visual link and the unifying element for all the diverse buildings.

We went a step further in drawing up this plan. The river level fluctuates from spring to fall by about twenty feet. I proposed that we not water-proof the bottoms of the canals and lakes so that the level of water in the islands would fluctuate with the river – it would go up and down twenty feet. That was a very exciting thing. You could build a series of terraces, the buildings being at the top terrace, which was the high water level in spring; and throughout the summer the water would slowly recede, revealing more and more terraces. We expected more visitors as time went by too. The highest number of visitors and the lowest water level were expected in July, August, and the beginning of September, so we would have more space as the number of visitors increased. The Expo site engineers were quite concerned about the technical problems this would pose and eventually opted for partially waterproofed bottoms for the lakes, and pumps and dams to keep the level constant.

By then I was no longer working on the master plan. Work had started on Habitat and I could clearly not continue with both. This was a painful decision, for you become possessive – you have that uncontrollable urge to stay with something until it becomes a reality. In developing the plan further Adèle Naudé, Miller, and Staples had modified the scale of the large bodies of water. They had become more like the canals in scale, relating to the scale of the roadways and the walkways. I had always been concerned about this question of scale because I felt that the hierarchy of scales, especially the larger bodies of water, was what would give the entire exhibition a sense of location, telling a person he was in one spot and not in another. I was concerned with the implications of a gridiron plan of roads and canals all the same size. But then, the essential elements of my initial plan had been preserved and it was rewarding as Expo took form to see to what extent it had succeeded in tying together the multitude of buildings into a continuous unified urban entity.

Expo was in quite a turmoil in those days, with the eight or nine of us young architects and planners working under Sandy in the midst of the rumpus. Then the resignations started flying; first the commissioner general's and deputy commissioner's, then Robillard's followed.

With the resignations came new appointments: Pierre Dupuy as commissioner general, Robert Shaw as deputy commissioner general, Colonel Edward Churchill as director of installations taking over and extending Robillard's role, and Edouard Fiset as chief architect. Pierre Dupuy, the commissioner general, had been Canadian ambassador to France for a long period. One day shortly after his appointment I came across a confidential memo in which he proposed that Beaudoin, the Beaux-Arts planner in Paris, should design the Expo master plan. He would come to Montreal with a group of assistants and take over.

We young planners got very upset. We felt that a man from Paris who did not know our city and who was out of touch with contemporary thinking was inappropriate. Our group prepared a carefully worded letter that stated our objections to having Beaudoin and his staff undertake the master plan. It was addressed to commissioner general Dupuy, and stated that we would resign unless the whole idea was abandoned. That was a pretty tough move to make and so we thought at that point we had better go see a lawyer. We contacted Claude-Armand Sheppard, whom we had known as a vocal McGill law student and a defender of underdogs, and had a meeting with him that night. He wasn't very encouraging. He asked, in a cold matter of fact way: "How many of you have French names?" Well, Adèle Naudé had a French name, but she was

South African, and the one French Canadian on the staff didn't sign the petition. Sheppard said, "You don't have a chance, they'll just let you go." He felt we were taking a big risk. But for us there was no other way. We felt like the protectors of the realm. We had to save the exhibition.

But Churchill was rather impressed with our move, while Sandy was right in the middle, hanging loose between management and us. Since he hadn't threatened to resign with us, management was looking to him to settle the dispute. That Saturday, two days after our ultimatum was submitted, Sandy asked us all to come up to his country house in the Laurentians to discuss the whole subject. We arrived and told him that our position was unalterable; if Expo was going to hire Beaudoin to make the master plan, this was the end of the exhibition so far as we were concerned.

Sandy got Churchill on the phone and they started negotiating. At one point the situation was so tragi-comic that I doubted Churchill was on the other end of the line. I thought Sandy's sense of ceremony was rising to the occasion. But Churchill *was* on the other end, and a settlement was negotiated. Beaudoin would be allowed to go through with his presentation, we would withdraw our letter as if it had never been written, and the Beaudoin submission would be phased out politely and slowly.

Beaudoin arrived a few days later with a scheme that displayed such a lack of understanding of the city, in terms of where people came in and where people left, where the subway alignment was and other such mundane facts, that it just came to a natural end.

A positive thing came out of what Churchill came to call "The Palace Revolt." Shaw, Churchill, and the rest of the new management were impressed; they had a group of people with strong ideas and they had better find out what work we had done to date. They took three days off for us to brief them and we conveyed in a marathon presentation everything that had gone on – the master plan, theme pavilion, Habitat, transportation, urban design, graphics, street furniture, landscaping.

In retrospect there was something charming about a group of young and quite naive designers working away at the Expo offices while all the political storms were thundering around us: English-French; Ottawa-Quebec-Montreal; industry-dominated or theme-dominated; profit-making or subsidized. It is to the credit of the country that at that moment the enormous task of planning the exhibition was not just sliced up into two or three big chunks, and farmed out to the great consultant establishments, as most government work is in the end.

In those early Expo days the organization was loose; there was little hierarchy. As a group we were all working together, and, as in all group or team work, relationships and responsibilities evolved as part of the dynamics between us. I found myself in a special position. On one hand I had pretty clear ideas about the basic planning of the exhibition. It had become an extension of the work I had done in the past three or four years. On the other hand I was the only one of the group who had previously worked very closely with Sandy. We had a *modus operandi.* He trusted me, in fact, even demanded and expected me to produce, and what I produced was compatible with his images. Because of that I found myself in the first eight weeks working practically continuously, and apart from the group, in Sandy's office, while Sandy was storming in and out of the room, bringing news of the latest meetings and negotiations between the powers that were.

It was the first time that I had given any thought to the whole question of team work. As students we all talked of team work as a positive thing, in the tradition of the Bauhaus. Out of that came the attitude that teams do better than individuals. Here I learned that when teams were made up of unlike individuals of different disciplines they complemented each other, but that the design process did not always lend itself to a homogeneous sort of team. Ten hands could not hold one pencil and push it in the same direction. I found myself latching onto that pencil with much pleasure and some sense of mission.

Soon after his appointment Fiset, the chief architect, appointed three Montreal architects, Guy Desbarats, André Blouin, and Fred Lebensold, to consult on the master plan. The motivation of Churchill and Fiset in taking this step was to gain broader support for the master plan from outside the corporation so that it could withstand whatever attacks might be launched against it when it was submitted to Parliament and the other agencies. But Sandy felt it personally as an expression of non-confidence. In any case, Sandy was finding it increasingly difficult to function within the new management. From his point of view the situation was intolerable; he felt his authority was being infringed. The new management felt that the loose organization through which the exhibition had functioned so far could not continue and a much more rigid hierarchy had to be established.

After a spell of continuous tension Sandy resigned. This was on December 3rd, 1963. The next day the three consultants came and joined the team of eight. The first step was to review all that had been done. The final master plan had to be submitted to the federal cabinet by December 20th. There were fourteen days to finalize all the loose ends. On December 6th, 1963 following a series of meetings, I consolidated the ideas and plans into a charcoal sketch that formed the basis for the formal presentation.

5   An immodest proposal

At the same time I was pushing ahead with Habitat.

Jean-Louis Lalonde, a Montreal architect who had become involved in Expo as a representative of the cement companies of Canada, indicated he could get financial support from them for a feasibility study of a housing exhibit. We worked out what it should contain, how it should be undertaken, and so on. At the same time Jean-Louis felt that the cement companies would probably want an international competition so as to get some world-famous architect for the project. But I was thinking singularly in terms of my thesis and had already for several weeks been working on its application to the site of MacKay Pier.

The thesis was basically a vertical structure. Working on the master plan for Tel Aviv with Tyng and Rinehart, I had come to see the need to mix residential with other uses; now I wanted to incline the structure to form a three-dimensional membrane integrated with the public spaces, essentially using the thesis system as a building method. I had never decided what the structural material should be. It was just a cellular, three-dimensional modular housing system. I made very clear when the cement companies offered twenty thousand dollars toward a feasibility study that it should not be tied to the use of concrete. They agreed.

The name "Habitat" was invented at that time, too. It was Jean-Louis Lalonde's idea. It said the same thing in both languages, French and English. (It was also the name of the CMHC magazine that first published my thesis in Canada and with which it was identified.)

We had the money from the cement companies but we didn't quite know how to use it. I realized you really couldn't do very much in the way of a large housing exhibit with no budget or funds except for the feasibility study money, so it seemed the only thing to do was go to Ottawa and see Central Mortgage. I knew several people there from the days of the travelling scholarship: Ian

Maclennan for instance, who had been its chief architect and had become a vice-president. I called him and said we would like to see him.

It was, of course, quite irregular for a lowly civil servant in the Canadian Corporation for the 1967 World Exhibition (Expo's official name) to ask for a meeting with the president and vice-president of CMHC, but because of my relationship with them and because Expo was such a young corporation and had not yet developed a regular hierarchy, it was possible. A few months later when I wanted to see anyone outside the corporation, say the head of the National Harbours Board, I had to go through channels – the management of Expo. But in those days I picked up the phone and talked to anyone. So Lalonde and I went to Ottawa.

Ian Maclennan is one of those men who make Canada tick. He is another without whom there would not have been a Habitat. He is aggressive, frank, and, unlike many civil servants, very outspoken. He charges into meetings with the fervor of a college debating champion. I always feel the pressure of his convictions when he takes a position.

Very few people at that time stuck their necks out for Habitat. It was a risky project, it was maybe not possible, it was the kind of thing that could easily tarnish you if you became involved. I was fascinated to see how people responded to it and were, or were not, prepared to support it. The ordinary civil servant who plays safe would not have supported it at the time. Ian Maclennan does not play safe. He goes by conviction.

Ian got the chief architect in, and the president and two or three other vice-presidents were there. It turned out to be a very high-level meeting. I had prepared a whole series of sketches which incorporated all of MacKay Pier for the housing exhibit.

The idea of building Expo around themes was still very strong; there was still the hope that national pavilions would not predominate and that all countries would collaborate on theme exhibits. I proposed that we build a total urban structure housing two thousand families, and that the public and commercial areas be national exhibits. One country would take the school, another the medical clinic, a third the theater, all as *permanent* buildings. There would be none of the sacrilegious waste of building temporary pavilions and then demolishing them. All the structures would become part of the living community after and even during Expo. It was much more than just a housing exhibit; it would be a community which was being built by the nations.

At that first meeting with CMHC in Ottawa, Habitat could have died. It was the first of a string of critical situations when Habitat was poised between "Go, No-Go", when an idea was confronting the system and struggling for survival. Ian Maclennan could have said it was a pipe dream. It would have been difficult to know what to do except make some more plans as others did. But

Maclennan said to his colleagues, "Well, they've got an individual who is in a position of responsibility in another crown corporation planning the exhibition. We would like to see a housing exhibit. If this is built it will set housing in Canada fifteen to twenty years ahead." The remark became a slogan that popped up frequently at later meetings.

That was why Central Mortgage was prepared to back us. But Central Mortgage had no funds available (though later they contributed two hundred and fifty thousand dollars toward Habitat's design costs – to me an important symbolic act). Maclennan said, "You won't be able to go very far unless you have a really hard-headed developer working with you. I know just the man." It was Stewart M. (Bud) Andrews, who was a vice-president of Webb & Knapp, Zeckendorf's Canadian development arm: he was responsible for the development of the much-hailed Flemingdon Park project in Toronto. Maclennan picked up the phone. Andrews was in hospital having his appendix out. Maclennan set an appointment for four days later in Toronto when Andrews was due out of hospital.

At that time Habitat was to be an inclined structure, not quite regular pyramids, but open-ended half-pyramids leaning on each other. All the community facilities were below. Since I had not then decided whether the units would be load-bearing or inserted into a frame, in the sketches we showed the alternatives: one, a steel frame with units plugged in; the other with load-bearing units.

We went to Toronto and met Andrews and his associate, Eric Bell. They were very excited by the scheme. I showed the sketches we had prepared for CMHC, my thesis, the publications of it, and the explanation. They immediately agreed to work on the feasibility study.

The Expo master plan was just being completed to go to Ottawa. On it, stretching from Victoria Bridge to the tip of MacKay Pier, was a community of fifteen hundred families. Guy Desbarats, one of the consulting architects, felt it was quite wrong to put a specific design on the master plan. It should be an area marked "housing exhibit", not a design, because that would prejudice the situation. I said, "I want to prejudice the situation," and I insisted that the plan contain my Habitat design.

I took it to Edouard Fiset, the chief architect. He had just been there a few days. He said, "A housing exhibit on MacKay Pier does not make sense." I insisted he look at the plans. I had a big model, drawings, sketches. I remember the moment. He looked at it all and finally said, "Well, that's a completely different story. Yes, I can see that." It was another of those "Go, No-Go" moments. That afternoon Fiset gave me authorization to hire four or five people to work on Habitat. I called my friend, Dave Rinehart, who had by then left Lou Kahn's office, and invited him to join me. He eventually stayed with Habitat almost to the end of the job. The other four architects were McGill classmates.

When the master plan was ready, a comprehensive budget of everything shown on it had to be made. The Foundation Company and some other consultants were hired to prepare it. Going over the master plan, they came to an area marked "Habitat 67." They looked up the budget allocations and there was no money for such a thing. Colonel Churchill, knowing almost nothing of Habitat, took the master plan to Robert Shaw for a final review before it went to Parliament. Shaw looked at the Habitat area and said something to the effect that it was not budgeted for and therefore should be off the plan. (I learned all this only later.) Churchill, who can't explain his reasons to this day, disagreed with Shaw. "I think it's a good thing," he said, "I can see that it would make the difference between a real exhibition and just a fair. I insist that it stay on." Shaw agreed.

This meant that when the master plan was approved on December 20th, 1963, Habitat (at least as something on a drawing) was officially approved by the Parliament of Canada. I don't think anybody at that time realized the implications.

But it had serious ramifications. For example, there was resistance to Habitat from the National Harbours Board. The Montreal port manager, Guy Beaudet, was the man who had originated the island idea and suggested it to Mayor Jean Drapeau. It was a stroke of genius. His motives, at least partially, were to try and get the exhibition out of his harbor so he could go on expanding without too much difficulty. He wanted nothing permanent on MacKay Pier, which the Harbours Board owned. Having Expo leak back from the islands onto the pier with a permanent structure like Habitat certainly made him unhappy. Yet we felt that if Expo was to change the city, the islands had to have a bridgehead on the mainland. The need for Montreal to open up to the river had priority over the needs of the harbor which could expand down river. With the authorization of Parliament this became an approved land use and that took care of the National Harbours Board.

Expo was becoming an interesting prototype of the relationship between ideas and creativity and a rigid organization with its hierarchy and bureaucracy. There is no doubt that an undertaking of that magnitude, the spending of one billion dollars in construction over a period of three years, could not have been done without the most highly efficient organization. It required department heads and deputies and assistant deputies and assistants to the assistants; channels of communication such as standard memorandum forms, application forms, briefing procedures, purchase orders, monthly, weekly, and daily co-ordination meetings; inter-departmental, super-departmental, inter-governmental, and inter-municipal committees, and on and on.

It is equally true that if this rigid organization had existed in the early days of the corporation, much of what we admire and appreciate about Expo 67 would not have been there. Had Expo been in full-blown existence, our small young planning group could not have come about and would not have survived. Even later on, when Expo became a corporation with thousands of employees, the development of the important ideas – the organization of the theme, the design of the street furniture, the conception of the great exhibits – took place not because of the organization but because the hierarchy was short-circuited, because a direct link was established between the few individuals responsible for the development of an idea and the two or three of top management who made the decisions and were responsible for communicating them to the governments.

The lesson of Expo is to find that secret formula by which a clear organization exists, capable of carrying out complex undertakings efficiently and under control, without stifling the kind of communication and informal organization that is required at the conceptual level. I suppose this problem cannot be disassociated from the broader urban question: Can we have large scale planning and complex technological processes in the environment without paying the price of stifling individual choice, variety, and identity?

While Parliament studied the master plan we proceeded hectically on the feasibility study. We needed a good engineer and I suggested Dr. August Komendant, an engineer who did much of the structural engineering for Louis Kahn's work and whom I had met in Kahn's office. I felt that he, more than any other man I knew, would be capable of dealing with a structure that might or might not turn out to be concrete but that was, in any case, going to be highly complex. The following week Bud Andrews, Eric Bell, Jean-Louis Lalonde, Dave Rinehart, and I went down to visit Komendant in his office in Montclair, New Jersey. We spread the sketches and drawings on the floor; Komendant took out his pipe and started sucking on it. Three hours later, in his old Prussian style, he said, "Yes, it can be done."

Komendant is one of the most Germanic people I have ever met, even though he's Estonian, not German. He has a strong German accent. He studied at one of the great German universities and spent a good part of the war years in Germany. After the war he became chief engineer for the American High Command in Europe and one of his tasks was to study war-damaged buildings: buildings that had beams, walls, or columns knocked out but had not collapsed. At that time, he told me, he gathered much knowledge that extends beyond accepted theory.

There is something about him that declares authority, his hair combed neatly back, his heavy black-rimmed glasses and the constant action of his pipe. (That pipe became part of the Habitat environment during construction.) He is extremely dogmatic, stubborn, and autocratic. He doesn't have an organization of hundreds of engineers; he has two or three people working in the basement of his house in New Jersey. No draftsmen; he does his own drawings. He used to arrive on the day of a deadline with a set of drawings and stick his finger out and show me the blisters on it. He designs and computes as he draws; often the contractors could not read his drawings because he did them in a kind of personal shorthand.

Without him, Habitat would not have been there. After that famous "Yes, it can be done," there was a continuous stream of engineers who said it couldn't be done, people who were working with him or working for Expo or other agencies, but he consistently said it could and explained why, and did it.

The relationship between architect and engineer is a complex one. There is that dependency on each other, resented by both and yet accepted. There is that natural tension of any relationship which is rooted in inter-dependency. This was even more so in Habitat. The conception of environment, the conception of structure, and the conception of construction were one and inseparable, and it took some pretty intense exchanges to bring about the resolution of all the factors that had to be contended with. For instance, how can you group the dwellings in a rational way from the point of view of the house designs, and at the same time arrive at a grouping that lends itself to the rational analysis of the stresses? Komendant felt the stresses physically. As he sat and explained the structure, you could feel them going through his body. Often when he said "Yes, you can do it," coming to meet the challenge of the impossible, he could have said "Yes, you can do it but you should not." Without his attitude Habitat could not have been done, not in ten months.

At that point we made a very important decision: the housing modules would be load-bearing as well as space-enclosing.

For my thesis I hadn't been able to come to a decision on this question. I didn't have the technical knowledge to make the judgment. I developed three systems: one had frames rising thirty storeys high with plug-in units lifted on a lift-slab method; another was a system going up to twelve storeys with load-bearing units; the third system used panels.

An early drawing by Le Corbusier shows a frame and a hand putting a box into it and there are many recent studies of space frames with plug-in units. It's the obvious, simple solution: put up a frame and plug things into it. It was the first thing I thought of doing in my thesis. It's also the obvious solution to mass producing, because the plug-in units are all identical. It's the simplest solution conceptually, because structure is separated from the shell of the house. You can consider the optimum structure separately and develop a geometry for it, and then you can consider the optimum house. You have considerable freedom in grouping houses. You can have windows anywhere, it is a freer system.

Yet it's redundant. By this I mean that you're doing two things separately. The frame has to be stiff, therefore you triangulate it. Yet your units would give you that stiffening in themselves if they were part of the structure. The standard question after Habitat was, "Wouldn't it be simpler to have a plug-in unit? You could have real mass production." It is the easy way out, but I don't think it's the superior way. The plug-in system might become cheaper, and better, if we were building the units out of a material that weighed the same as foam plastic and the frame out of exposed steel, aluminum or cable structures. Where the weight of the plug-in unit is small in comparison with the rest of the structure, the redundancy becomes negligible. But we are fifteen to twenty years away from that technology. At least, so we thought in 1964.

With the technology then available the units would have had to be concrete and the frame, if it was metal, would have had to be fireproofed with concrete. What's more, if the units were to be concrete – and this seemed the best choice for many reasons – they would have had to be strong enough to resist stresses while being lifted into place. For that you would have to make them much stronger than they had to be merely to support themselves. Why shouldn't they do a little more? The redundancy of two such heavy systems seemed wrong, and Komendant then made the judgment – which I agreed with – that, given the use of concrete, it would be a superior system if the units not only enclosed space but were load-bearing as well.

I had promised Central Mortgage at the Ottawa meeting to be back in eight weeks. Time was already impossibly short. In our group there were about six architects, an engineer, and the developers who were going to prepare cost estimates. We worked day and night for eight weeks.

Out of this process evolved Habitat, the first proposal – nine hundred and fifty housing units in inclined rhomboidal planes leaning on each other, pedestrian streets, inclined A frames with elevators and passageways penetrating them, and a complete commercial and cultural center below. The cost estimates came to forty-two million dollars (about forty-four thousand dollars per unit).

It was an incredible eight weeks. The project was gaining momentum. The cement people were getting interested, people in Expo were becoming aware that there was a group working on some scheme downstairs. Ed Churchill, before he went home around midnight every night, would walk by, just look at the drawings pinned on the walls and with a smile walk away, never letting us know what was going on in his mind. Industry was being brought in, the precast concrete people, elevator companies, and various contracting companies were being asked questions and opinions, the word was going around town that something was happening on a very big scale. In the final four or five days I wrote a sort of manifesto declaring what Habitat was all about; Andrews and Bell wrote a second half, an assessment of the rents that would have to be charged, the cost of construction, how many units could be marketed every year, and other developmental questions. Their cost estimate turned out to be relatively optimistic later on, but there were many technical problems they could not have anticipated at the time.

On Friday evening February 21st, 1964 the feasibility study, a set of drawings in full color, and a model were delivered to Churchill's office. We hit the deadline on the day. We had made it.

The study was signed by me and counter-signed by Bud Andrews. Lalonde felt it should have been submitted from the cement companies to Expo, but I disagreed. It was my design, and I was not paid by the cement companies, nor were the other architects on the team (though Andrews and Bell and Komendant were paid out of the cement companies' twenty thousand dollars).

Churchill spent the weekend with it. On Monday morning he poked his head through the door and said, "That's a fantastic thing. We've got to make it go." Half an hour later he got a very angry phone call from Louis Lapointe, president of Miron Compagnie Ltée and chairman of the committee of the cement companies: this was an absolute infringement of the rights of the industry that had paid for the study and owned the design, Churchill had no business accepting it from me, it was absolutely wrong to have it submitted internally within CCWE, and the cement companies wanted to see it, review it, see if they agreed with it, and then submit it themselves to Expo. Churchill said Andrews and I were officially presenting it to the corporation at eleven o'clock and if Lapointe wanted to be present he was welcome. Ten minutes after the meeting started Lapointe stormed into the room, repeating what he had said on the phone.

This was another moment when Habitat sat poised between life and death. At that point Churchill could have backed down before Lapointe's pressure. He could have said, "It's your property, you paid towards making it, and you have some rights to it . . ." or "What do you think we should do with it?" Instead, he, turned round and asked, "Are you prepared to build it? Are you prepared to finance the whole project?" Lapointe said, "No." Churchill said, "When you give money to the government you give it without any strings attached. The government owns what is done with the money you have donated. This is our plan. The Corporation owns it."

That was when I realized how strong Churchill really was. He had dealt with the private sector as a government official; there had often been attempts to push him around before, and he wasn't taking it. Right there he saved the project from drifting into the potential problems of the cement companies' uninvolved involvement.

Ed Churchill is unique. I'll never forget the first day he came to Expo. A man with a name like Churchill, a colonel from the army engineering corps, from Ottawa: You'd expect the Anglo-Saxon major type. Everybody was saying, "This is the end of Expo. With an army engineer running the show, what's going to happen?"

The difference between him and Claude Robillard, whom he replaced, was evident from the beginning. Robillard had his office designed by Jacques Guillon, the Montreal industrial designer. It had a charcoal carpet, beautiful ash furniture, soft orangey leather seats, stainless steel and glass tables; one of the most sophisticated and beautiful rooms I had seen in a long time. There was French-Canadian finesse all over the place. Then Churchill came rambling in and took over the same office. Within a few weeks the papers started piling up, the carpet got wrinkled, the intensity of work showed all over. For relaxing and thinking he brought in a big blue reclining bed which didn't match the colors, a little refrigerator got shoved in one corner. He was surely in those terms an unsophisticated man.

He made it clear he was not going to take any chances on the schedule. He was going to have Expo ready on time. Everyone assumed that he would save money and ignore the undefinable, that which gives things soul, anything that they, the so-called Expo intellectuals, considered good . . .

My experience with Churchill in the following three years was that he compromised less and stood by his guns about such things as quality of design and the importance of the human element in the end product more often than many of the Expo intellectuals.

Churchill is in his fifties, short, very broad shoulders, thinning curly red hair, blue eyes, a big grin even when he is angry. He is a very gentle person in spite of his reputation as a bulldozer. Once Churchill gained confidence in an individual, he would back him up completely. Two or three years later, when our relationship had become closer as a result of our work together, I would make a recommendation to him and though he was one of the busiest men in the world at that time, he would listen to me. Sometimes I had to walk down the corridor with him from one meeting to another to get his ear for ten minutes. If it sounded right he would ask me a few questions, get an understanding of the situation right away, and then back me up. I can say without reservation that if it were not for Churchill there would be no Habitat. It just would not be there. Not only that, but the fact that it's there with so little compromise is thanks to Churchill.

In the end, of course, the cement industry had no complaints. Habitat was built in concrete. It was the most spectacular concrete structure at Expo and one of the most spectacular concrete buildings anywhere. They had put up the money hoping to promote their material. They had no intention of doing any more. Lalonde felt quite hurt at that time. He had started a project hoping a great international competition would be called, and I insisted on designing it. Quite apart from my obsession and conviction about Habitat I was sure that any big, vague, international competition would lead nowhere. I felt that what I had put down on paper had a validity that gave it the right to come into existence. But without the cement companies' money to hire the developers and the engineer it would probably have been "No-Go". At one point Churchill even offered to pay back the twenty thousand dollars, but of course they did not want that. A few days later I made a presentation to all the presidents of the Canadian cement companies. There was fairly long applause at the end. No cheque or money to build it, but applause.

Another "Go, No-Go" point: shortly after Churchill arrived at Expo he said he felt that if Expo was to be a success it was important that a group of the best architects in the country be involved in an advisory capacity. He also felt it would be wise politically and the exhibition would be in a much stronger position to deal with criticism or opposition to some of its actions. Among the fifteen members of the committee were John C. Parkin, John Bland, Geoffrey Massey, Etienne Gaboury, and Doug Shadbolt. When Fiset said we ought to make a presentation of Habitat to the architectural advisory committee and get their comments, my first response was, "My God, that will be the end of that." But he insisted. He said he thought it worth the risk. One week later the advisory committee came together. Parkin was the chairman. I brought all the photographs and the model which had just been completed and gave a half-hour presentation – the problems of mass housing and how we were tackling them, how the structure worked, and the idea of factory-produced housing.

It was a strange experience. There was Doug Shadbolt, my professor, and John Bland, the dean of my school, and many of my "elder peers." When I completed my presentation there was a momentary silence; my heart was in my boots. Then John Bland said, "I'd like to move that the architectural committee congratulate the Expo management and the architect for such an imaginative scheme and wish them the best of luck in realizing it." I believe it was John Parkin who seconded the motion, which was carried unanimously. It would be interesting to speculate what would have happened if they had not endorsed it so strongly, because quite soon afterwards the first rumblings of professional criticism started, and the architectural advisory committee's support proved to be an important defense in the hands of Churchill and Fiset.

The steel industry had been hearing what was happening down at Expo – a forty or fifty million dollar project in concrete – and one day the chairman of the steel advisory committee walked into Churchill's office and insinuated that because the cement companies had paid for the feasibility study it was being done in concrete. Churchill said, "They spent some money, why don't you? Why don't you show us how to do it in steel?" They retained Joe de Stein, a Montreal engineer, and Eric Arthur, the Toronto architect. Their report included a series of assessments of Habitat itself and how one could do it by giving the boxes steel frames and spraying gunite on them. Forty thousand dollars later it reached the conclusion that "properly designed within its present concept, Habitat is more appropriate in precast concrete." That, unfortunately, finished the participation of the steel companies in Habitat.

Later on we had a great deal of difficulty in getting help from many of the large industries. Always there would be strings attached and always complications. As Habitat came closer to reality interest in it grew and so did the pressures surrounding it. We would hear rumors of various studies being made as to how to modify the buildings to use more aluminum – or more wood – or more glass – or any one of many specific products. We were getting to sense that with many millions of public funds being expended it was going to be difficult to keep decisions at the level of simple logic.

The big question was still, "Where is the money to build it to come from?" Habitat would cost forty-two million dollars but its market value, in terms of the revenues it would generate, would be about twenty-two million. The other twenty million had to be gotten somewhere else.

The twenty-two-million-dollar market value was calculated on the basis of local rents, and maintenance and management costs projected for this building in this location. Andrews and Bell worked out the potential net revenue, about a million and one-half dollars a year. A normal mortgage return then would have been six or seven per cent of capital investment. That gave a market value of twenty-two million dollars.

For the other twenty million they had two plans. One was to call Habitat "research." Under federal tax laws industries are permitted to claim approved research as a one hundred and fifty per cent tax deduction. If they spent twenty million dollars on research, they could claim thirty million as expenses on their income tax returns. Thus, the government is indirectly subsidizing research. The second plan was derived from a legislative formula for preserving the ship-building industry in Canada under the pressure of world prices. Corporations could build ships for a certain cost, sell them on the world market, and claim the difference as a tax write-off. If they built a ten million dollar ship and sold it for five million, they could write five million off their tax. The government pays the difference by not collecting due taxes.

The research formula was favored because Habitat obviously was research. (The chemical industry has research; why not the construction industry?) The procedure was that the National Research Council had first to agree that Habitat was building research. We made a full presentation through Central Mortgage to the National Research Council. But no, they would not accept Habitat as research. They were concerned that if they did accept it, any developer or builder with a building that did not quite conform to regular practice could ask for the same concession. It would be setting a precedent.

This was a great mistake, a basic misunderstanding of the whole problem of the construction industry. It would have been a precedent – a significant one – to encourage builders and developers to think up projects that would advance the industry. I'm sure one could set up regulations to separate the genuine projects from the phonies. Later, when Habitat was under construction, we kept getting visitors from the National Research Council who looked at the building and noted the experience gained. By their own actions they admitted it was research. They even changed the National Building Code where we had won concessions that proved workable.

It would have been a more radical precedent to apply the ship-building formula to housing construction. Yet we had heard from Ottawa that this would be considered as a special case, and Expo made a series of presentations to corporations that had sufficient income to benefit from this kind of write-off.

(Obviously, a company had to have a net annual profit of over forty million dollars and be paying tax at fifty per cent, to write off twenty million.)

No developer, financier, or corporation could afford to make a commitment to build Habitat without more detailed information. Detailed architectural and engineering drawings had to be done and more cost estimates had to be made. I was asked to estimate what this next phase would cost and came to the conclusion that it would take a quarter of a million dollars. No industry was offering that kind of feasibility money. Churchill and Shaw went to the board of directors of Expo and they approved a budget appropriation of two hundred and fifty thousand dollars.

This could have been made available to me within Expo, but it would have meant building up quite a staff. Another possibility was to hire an architectural firm and make me the chief designer while I remained an Expo employee. Churchill, who had dealt with consultants for years, knew the problems arising when the owner and designer are one organization and when the owner's consultant is responsible to the owner's employees. He felt, and Shaw concurred, that since I had originated the project the proper thing was for me to resign from Expo and open an office in a joint venture with another firm. He called me into his office one day and said with a straight face: "Moshe, you are fired." I didn't have an organization. I had never had my own office. But I resigned, and the board of directors approved my resignation and my appointment as consulting architect to Expo, all on the same day.

Two days later the world came tumbling down on Nina and me. Our two-month-old son Dan suddenly died in what is known as a crib death, and then nothing mattered. Everything just stopped and was in darkness.

6   In the balance

A number of large architectural firms that had experience of joint ventures with other designers were considered by Expo. The firm of John B. Parkin Associates was proposed. I met with John C. Parkin, the partner in charge of design, and told him what my terms were. He told me his, and they seemed acceptable. I made it clear: I had commitments to Komendant as an engineer; I had people who were to remain in positions of responsibility, Dave Rinehart particularly; I wanted full design control of the building; all decisions for hiring engineers and other consultants would be made jointly and so on. The agreements were outlined in a letter, but we had not signed a contract. We agreed that the work should be done in Montreal. They were to send people down from their Toronto office.

But the Parkin people just didn't show up. I was getting nervous and started hiring my own. In a short time I hired twenty people. I then found problems were arising with their office.

It appeared that John B. Parkin, the senior partner, felt differently about some of the points we had agreed upon. I had prepared a contract which he found unacceptable. He felt they ought to do the engineering. I was nervous about that because of rumors that there had been friction between Parkin and Viljo Revell over the Toronto city hall on this point, and because I felt a moral and practical commitment to Komendant.

They felt uneasy about some of the people in my office because they had long hair or didn't wear suits. The office had evolved to a relaxed, unregimented place. I didn't feel an architect, a professional, should get his time sheet signed every evening he was going to work overtime. I felt it was up to him. These small things became important.

I went back to Expo and said I couldn't continue with Parkin. I assume Parkin also went to Expo. All around, they must have felt the entire project much too risky. Expo said the decision was mine to make but they felt it would help them, and the job, to have me associated with a reputable firm, even for such purposes as professional insurance. I had no objection to that. I had hoped in fact, that a joint venture would help me in dealing with administrative matters, running an office, finances, and so on. But it didn't work out that way. In the final analysis it was good. By the time those three months of negotiations were over, I found I had built up an office of my own. I was independent. Expo said they would be perfectly willing if I associated with another firm.

At that point I met Peter Barott of David, Barott, Boulva, a Montreal firm. I made very clear what my terms were—exactly the same terms I had made with John C. Parkin. They accepted them and that was the beginning of our rather good relationship.

Anthony Peters, who had been one of the original team of eight, was appointed Expo's representative for Habitat. He was in effect "the client." His official title was "Section Head—Habitat," directly under Edouard Fiset, Expo's chief architect.

I first met Tony Peters when he was working part-time for Harold Spence-Sales. Tony is an Englishman who came to Canada about 1958. He went to work for Sandy van Ginkel when I left for Philadelphia. When van Ginkel became involved in Expo his whole staff moved over, and so when I went to Expo in 1963 Tony was there on van Ginkel's team. Tony sat in on our weekly job meetings, and processed the endless flow of paper work. Later on, when Habitat was completed, he was given the job of running it as an exhibit. Now he's working for Sandy van Ginkel again.

Tony has a very shrewd understanding of the total structure of things; he understands the politics of a situation. He had a difficult task with Habitat because, though we were friends, he had the responsibility of saying, "Stop doing that, it's going to go over the budget." He was constantly subject to all the Expo pressures and I am grateful he managed to shield me from so many. He was involved in situations where federal and provincial agencies were constantly questioning the project and he had to deal with that volatile energetic group of people who made up our office.

The office was new and I was twenty-five. Everything had to be learned the hard way. Since I already had a substantial staff, David, Barott, Boulva put on only three or four people, in a team of about thirty. Again this was all for the better in terms of independence. There was no attempt to take over the job. Their firm was very busy with its own work. They were pleased to give whatever assistance they could, but did not feel possessive about Habitat.

About that time we had an eventful visit. The Habitat design drawings had just been completed and released by Expo to the press and we were starting our working drawings. One day I received a call from one of the public relations people at Expo: "Could I come by? I have a visitor here and I would like to show him your model and drawings." The visitor turned out to be a small bald man with large glasses who in some ways, in the intense communion of meeting his eyes through the lenses, made me think of Lou Kahn. The PR man said, "May I introduce to you Mr. Buckminster Fuller. He's the one who designs the domes, you know." I directed the PR man to the two or three Fuller books on my shelf. (I had been interested in Fuller's ideas and writings since university.) Everybody in the office of course became very excited, and I took Fuller to where the models and drawings were and started describing the project to him. After I had spoken for maybe three minutes he said, "You need say no more. I understand what it's all about." He added something to the effect that he appreciated how difficult it was to get it that far. Then he left.

I didn't hear from Fuller again directly until a year later. Expo had just opened and his U.S. pavilion was a big hit. I received a letter from him and attached to it was a press clipping from the Toronto *Telegram*. The heading of the article was, "Buckminster Fuller Blasts Habitat, Pats Himself on Own Dome." Fuller's letter started: "I'm sure you will agree with me that it is not a pleasant thing to call any man a liar, but this reporter is a liar." His letter went on to tell me how he felt about my work. At that time I was subject to considerable criticism from many in my profession, and the letter was a very important reinforcer of morale. (I was to meet Fuller again and spend considerable time with him in Israel in 1967 during the International Congress of Engineers and Architects. We went to Jerusalem and several other places together.)

It's a strange thing to say about a man who is known mainly as an architect and builder, but if I have a political mentor it is Buckminster Fuller.

We completed the preliminary working drawings and the first cost estimates came in. They were around seventy million dollars, compared with the expected forty-two million! We started making modifications to bring it back down to forty-two million. That meant we had to cut out thirty million dollars' worth of construction, nearly half the estimates. But it wasn't quite as bad as it sounds. The seventy million was a rough first estimate, and they are usually very conservative. We went over the plans and estimates, discovering where and why they were priced so high, refined the design, made it more efficient. We also simplified some things: the pedestrian streets were to be heated and enclosed in plastic, so we changed the enclosures to shelters, and eliminated the heating; the elevators were changed. We did a whole lot of things like that and brought the estimates back to the original figure.

We were still searching for money. On the initiative of Expo and the development consultants, Andrews and Bell, I made nearly a presentation a day for two months until we had seen the presidents of virtually every large corporation in the country: William Zeckendorf who came in from New York, the presidents of the Royal Bank, Montreal Trust, General Motors of Canada, Stelco, Inco, Alcan, Domtar, Imperial Oil, Power Corporation and many others.

The exposure the idea was getting was incredible, and as a result three offers came in. Power Corporation put in writing that if given the ship-building formula tax write-off, it would be prepared to build the whole project. A subsidiary of Imperial Oil also made an offer, and so did Lionel Rudberg, the developer responsible for CIL House and some large apartment buildings in Montreal.

With these three letters, the working drawings, and the cost estimates made by the Foundation Company of Canada we set off for Ottawa – Shaw, Churchill and their staff; Andrews; Fraser Elliott, a noted tax lawyer; and myself, packed in a small two-engine chartered plane – for a meeting with the Cabinet committee. I remember Churchill saying on the way there, "You're twenty-five and you're going to make a presentation to the Cabinet of this country. Isn't that absolutely wonderful?" and he meant it. It was a great experience, a great moment.

Mitchell Sharp was the minister in charge of Expo. The presentation was made to him; several other ministers were there as well as people from CMHC. It was well received as a concept. I think it excited everybody. I remember Jean-Luc Pépin, then parliamentary secretary to Mitchell Sharp, shaking my hand and saying something especially warm. Those present felt it would be good for the country and good for Expo. But the power house at the meeting proved to be Robert Bryce, the deputy minister of Finance. What he said amounted to: "We don't think we want to make a precedent by using the ship-building formula. What would you do if you were just given a straight budget of ten million dollars?"

I said it would be absolutely impossible. Half of the ten-million-dollar budget would be spent building the prefabricating plant and tooling up before construction started. That would leave only five million for construction. We couldn't build more than about a hundred and fifty housing units – a very small number. The unit cost would be astronomical, triple the proposed unit cost for the original proposal. What was more, we couldn't get amenities to support such a small population, and it would become an isolated community.

At the time I didn't think the project would be reduced in size. I repeatedly stated it was impossible to reduce it. Bryce said, "Well, that's too bad, because that may mean the thing is dead." (I think the decision was made very shortly after not to apply the ship-building formula, but I didn't find out until later.)

Chatting in the plane on the way back, Bob Shaw jokingly asked, "If they say 'No', what will you do?" I said, "I'll come back to Expo and get involved with the master plan again." Nobody really knew what would happen. Our spirits were high but we were quite tense.

Meanwhile we went on with the work in more detail, studying and refining toward the final working drawings. Two months later I was called into Churchill's office. Churchill said, "We've got instructions from the Treasury Board. They are not prepared to go with the formula. They are offering ten million dollars for construction and one and one-half million for design and development. They want to see what we can do for it and if they are satisfied we'll get a go-ahead with that budget.''

I was in a state of shock. It had never occurred to me through the whole struggle that my project would not be accepted in its entirety. I was convinced of its feasibility and had an obsessed sense of the inevitability of its realization. The set-back took me completely by surprise. Had I expected it, it might have been easier to understand.

My immediate reaction was, "I won't do it, it would be irresponsible." For two or three days I just sat at home, went out to the movies, drifted. We had been working at a hysterical pace, and of course nobody in the office was aware of what was happening. I couldn't bring myself to tell them.

Thinking about it afterwards, pondering that unanswerable "Why?" I believe there were a number of reasons that influenced the government to decide on a modified version. Anything above ten or fifteen million dollars would have required an arrangement with private enterprise and they were not going to enter any such joint venture. Their final decision was safer.

To give money for housing is a dangerous thing politically. I was told after that Cabinet presentation: "If you would only call it an exhibit we would have no trouble, but being housing it's a problem." A government could have voted fifty million dollars for a tower or a symbol or an exhibit and there would have been no difficulty but the same money voted for housing – even housing research – became a major political problem. If they gave housing to Montreal even within the context of an exhibition, then why not to other cities? A pavilion that happened to be a housing exhibit was, they decided, politically easier. As it turned out it was not. It still got all the criticism, all the attacks that are always made whenever government gets involved in any form of housing.

Another factor that I prefer not to think about too much, but I'm sure was very immediate, was that while I was working on the original Habitat proposal, Montreal's Mayor Drapeau came up with his proposal for the Paris/Montreal thousand-foot tower that was to cost forty-two million dollars – exactly the same as Habitat. Drapeau was spending most of his energies in those days trying to get it going, and I'm quite sure the City, which was a major partner in Expo, wasn't pushing Habitat; they were pushing the tower. They thought of the tower as the major symbol of the exhibition, as an Eiffel Tower or Seattle Needle, even though it ignored the Montebello conference decision. Habitat too was thought of by those who supported it – particularly in its original form – as a major symbol of Expo. I'm sure Churchill and Shaw felt it was; they said as much. You couldn't have two major symbols. Well, you could, but it was unlikely. There certainly wasn't enough money going around to do both. I feel that this distraction of Mayor Drapeau while pursuing the tower was at least indirectly responsible for Ottawa's decision.

The conflict between Habitat and the tower came up again later when the City called for bids on the tower at the same time that bids were called for Habitat Phase One. Most of the large contractors in town had to decide whether to bid the tower or Habitat. They couldn't do both. So Anglin-Norcross and the Foundation Company chose to bid Habitat and other contractors bid the tower.

Everyone in Expo became either Habitat-supporters or Habitat-haters. There was no neutrality. The ratio was two to one against. Churchill's secretary, Yoland Beaumier, was one of the supporters. I told her I wasn't going to do the reduced version and she gave me a long lecture about how ridiculous that was, the government didn't care about the unit cost, why should I? I went into Churchill's office after that and got another lecture from him. I could prove most of the things I wanted to prove, he said. It still had the scale to live as a community.

I felt very low. I realized that even though I could announce once a day for the next five years that the unit cost had been tripled by cutting the project's size, it would not be listened to. People would keep pointing at the unit costs and saying, "The concept is ridiculous because of the unit cost." No amount of explanation would be able to overcome that kind of criticism.

I insisted that if we built a small Habitat, the balance of the land on MacKay Pier had to be zoned for housing and commerical use so that after Expo the community could be completed. I could not envisage a hundred and sixty families being isolated there. So few people can't have a school, can't support shops – and if the National Harbours Board were to take it over and build warehouses next to it the thing would become a complete nightmare. I didn't care if the future extension would be designed as Habitat as long as people lived there. The zoning was agreed to. Then, after great inner deliberation, I decided to do it.

7   Further threats

But I did not give up completely. I still felt we had to build a project big enough to create large public areas below with an integrated commercial center because that was what Habitat was all about.

Instead of pursuing the idea of doing the ten-storey or twelve-storey section, I still attempted to keep the large rhomboids, twenty-two stories high. The minimum would be three rhomboids to support each other, and that meant twenty million dollars. I drew up a twenty-million-dollar scheme in two or three days of intensive work and went back to Churchill: "Well, we can do something, but it is going to be twenty million dollars."

Churchill spoke to a representative of the Treasury Board and called me half an hour later. He said: "Moshe, you just don't understand. It's eleven and one-half million dollars or nothing." Only then did the decision dawn on me in all its implications. I started to work on a modified scheme. I was given four weeks and a new design budget of forty-five thousand dollars to make a presentation of what could be done for eleven and one-half million.

The original design had two parts, a ten-storey section and a twenty-two-storey section where the commercial center was. What the government expected was that I would just do the ten-storey section and forget the other one.

I decided to place the building at the northern end of the pier because that's where the best view was. I redesigned it completely to create some notion of the public space that was in the original twenty-two-storey section. With the same modular box units, instead of cellular columns in inclined planes, I developed a cluster geometry. That was a basic change. Clusters of eight boxes would be piled one on top of another.

Once the actual construction budget was officially appropriated, the vultures really began to circle. I think the most dramatic example was the Y67 affair.

We had been in contact with a number of manufacturers and industries. Francon were sitting in on our job meetings as precasting contractors and advising us. We received word that the Camus Company, who are the largest prefabricated system builders in France, were considering extending their operations to Canada, and were very interested in looking at Habitat to see whether they could act as our precast contractors and help us technically. They hoped to use that as a kind of entrée to the market. We, of course, responded very favorably. Camus was a very large company, with a lot of experience in their kind of precasting.

A couple of months before the deadline for presenting the revised project to the government we had a phone call from their local representative, saying that Mr. Camus himself was arriving from Paris with his assistant, some general, and would like to meet with us to discuss participation in the project.

They all arrived, a very distinguished party, a great big tall general with a big mustache and Mr. Camus himself, two or three assistants and the local representative. We had asked Komendant to fly to Montreal especially for that meeting and to describe the progress of the work and the system we had in mind. They asked us to make available to them all our drawings, feasibility studies, cost estimates, the works, which we did. Everything. They said they would study it and come back to us about a month before the presentation had to be made and tell us in what way they could participate, help us, and act as contractors.

A few weeks passed by and we heard nothing. Then one day Eric Bell, of Community Development Consultants, came into the office and said he had heard rumors that Camus had commissioned local architects to design a scheme using their panel system and that they were making overtures to the government to dump Habitat and give them the budget to build their own so-called experimental project on the same piece of land, and because it was a conventional structure they would get more units per dollar than Habitat. I found the whole thing too fantastic to believe and dismissed it.

But a week later Eric Bell came back to report that Camus had offered to retain Andrews and Bell as their consultants to submit their design to the government to replace Habitat. I was shocked. What made it even worse was that instructions came down from Ottawa that the Camus submission was to be looked at very carefully. We heard that the French ambassador had made a special presentation to the Minister of Trade and Commerce. This coincided with a big political fight about the Caravelle and the DC9 aircraft. Air Canada was going to buy some short-range jets and pressure was being applied on behalf of the French Caravelle, even though economic analysis showed that the DC9 would be a superior plane for Air Canada. So there was a parallel situation in which diplomatic pressure with political overtones was being used.

Andrews and Bell found out that Camus were hoping to present their project in

Ottawa four or five days before our presentation was scheduled, and suggested we should move our deadline ten days ahead, to get to the government before Camus had a chance to make their presentation. That was pretty tricky, because we had already been working fourteen and fifteen hours a day, even Saturdays and Sundays. To move the deadline at the last minute would take an almost impossible effort. Nevertheless we decided to do it. We worked like dogs and got the presentation ready for the revised date.

Representatives of Central Mortgage, Expo, and Treasury Board came down to Montreal. I had a new model and new drawings. The meeting was in my office, in the open so all the staff could hear what was going on. The Ottawa people looked at it. It wasn't what they expected. They had expected a piece of the ten-storey building from the original scheme. They liked it. On October 28th, 1964 they told us to proceed with the plan for a hundred and fifty-eight units as they had seen it.

Three days later Camus made their presentation. It arrived in the form of an eleven by twelve leatherette-bound book, at least two and a half inches thick, with many dockets in it presenting the design, the system, the economics. It was very lavishly printed using the finest Swiss graphics, expensive paper, and fancy binding. The written portion of their report was a paraphrase of our feasibility study. The project was called Y67 (why indeed!); a series of apartment towers cantilevering outward in the shape of a Y gave the project its name. These apartment buildings were projected to run all the way down the MacKay Pier on the Habitat site. The architects were Papineau, Gérin-Lajoie, Le Blanc, a Montreal firm, who must have known that the project was being proposed for a site already approved for Habitat.

Shaw and Churchill handled it very carefully. They asked Tony Peters, Expo's project architect for Habitat, and his staff to make an evaluation of the proposal. Churchill called a meeting with Camus' architects and representatives and listened to the presentation. It was rejected after Tony wrote a comprehensive report on why it was thought to be inappropriate. The funniest part of it all came seven months later. Tony called me one day and said, "You know what we just received? A bill for a hundred thousand dollars from Camus."

Shortly after we got the go-ahead on the working drawings for Phase One, Peter Barott died of a heart attack. He was forty-two. He was the partner in David, Barott, Boulva who was working on the project. I was very fond of him.

We were hiring engineering consultants and discovered that many were quite skeptical about the building. We lost two or three along the way, and the one who did stay with us was questioning everything in a way that was detrimental to the progress of the job.

The difficulty with Komendant's concept was that there were three structural elements in the building: the boxes, which were load-bearing; the pedestrian streets which were also beams carrying both horizontal and vertical loads, earthquake and wind loads; the elevators and stair towers. The whole thing was one continuous, integrated, three-dimensional structure, technically known as an indeterminate structure. Loads are transmitted in complex patterns. Higher mathematics and limit design had to be used to determine what would really happen.

With a beam on two posts you know exactly how much load is coming onto each support. But here, we were not designing for a single condition because the structure did not behave as a simple structure. It was one of the most complex structures to analyze ever built. Komendant in his old-fashioned way did not use computers. We had difficulty in getting others to accept the validity of his computations or even to understand his approach, and since they were to share the responsibility it was no good having them say, "You can't do that." If one thought of it as a post and beam building, it really didn't work.

I realized that every building has to be submitted for a building permit, that probably the engineering department of the City of Montreal or Expo wouldn't be able to assess the structure, and that we were going to have a problem. I discussed it with Tony Peters and we proposed that Expo hire a special committee of distinguished engineers to review the building. There was Professor J. O. McCutcheon, the chairman of the civil engineering and applied mechanics department at McGill University; Professor G. K. Kani, a noted structural engineer from the University of Toronto; and a third member. They had one brief meeting with Komendant when he was doing his preliminary studies and two or three other meetings with his local collaborator. When the report came in it said that the building as designed would collapse. To make things more difficult, we were just about ready to move in with foundation drawings and complete them so that we could start calling bids. Expo was making commitments, e.g. we had ordered a crane because if we hadn't we wouldn't have got it on the site in time.

The report commented on Komendant and his collaborators and recommended that "competent" engineers be hired to handle the job. There were a number of criticisms: no expansion joints were provided; and *certainly* one could not make an earthquake analysis without an elaborate computer program, which would take months.

I read the report and said to Churchill, "If you give me that officially we will have no choice but to sue the committee for libel." I felt that even though not all the information had been available at the preliminary design stage, they had not asked questions; they had merely made a negative report on incomplete evidence. I could have understood if they had raised questions or wanted more information, but they just categorically said it wouldn't work. Churchill didn't give me the report. He wrote a letter to our engineers paraphrasing it, turning their statements into questions: "How do you intend to deal with earthquake design? How do you intend to handle expansion? Can you give us more information?"

This was the point where Habitat was closest to being called off. Many people in Expo opposed it. Gilles Sarault, Expo's chief engineer, was even refusing to sign the plans that were being produced. Politically it was becoming more and more difficult. The city was getting nervous about the criticism. It seemed as though everybody was saying Habitat would never be built – than a committee of the most distinguished engineers in the country says it won't even stand up.

Churchill said, "We have Komendant's word against these engineers, and Komendant obviously is a man with a world-wide reputation. What has he done in an earthquake zone?"

I said, "He has done the Salk Institute for Biological Studies, in San Diego."

"Who collaborated with him there?"

I named the firm.

He picked up the phone, got the firm's principal, told him the situation, what the committee was saying.

"How do you find Komendant? How do you consider his judgment? His ability to handle earthquake design?"

The answers satisfied Churchill. He said, "I want Komendant to answer my questions – and then we'll go ahead with it." Shaw made the decision with Churchill. The courage that took was remarkable.

The collaborating engineers were not producing drawings, and finally we had to replace them; Expo made them resign. Churchill and Shaw knew the Montreal firm of Monti, Lavoie, Nadon, and they were brought in. Monti spent three days, went over Komendant's computations, got on very well with him, wrote the report answering the professors' "questions," got the job, and off we went. By that time, we had already awarded the contract for the foundation on the basis of Komendant's preliminary structural drawings. For the rest of the job the contract stipulated that we would increase or decrease the payments according to fixed unit prices depending on how much concrete or steel was finally used.

Things were not settled with those professors for many months. The building was almost complete – one section was at full height – when Churchill thought that the matter should be officially closed. Monti was called in to meet them and said, "Well, gentlemen, it's up. I think that answers your report."

That was almost the last time Habitat hung in the balance.

As the project became more widely publicized a number of anti-Habitat crusaders emerged. By far the most vocal critic was Paul Trépanier, the mayor of the town of Granby and a former president of PQAA (the Province of Quebec Association of Architects). Trépanier's criticism intensifed when the working drawings started. The closer the project came to reality, the more intense his criticism became. He gave a series of speeches to service clubs and interviews to newspapers. The crescendo of his criticism was a speech to the Canadian Club in which he called for a Royal Commission to investigate why such an "Insane Project" – the headline in the papers said – was being supported by Expo and the government. They were subsidizing millionaires' housing, he said, at the taxpayers' expense. The papers had a heyday with headlines, and I must say that I was becoming increasingly irritated.

Expo's way of handling it was very wise. They had scheduled a press conference to announce the award of the construction contract to Anglin-Norcross. They moved it forward and, three days after Trépanier's great attack, simply announced that they had awarded a contract to build Habitat.

But I got quite upset and when reporters called to ask for my comments, I said at one point that I would have to look at what he said, but that it seemed to me I might sue him. They had a ball with that. Eventually, I decided not to, but I felt it was proper for me to write the president of PQAA, because the statutes of the Association at that time forbade an architect to criticize a colleague in public.

Really I felt the statute was wrong in the first place. I've been saying for years that as long as architects are prepared to act under their own names, they should be able to say whatever they wish about the work of another architect. So, I didn't want to refer to a statute I disagreed with and I simply asked if PQAA itself wanted to intervene in the case. I was given a negative answer. I now regret that I bothered writing PQAA or even commenting to the newspapers, but at the time I felt very threatened, because there was always a chance that Trépanier's criticism could have killed the project.

Before the bids were called we had estimated the job at twelve and one-half million dollars, slightly over the budget. We had a bet and everyone in the office put in a dollar – a total of forty dollars. I had a separate bet with the estimators and developers. I estimated it would come in at twelve million and the estimators themselves thought that it would be fifteen million. Some guesses went up to twenty-two million. I won both bets. It came in at slightly below twelve million dollars. There were three bids, Anglin-Norcross Quebec was lowest, followed by the Foundation Company a hundred thousand dollars higher, and a third bid of eighteen million dollars. That meant a revised budget of thirteen and one-half million including design. Had they come in any higher it would have killed the project. I knew the government would not go over thirteen and one-half million.

8   On the drawing board

The total package of drawings for Habitat was done in six months, between November 1964 and May 1965.

There were about two hundred and fifty architectural working drawings in the final set; at least an equal number of structural, mechanical, and electrical construction drawings; thousands of shop drawings; innumerable design sketches and studies.

The shop drawings had to be co-ordinated by us and checked by both the consultants and ourselves. Francon the precaster, alone, had four thousand, and there must have been at least two or three thousand more from the other subcontractors. Each one had to be submitted in sixteen copies to my office. In some cases we had to mark changes in red sixteen times and then return copies to Expo, to Anglin-Norcross, to the sub-contractors, and to all concerned.

These drawings are made by the manufacturer or contractor for something detailed by the architect. For example, we made working drawings of a window and the manufacturer made shop drawings of it which we had to check to make sure it conformed with our design. In the case of a shop drawing for heating ducts, the mechanical engineer had to make sure it conformed with his requirements, and we had to make sure it didn't conflict with the structural engineering drawings or with the architectural finishes.

When I left Expo I decided to stay in Place Ville Marie, where Expo had its offices. One wing of the thirty-eighth floor was unoccupied and I took it on a short-term lease, unpartitioned, and set up there. We had a very beautiful view of the site of Habitat. In a short time our office built up to about forty architects, draftsmen, and students. I insisted from the beginning that the engineers work with us in the same office, so even though we were separate firms they moved their Habitat staff right into the same office, and so did Community Development Consultants. We were all in one huge space, with a few partitioned offices within it.

97

The most important person on my staff was Dave Rinehart. He came from Philadelphia right at the beginning, while I was still employed by Expo.

The next group of people to join the office were Montrealers, mostly McGill graduates, some classmates and others I happened to know from school. Irwin Cleve, who was assistant chief architect with CMHC and was leaving them, joined the office, too. From David, Barott, Boulva the key person who became very important to the project was Jean-Eudes Guy. Dorice Walford, who wasn't as actively involved as Jean but sat in on our job meetings, was a great help. Then there were a number of young American architects, recent graduates, several of them attracted to the project from Philadelphia, who knew either Dave or me from our days there.

Doug Shadbolt recalled those days recently when introducing me at a lecture in Halifax: "A group of remarkably young people produced a remarkable set of drawings." I never thought of it that way until he said it, but it is an accurate statement. The office was very young. There were few experienced architects, myself included. I hadn't built a building before, nevertheless we produced what I have been told by several people was one of the best set of working drawings put together, in terms of accuracy, clarity of expression, and quality of detail.

It was during those working-drawing days that our son Oren was born.

One of my problems was that I was young and many of the people working for me were older, and the pressure of the schedule meant that I had to exercise considerable ruthlessness in making decisions. I was twenty-five when I left Expo and Dave was thirty-two. Irwin Cleve was in his late thirties, and the recent graduates were slightly younger than me. And that did create some tension. Although my inclination and my temperament is to hear out every proposal and discuss it until a conclusion is reached by consensus, there were many occasions when the mere pressure of time meant that I had to make a decision and just impose it. It was a painful process and a role I did not enjoy.

The landscape drawings are an example of that. There were many different and quite strong opinions about them in the office. Komendant, who wasn't involved with landscape at all but often volunteered opinions anyway, kept saying, "We must leave this structure pure and uncluttered. We must have grass only." Dave Rinehart and Lois Sherr, a friend working with the Expo landscape group, felt doubtful about my desire to make landscape and building one.

The MacKay Pier peninsula was man-made. It was fill, rock put there by man. It wasn't a rolling natural hill with grass and trees. There was no vegetation. I felt, therefore, that it ought to express the feeling of a man-made garden, and it was quite proper for the geometry of the building to extend into the landscape, so that the building would apparently stretch from the St. Lawrence River to the Montreal harbor, from one body of water to another. The retaining wall on the harbor side, the road, the terraces, the different levels, the building itself, the plaza, the spray ponds, the pools, and the wall along the river were all one structure and Habitat was part of it. I wanted plant-life to be a dynamic part of it too, changing through the year. In spring, certain terraces would be red; then those flowers would wither away and other terraces would become yellow; later other terraces would become blue – constantly changing patterns.

The arguments went on and on, and all the time the pressure to produce the drawings was growing. I would make sketches and because of the controversy people would not develop them. At one point I decided to sit down and draw it myself. I took a large role of paper and spent two days and a night drawing the whole thing up – every level, every terrace – and colored it with pastels to express the texture of planting, the grass, the flowers in each area. All this was drafted into working drawings and built as it was in the sketch.

On the whole the spirit in the office was incredibly good. People worked every day and every night, Saturday and Saturday night and Sunday night, for three or four months. I found the pressure to keep up with the two-fold job of running the office and working with people on their particular drawings and details so enormous that I couldn't find time to sit and think out basic questions. I got into the habit of coming into the office at four o'clock every morning, and after a while Dave started coming in early too. I would work on my own from four until nine, when everybody else came in, and then I would work with them or give them sketches that I had developed earlier in the morning. Dave and I would invariably stay until about eleven o'clock or midnight every night. We literally got by on four or five hours' sleep a night for a very long time.

It was not all smooth sailing. Here was a group of very devoted people, each giving a project all he had, all that was in him and each also in his particular way feeling possessive of the part on which he was working. Add to this the intensity of day after day and night after night of working together under severe pressure and our occasional family flare-ups were understandable.

Those who had more responsibility were in the most difficult situation. Dave Rinehart, Jean-Eudes Guy, Al Meyer, and Irwin Cleve were each responsible for certain areas. Al was in charge of developing the house plans, Jean of the specification and the material selection. Dave had all the public areas in the building – the streets and the elevators and so on. Irwin Cleve was in charge of detailing the interiors of the houses. Each had a number of younger people working with him.

Had the office been a highly regimented place with a clear hierarchy, the organization would have worked quite smoothly. I would have discussed each aspect of the building with the associates and they in turn would have worked with the groups responsible to them. But such a rigid hierarchy was contrary to the entire spirit of the office and individuals took more or less responsibility depending mostly on their temperament and initiative. I worked with everyone in the office, often to the great confusion of those who were responsible for the work in a particular area of the building. What I had learned from Lou Kahn was also becoming clearer, every detail was part of the whole and the success of the environment as a whole depended on all its parts. It was this lack of organizational hierarchy with its apparent inefficiency that made it possible for such a large group of people to work together and to produce something that had unity.

I suppose that these group dynamics are common, but for me it was a new experience and the source of much pain. In the case of Dave Rinehart there was a much more subtle relationship. Dave was older than me. I discussed ideas more with him than anybody else. He was I felt, the most creative man in the office. He was the one whose opinions I trusted more than any other architect I knew. All this made it tougher, because there was I in the limelight for what was coming to be known as a very important building.

I feel today that it was the assertion of our affection and our commitment to the project, the idea, that possessed us, that made it possible for us all to overcome problems and work together.

During those four or five months there was hardly time for any personal life. But after the excitement of the bids coming in and the construction starting, things loosened up a little. Once the construction was underway I went to India for three weeks at the invitation of the Indian government. Another very enjoyable experience was the Montreal International Film Festival competition for a fifty-second film on the theme Man and his World. The first prize was ten thousand dollars and there were nine silver medals. I was on a jury of five. The others were Pat Watson, the TV personality of *Seven Days;* Claude Jutra, the Montreal film maker; Geneviève Bujold, the actress; and Wolf Koenig of the National Film Board of Canada. We spent three days and three nights looking at the two hundred and sixty-five entries. It was, as Claude put it, instant friendship for all of us.

Then the Montreal Film Festival people did something very nice. They invited the ten top winners, who were from widely scattered parts of the world – a Russian, an Italian, a Japanese, a Czech, a couple of Canadians, a couple of Americans, an Indian, and an Englishman – and treated them and the jury to a weekend in the country. We went out to Sun Valley in the Laurentians in the middle of winter. There was wonderful wine and good food and sleigh rides and skidooing and walking in the snow. No movies. It was very nice. This was before the opening of Expo, and at that point life became very exciting in Montreal.

Confronting the system

The process of realization of a building environment, really slugging it out, is the final test of any idea.

When I look at theoretical new town plans, housing proposals, I'm very conscious of what they have yet to go through before becoming physical reality. An abstract concept can ignore the existence of gravity, rely on miracle materials or be unrelated to the realities of economics. Yet I can think of no other profession where realized concepts and academic proposals are compared and discussed as if they were one and the same thing.

The building of environment depends on a great number of people physically participating in its realization: contractors, laborers, craftsmen. Therefore all technical solutions and detailing have to be in the context of what these people can or cannot do. You're dependent on the organizational structure of the business world, the industries that supply material, what they're prepared to do, what risk they're prepared to take. You're dependent on government because the city and sometimes the province and even the federal department have to approve the drawings. When they grant a building permit, they're accepting part of the liability for it, they're saying: "This is sound and safe." You're dealing with the whole legislative bureaucracy and tradition. You must either work in the context of the existing legislation or change it; you must build in the context of building codes and zoning laws.

Codes are established to set standards but their original intent is often forgotten. The code may say that a concrete wall, in order to withstand a severe fire, should be a minimum of eight inches thick. If you can show that a four-inch wall of new design could do the same, then you have satisfied the intent of the code. But too often that does not mean that you will be permitted to build the thinner wall.

In many cases, the code is really protecting a particular union practice. The code may refuse PVC plastic piping and insist on copper or cast iron. That may have a lot to do with the lobby of the plumbing union, or for that matter the copper manufacturers who would lose a substantial number of man-hours or material sales if PVC piping were introduced. New York building practice is notorious for such rulings. Every plumbing connection is described by the code. Often it has less to do with the performance of the plumbing than with the way plumbers like to work. *Performance codes* are much more meaningful than codes where the performance is translated to data and the data become the statements of the law. We are a long way from establishing uniform and versatile performance codes on this continent.

Zoning, on the other hand, attempts to establish certain environmental standards for such things as daylight or the separation of land uses. As it deals with environment, it is much more susceptible to value judgment and is less precise in definition. That a building should resist hundred-mile-an-hour winds is a very definite statement, and it can therefore be assessed. How much daylight a house should have is a less tangible thing. Zoning laws tend to be vague. Often, as our values change, such laws become an obstruction.

For example, for years it was impossible to put a shop in a housing project in Canada because in the early part of the century it was considered that a commercial function would be a nuisance to the tenants. When the Jeanne Mance public housing project in Montreal was being built in 1960 it was a major battle for CMHC to get one little shop on the ground floor of one of the buildings. In contrast, health regulations may require that each room have a set minimum of window area, but these requirements are so minimal that they are not an effective guarantee of environmental quality.

Habitat had to challenge the system at each of these levels. It had to challenge industry, the practice of labor, the by-laws, and the state of the building art of the time.

Habitat is a collection of statements of intent. Very often the intent was not fulfilled, but suggested. We had certain concepts of how the mechanical services of a dwelling should function, for example, and we developed systems that approached that concept, only to find that circumstances put it beyond realization.

The modules were a major challenge. The building is made up of boxlike modules of identical size. The modules are factory products, and we grouped them in an intricate three-dimensional structure.

Establishing the size of the module was a long process. If it was to be the size of an entire dwelling, it would be too heavy to lift. Another disadvantage was that there would be very little flexibility in design; a module a quarter or a third of a house could be combined in many permutations to achieve a variety of house types. Next we investigated small modules, a room size, sixteen by sixteen; the problem there was that then we would need a large number of connections, and connections are where the money is; it would also increase the number of crane lifts. So we reached the conclusion that the module should be a complete one-bedroom house or one-half, one-third, or one-quarter of a larger house. That meant a module of about six hundred square feet.

What shape should it be? A square did not lend itself to grouping. If it was oblong in plan, modules could be connected in a variety of shapes, including two-storey houses. The shape should also ensure that the point of connection be standard, to simplify the preparation of drawings and erection procedures on the site.

We concluded that the plumbing should be contained in vertical cylindrical shafts, located outside the modules. This suggested the modules should overlap one another rather than fit flush, to create a continuous space for the pipes. It also suggested the size of the overlap – three feet six inches to accommodate a three-foot shaft. After considerable trial and error we established a three-foot-six-inch grid as the dimensioning matrix for the entire system.

It was essential that the box could be hoisted into place and left there safely in equilibrium even before being physically connected. So if one module was set crosswise on another, the center of gravity of the top one would be within the walls of the lower one. This meant that the length of the module had to be twice its width plus the overlaps.

In turn, the width had to be seventeen or eighteen feet in order to accommodate a stair running across the module from one floor to the other. Five of the three-foot-six grid units gave us a seventeen-foot-six module width. With an overlap of one grid unit we could have a length of eleven grid units, or thirty-eight feet, six inches. This gave an area of just over six hundred and seventy square feet, or about six hundred and forty square feet of floor area inside the walls. We considered this the minimum size for a one-bedroom house.

Those were the major considerations in setting up the grid, size, and proportions of the boxes. But the complexity of dealing with a building as a system is that one decision, such as the three-foot-six grid, affects every dimension in the building. It not only affects the size of mechanical shafts and the stability of the module during construction but also the size of rooms and the possible house plans; it affects the angle of inclination of the face of the structure, the placing of windows, the size of public spaces below, the size of gardens, everything.

I was aware even as we were fixing the grid and the module, that we were making some serious compromises. One was that since the dimensional system was for the outside of the boxes, the wall thicknesses had to be subtracted when we were dimensioning the inside of the house. That meant that the inside of the house was made up of a certain number of three-foot-six grids except at the outside walls, where it was three-foot-six minus the wall thickness. That threw everything off. We couldn't prefabricate the interior components to a fixed grid and still make them work everywhere. If partitions or floors were manufactured in three-foot-six panels they had to be chopped off at the edges of the box.

I was unable at the time to work out a dimensioning system that worked both inside and outside the house. Yet a comprehensive dimensional system is critical to the success of any building system. I think eventually one could find a system that works both inside and out, co-ordinating both structural and interior components.

Once we established the module there came the question of material. We thought about various plastics, fiberglass, and combinations of materials. But the plastics were too expensive, they were unpredictable technically, and above all, they melted at low temperatures. We considered steel too. Sheet metal had to be fire-proofed and, once fire-proofed, it became extremely costly and heavy. That led to concrete.

Concrete, unfortunately, is a very restricting material. It can take hardly any tension, it's relatively heavy and porous, and the most advanced methods had to be used in order to be able to construct a complex three-dimensional building at all.

Habitat's form, which was largely dictated by the relationship of houses and gardens, sunlight, and the desire to express the identity of the individual house within the group, was just possible in concrete, but it anticipates materials that are lighter, stronger in tension, have a watertight surface, and are easily moldable.

Working on Habitat I became increasingly aware of a basic shortcoming of the building industry. Its whole tradition is to build with what materials happen to be available. Every other industry defines its requirements and then develops the material best suited to the problem. They don't design an aircraft with steel just because they happen to have steel handy: if they come to the conclusion that they need a metal that's lighter, then they perfect the manufacturing of aluminum. When they discover that aluminum is going to melt at high supersonic speeds, they develop a material that has a greater heat resistance, like titanium. Dupont for example, came to the conclusion through market research that world resources of natural leather were very limited and that a synthetic material with the qualities of natural leather would be highly marketable. They poured in something like twenty-five million dollars over a period of several years to develop Corfam. Rocket nose-cones required a material that could resist very high temperatures and to that criterion Corning Glass developed Pyroceram.

I would say that as a rule industry, where it has the resources and organization, develops materials to meet a given specification. Fifty years ago, as Buckminster Fuller describes it in *Nine Chains to the Moon,* the tremendous demand for better weapons in World War I created the pressure to develop steel alloys that were harder and stronger than carbon steel. After the war they benefited the automobile and other industries. Where the pressure exists, an effort is made. But because of its organizational structure, its method of operating, and its fragmentation, the construction industry has neither the circumstances nor the resources to do the same and consequently has always used leftovers; it has used steel, aluminum, fiberglass after they were developed elsewhere. I don't think technologies are directly transferable from one industry to another. Each realm of manufacturing has its own specific needs. It can't just borrow – yet that's what the construction industry has been doing.

The material we needed for Habitat would have been about one fifth the weight of concrete, with a tensile strength double that of mild steel, so that you could hang twenty tons on a strip with an inch-square cross-section. It would have compressive strength and density where buckling is not a major design criterion, its relative lightness making its cross-section thick enough to give it that strength. Its lightness would also give it an insulation value equal, say, to foam plastic, and yet it would be completely moldable by simple processes. Its skin would be impermeable to water. I am not describing a "miracle" material. This material exists even today in the laboratory, in the hydrocarbon family of polymeric materials. All we have to do is find a way to manufacture it cheaply.

But in 1964, the decision was that Habitat had to be concrete. It was a 1964 decision. Today I am building in Puerto Rico with walls half the thickness of the Habitat walls. Even with regular concrete there is considerable latitude to the state of the building art. This is only six years later – which gives some idea of the pace at which building practice can change.

The modular boxes had to be as light as possible. The fire code required reinforcing steel to be covered with at least two inches of concrete to give it a four-hour fire rating and that suggested a five-inch wall if it was to be all concrete. In the first discussions with Dr. Komendant and the other engineers, the precasters insisted that they couldn't pour ten-foot-high walls five inches thick with the kind of reinforcing we had in there. They feared the concrete wouldn't go to the bottom, that it would leave great pockets of honeycombing, but they eventually found that they were able to do it. Four years ago we were told we couldn't do five-inch walls; today we're being told we can't do two-inch walls. The fact that we've done both is all an expression of the immobility of the building industry.

The contractor naturally reacts by saying "No" because he's afraid to lose money. Usually he's on a lump sum fee. He looks at a drawing that calls for five-inch walls, and he usually has neither resources nor time to test it in the field. The trade unions resist change because they always think in terms of the number of hours of work for their particular trade. If you could connect plumbing parts with a magic joint it would cut the number of man-hours for plumbers by one-half or one-third, and so the unions resist. In contrast, I don't think there are many examples where the auto workers' unions have had a drag effect on how cars were to be made. Yet there are dozens of examples where construction procedures were dictated by the unions without regard for economy.

The modular boxes are tied to each other with steel rods, which being under tension, put the concrete under compression. Robert Shaw has a nice description for post-tensioned concrete. He compares it to the toy dolls that stand erect when you pull a cord and flop down when the cord is loose. The tension in the cord keeps the doll together and upright. This is basically how Habitat stands up; except that it is even more complex since each pair of boxes is post-tensioned to act that way rather than all the boxes being tied to each other by one continuous tension cord.

As all these major decisions were being made, the Habitat team was being further built up. I considered that the architects, the engineers, the technicians, those that industry assigned to the job, ought to be working in the same place. I felt you couldn't separate the process, and I succeeded in getting all of them to agree to work in my office. The mechanical and structural engineers, the representatives of the contractors, bathroom and partition manufacturers, actually came to the office and worked with us. There were close to a hundred people in one room. I doubt such a thing had ever been done before on a housing project.

But here too, in our relationship with industry, we were inhibited by accepted practice. The problem with calling public bids is that no one is prepared to risk doing work or research before he gets the job. The result is that when designing the products for which you're going to call bids you don't have the benefit of the know-how of the man who's going to make that product.

We circumvented this in two ways. On certain components I was able to get help from industry on a strictly voluntary basis. The precasters, for instance, sat in on our job meetings every Monday for several months before the job went out for public bids (luckily for them and us they were lowest bidder). This in itself was unprecedented and largely due to the circumstances of Expo. Secondly, we short-circuited things by modifying the bid procedures. Instead of drawing a product in great detail and then calling for bids, we described the product in terms of what it had to do and its general characteristics. We said a successful bidder should name the price for which he could both research and manufacture the product. The detailed design we would develop jointly after he had the contract.

From the outset I had hoped to have the bathroom, kitchen and partitioning system as pre-manufactured components. Fuller designed a prefabricated bathroom in the thirties for his Dymaxion house, and there had been attempts at prefabricated kitchens, but none had been commercially produced. The Habitat components, I felt, must conform with codes, or a revised code, and had to be within industry's capabilities.

The bathroom had to come as a complete room. We rejected metal because we realized the tooling cost would not be realistic for a hundred and sixty units. Eventually we concluded that gel-coat fiberglass was the best material. Expo suggested to Fiberglas Canada that they ought to contribute toward the research costs. Expo did not intend to pay more than the cost of a conventional bathroom and considered the difference should be covered by Fiberglas Canada because of the promotion the bathroom and their material would get. The president of Fiberglas Canada was very nervous about the whole affair. He was not convinced his material was good enough for bathrooms and several weeks elapsed before we could convince him that it was. We sent the material to the National Research Council of Canada and had them carry out extensive tests on the wear that would be expected over a twenty-year period. We determined that local damage by burning or breaking could be patched the way fiberglass boats and cars are fixed. And we were prepared to take a certain amount of risk.

We got only one bid for bathrooms, from Reff Plastics and Tielemans in joint venture. Reff Plastics were working on their own fiberglass bathroom at the time, by a happy coincidence. Tielemans had made various large fiberglass elements but not bathrooms. Before bids were called, Fiberglas Canada had finally said they would contribute a hundred thousand dollars to the project. Once the bid was in however, they went back on the informal agreement. It looked as if they were about to kill "Operation Bathroom," a project that we thought might revolutionize the market for their product. In the end they made a compromise offer to Expo of thirty thousand dollars. The bathroom was about to be abandoned when I went to Churchill and told him what was happening. The bathroom demonstrated the possibility of pre-manufacturing large interior components into a modular system, I said, and if we resorted to conventional bits and pieces – tubs and sinks and tile and cabinets – we would kill the demonstration of an industrialized building process. Churchill and Shaw met and the next day the budget was increased to fill the gap left by Fiberglas' reversal.

Once the bathroom contract was awarded, Reff Plastics proceeded with the technical drawings from which the molds were to be made. This was for me one of the most rewarding experiences of Habitat. We spent hours together going over the drawing. I was absorbing the background and experience of manufacturing with fiberglass. The mold – the negative form of the bathroom – was made by hand out of wood, plastic laminate and fiberglass. The gel-coat and fiberglass were sprayed on and then the bathroom popped off. I went down to Toronto once a week as the master mold was being made. Robert Zoebelein of Reff Plastics and I would get into the tub, sit in it to see if it was comfortable, make the soap dish, change our minds, remold it, fill it up, carve it out, try the towels. It was a trial-and-error process finally resulting in a room that appeared to be the kind of bathroom we wanted. After Expo, Zoebelein modified the bathroom to overcome the difficulty of shipping it. He changed it from two, to three sections that fit into one another so that it could be shipped in a small package. He put it on the market for something like five hundred and sixty dollars – one of the first success stories from Habitat! As the ministers and other officials came down from Ottawa criticizing the money wasted at Expo, we could retort that we had put a new Canadian product on the market. A year later the Crane Company bought out Reff Plastics and put the fiberglass bathroom on its international marketing network.

Following the same procedures, we described the kind of kitchen we wanted and how it should function. Again we set a maximum: the kitchens could not exceed one thousand dollars each. We knew that this couldn't be done and that only an industry that was prepared to contribute some of its own funds could bid. One corporation was prepared to do it: Frigidaire, a subsidiary of General Motors. They produced a very sophisticated kitchen, through relatively conventional in its manufacturing. I was told they put two hundred thousand dollars of their own funds into the program. Bud Andrews and I set the strategy for this project: to convince Frigidaire that the Habitat kitchen could be the means of going from the appliance business into the kitchen business. We met with the president of Frigidaire Canada and his chief engineer. As a result of a number of meetings with the technical staff, there was enthusiastic response, leading to Frigidaire's bid and our successful collaboration with them. It will be interesting to see now whether Frigidaire follows up and starts manufacturing whole kitchens for general consumption.

The importance of Frigidaire's decision to sponsor the kitchen cannot be underestimated. As a result of their public support, Habitat acquired a certain respectability with people in and outside of Expo who, until then, were very skeptical. If General Motors was prepared to put a quarter of a million dollars into this project as their participation in Expo, the project was obviously respectable.

When the time came to design the mechanical service shafts, my first sketches were for a metal shaft. Since the bids we received were over the budget, we decided to try out fiberglass. Now I was able to go to Reff Plastics, who already had the bathroom contract. We spent several evenings discussing the problem. They developed a system at a third the cost of the metal bids. We then called for bids, and of course they got the job.

What I learned in these ventures was the wealth of experience, the whole world of possibilities, that arises when you work with the people who make the product. Designing that shaft or the bathroom with the people who understood all the subtleties of making it was a completely different process from sitting in my office with a piece of paper and thinking what a bathroom should be, ignoring the potential of industry. It was a unique relationship and it produced a different kind of design. Habitat at its best was produced from such relation-ships. It convinced me that the set-up in which the architect is independent of the manufacturing process is totally obsolete.

10   Houses from factories

While we were designing the Habitat interiors I flew down to Toronto to see the Frigidaire assembly line. Since Frigidaire were going to build the Habitat kitchens they wanted me to see the way they should be assembled so this could be taken into account in the design.

It was enlightening. Here was a relatively complex product, a refrigerator, and yet it was assembled simply with few steps. The installing of a particular piece of insulation piping or wiring was timed to the second. Just compare that with a building site! Imagine an automobile assembly line where each step along the line is undertaken by a different company with its own financial interest and separate labor union! I'm convinced that no one is going to be able to mass-produce a house until the entire process is under a single corporate structure, and probably a single union too. Yet factory-made mass-produced housing is the magic word being whispered as the key to salvation.

Present practice is impossible. The client asks an architect to design something specifically for him. In making drawings the architect will specify various components out of catalogues. He is nearly always restricted to elements that are already manufactured. Then the contractor, who has usually had nothing to do with the design process, examines the drawings and makes his bid. Industry supplies raw materials and components and has little contact with the contractor. The various building material manufacturers make their components totally independently of each other. They do not develop a product with an overall view of the complex it goes into. It is an absurd industry, inefficient in comparison with any other area of manufacturing. The design process is done over and over again; the architect has to invent the wheel every time. The contractor, on the other hand, cannot put his own experience into the design process; he gets a set of drawings as a *fait accompli.*

From the time I started working on my thesis, I felt that the whole construction process had to be put into the factory, with all that implies. I studied what was

111

considered in Europe to be industrialized housing. All their systems in 1959 and 1960 were based on panel construction. The walls, floors, and ceilings of a house were manufactured in a factory. The rest of the building was more or less conventionally finished. This seemed a limited system, since even if you could perform a miracle and produce the shell at no cost at all, all you were doing was cutting the construction cost by twenty-five per cent because seventy-five per cent of the house isn't in the shell.

I concluded, any system that didn't permit you to take seventy-five per cent into the factory was automatically obsolete. I also felt that the limits on these systems forced the architect to produce a vertically stacked cellular beehive of an apartment building. All the components met at corners, and corners are always the weakest point in the structure. Only in the U.S.S.R. was there further experimentation: instead of prefabricating panels, they were prefabricating whole rooms.

So I came to the conclusion, as others have, that in order to take that seventy-five per cent into the factory, you had to deal not with panels but with volumes of space. You had to prefabricate cells of space in the factory, and put your mechanical services, plumbing, bathrooms, whatever else there was, into them in an assembly line procedure. You would then assemble the modules on site and, if connections were simple, you would have a ninety-five-per-cent-factory-produced building. This was the first very important implication of making houses in a factory.

It seems to me that dissection into space cells is going to be the single most important change in the building process in the next twenty or thirty years. It will be necessary to rethink much of the building that makes the city in terms of space cells.

Industrializing building is, however, much more than prefabrication; essentially it is a reorganization of relationships. In the automobile industry, design and construction, research, marketing, and servicing are an integrated process within a single operational structure. The group of people who design the car also design (at the same time) the machinery that makes the car. The quantities involved are such that the company can afford to build machinery to make the particular product. The design of a window, the design of the gaskets for the window, the design of the steel door the window goes into, are all done simultaneously, so they are really designing particular components for a very specific context, in a sense, a closed system. Then, since the automobile company is involved with servicing and marketing too, the designers must also consider operational economy. The large automobile companies can afford to spend millions of dollars – maybe ten thousand per cent of the sale price of the individual product – designing a car that will sell for a few thousand dollars. (Pre-manufacturing costs for particular models have been quoted at anything from seventy to two hundred million dollars.) Conversely the architect's fee is six per cent of the sale price, even though a building is so much more complex than a car.

One of the most critical reasons for reorganizing the industry is to create a capability for research.

Other industries have the ability, once they have decided to manufacture a product, to build prototypes, and test and improve them before they go on the assembly line. The British and French aircraft companies spent two billion dollars on development of the Concorde supersonic transport over a period of many years before manufacturing it. The U.S. expects to spend five billion dollars on its SST. But, if you suggested spending that kind of money building and testing prototype communities (you could build one prototype community in every state and every province on this continent for five billion dollars) people would think you were "unrealistic."

The design cost of Habitat, two million dollars, is building research. In a way the whole cost of design *and* construction, twenty million dollars, should be considered research. Just as the car manufacturers hand-make a test model so Habitat was a hand-made prototype of what eventually could go on a mechanized assembly line. Habitat was more hand-made than even a conventional building. We were following a process of trial and error, trying things out and changing them in the building. The contractor of Habitat estimated that whereas the efficiency of a car assembly line is eighty per cent in terms of the workers' productive time versus idle time, and the efficiency on the average construction job is thirty to forty per cent, on Habitat it was ten per cent.

I do not believe that careful pre-planning would have prevented that amount of wasted time. Most of the time we were learning lessons, not making mistakes. We were learning things that could not have been predicted without physically doing them, for real, in full size. We were stretching the existing state of the building art far beyond its accepted capabilities. For these lessons the Canadian taxpayers paid twenty million dollars.

Building Habitat highlighted the problems of industrializing the construction industry. Construction is one of the few industries that developed before the rise of modern technology. The automobile and aircraft industries developed their own organizational structures as they evolved with that technology.

In a sense, building Habitat was like trying to have an assembly line without the organizational structure of mass-production industry – we proved it couldn't be done. We were successful only in fragments. For example, forty years ago Buckminster Fuller pointed out that a bathroom was made up of five hundred different bits and pieces of pipe and tile and hardware, assembled by a number of people over a period of three to four days, yet the whole bathroom done in one single molding of one material, in five per cent of the time, could eliminate most of the labor and be a superior product without joints. Habitat's bathrooms were a belated realization of Fuller's statement.

It is dangerous to underestimate the difficulties of introducing mass-production, closed-system techniques into housing. A house is much more complex than an aircraft. An aircraft can be clearly defined in terms of physical performance. Passenger comfort is a minor consideration compared with the plane's needed ability to fly at certain speeds for certain costs and to land and take off on available runways. A house is a physical problem, plus a complex social problem, plus a complex psychological problem. A house has to be publicly accepted. It has to have what a real estate man would call "marketability." This basically means it has to satisfy certain requirements not physically definable. These requirements are also dynamic, and therefore less predictable. You could design a complete housing system and find that no one wanted to live in it. Therefore, there is great risk in investing two or three hundred million dollars in a housing system at present; which suggests that the risks should be shared by the tax payer, as they are in space and other research.

Another consideration is that aircraft or cars or appliances or typewriters are relatively compact. The price per cubic foot is relatively high. That means that you can manufacture typewriters in one place in the United States and ship them throughout the world without shipping costs becoming an appreciable portion of the total cost. Housing is much cheaper per cubic foot. A house which has a volume of ten thousand cubic feet may cost twenty thousand dollars, or two dollars a cubic foot. A car with a volume of five hundred cubic feet may cost three thousand dollars, or six dollars a cubic foot.

To take the extremes, there is maybe ten thousand to one hundred thousand times more value to the material per cubic foot in a satellite or a computer than there is in a car; and there is less per cubic foot in the construction of a street or a dam than in housing. Since shipping air is extremely expensive, the shipping costs become a much more critical factor in housing.

You probably could not produce a total housing product in a single location in the United States or Canada and distribute it throughout the continent because shipping costs would be too high. On the other hand, I should think you could manufacture eighty per cent of the house (in terms of cost) in centralized plants on a continental basis – bathrooms, kitchens, electrical systems, heating and cooling systems, everything but the shell – and distribute nationally, just as the car people make their ball bearings in Puerto Rico and all their engines in Detroit. You could manufacture the shells in, say, five locations on the continent and under today's market conditions distribute them within a radius of a thousand miles if you were using relatively light materials, maybe five hundred miles using heavier ones.

These two substantial differences between housing and most other industries explain why private enterprise up to now has not taken the business risk of tooling up for industrialized housing, and illustrate one of the chief problems they will face once they do.

If we apply factory efficiencies to the construction industry, the financial relationship between owner, designer, manufacturer, and contractor must also change. It has to be integrated, made into a single entity. I see no way in which meaningful technical advances can be made unless total integration takes place. You can't deal with thirty different labor unions on a single assembly line, yet that's what we were trying to do in Habitat. The implications are clear: The obvious, even if not the safest, North American solution is for the great corporations, which are already involved in making everything from space ships to toasters, to start making buildings.

If we could achieve this integration, the architect, who up to now has acted as an ivory-towered prima donna making sketches that the contractor will hopefully transform into a building, would become part of a much greater entity. Architects today are certainly resisting any such change. But I'm afraid they are going to be gradually pushed out of the picture. Today, architects in North America design only twenty per cent of all buildings. If they persist in their attitude this percentage will dwindle until only the odd museum and concert hall will be architect-designed. A new profession of industrial building designers will be created by the great corporations.

One thing that frightens most of us architects is the difficulty of preserving identity and authority in the new team. But I don't think we have any choice. This is what differentiates Buckminster Fuller from the architectural establishment of today: Half a century ago Fuller made the link between environment, technology, and industrialization. He stated in clear terms that if we use technology we will be able to provide more for more people using less material. Since this is what we are after, then we ought to use technology to industrialize the methods by which we build our environment. In contrast, Philip Johnson expressing a common view, could say to me in 1967: "I don't give a damn about technology, I'm interested in space." But when he says that, it seems to me, he's also saying that his interest in the environment is in creating certain isolated buildings of as good a quality as he can, but not in making that solution available to everybody. The difference in attitude is one of conscience or politics.

Technology today means mass production, the assembly line, large-scale organization, corporate structure – whether it's in Russia or the United States. It means automation. It means integrated production. In the field of environment, it also means a tremendous threat to human identity and aspirations. Not only architects, but the public too, are terrified of it.

People recognize that our technology basically means doing things in great numbers, which means repetition, which implies the kind of organization that operates on centralized decisions. Nothing more powerfully symbolizes the conflict between the individual and a centralized, numerically-oriented process than the concern with environment. The fear is that the environment will become stereotyped, repetitive, monotonous, overwhelming – a place where the individual will feel that he has lost his identity or, even more serious, has lost control. People make the link between mass production and monotony, even further discouraging the industrialist from going into mass-produced housing.

In fact, I think the public is right to be frightened of industrialization and all that comes with it. Russia is an example of what can happen when industrialization takes place. Building has been put into the factory, and because there is a lack of understanding or concern for the environmental problems that are caused by repetition, the Russians are creating a deadly monotonous Kafkaesque soulless environment.

Suppose housing were industrialized overnight, and a great new corporation called General Housing Corporation started making houses, with design departments to slather form over the utilitarian chassis – the way they make cars now. How would an ad for houses read in 1982, say in *Life* magazine?

Introducing the new Ranchera	Featuring, for 1982, touch-wrist lighting (you touch your wrist and the lights go on)
	the new aerolite finish, gold inside and outside
	hermetically sealed to filter poisonous smoke in the air (you can now remove your gas mask when entering the home)
	requires no daylight whatsoever – all the walls glow
A new feature	dial-view – select your own view! project it on the walls!
	Infra-blue automatic cooking, a new kitchen by Fisher.
Special bonus	With each house comes a special bonus of a one-year supply of pre-cooked food for the whole family, six menu selections to choose from.

Or, at the other extreme, we could read in the Washington *Post* in 1982:

Notice TW 6715, Department of Housing and Urban Development

Department of Housing announces that all heads of families born between January 1, 1952 and January 1, 1962 within the income range of $8,450 to $10,740 are now eligible to receive Dwelling Types H, J, or K which are available in zones B1, B2, and C. Applicants must fill in six copies of Form Number HUP 36.968: DC 16/54. The Department also announces that families of category XP14 who are living in Unit Types S, U, and V which were distributed in 1974 may now apply for installation of new washing-drying machines. Applications . . .

That is equally frightening. We already have examples of both sorts of announcement so we can't afford to laugh at them too much. I'm sure you could open up some government gazette in Eastern Europe and find a similar notice; and if we look at TV or magazine advertising in North America today and project those ads into housing, my examples do not exaggerate.

The real issues of the environment as we see them today would no longer be issues. We would not bother trying to organize a city plan that allowed every house to have daylight, we would avoid the issue by creating houses that need none. We wouldn't bother with pollution, we would avoid the issue by creating a hermetically sealed environment. Technology is process and is only the means to an end; it is no guarantee of anything.

If Habitat went on for five miles it would become intolerable, because unless other scales or orders of organization were introduced to give a hierarchy we would lose our sense of location and identity, our sense of orientation, which is the most essential part of any environment. What frightened me about the modern parts of Moscow was the lack of varying rhythm, the fact that you have a series of identical buildings repeating indefinitely in a neutral landscape. You never know where you are. You always seem to be in the same place. You have to rely on numbers and signs to find your way.

Without the introduction of a larger scale of organization Habitat would be no different from Moscow. This hierarchy is created by the interweaving of open and built-up space, by the transportation systems, the varying mixture of land uses. Rhythm is the essential ingredient of a sense of location. If we removed the black keys from the piano, the pianist wouldn't know where to put his hands. Architecture today tends to ignore rhythm, or rather has a 11111 rhythm. Curtain walls, suburbs, modular partitions, much of contemporary architecture is 1 1 1 1 1, a repetitive beat giving no sense of location. In suburbs, we try to create identification by superficial changes to make up for the monotony, whereas in the Greek village they didn't have to paint every house a different color, people recognized their own houses because difference was the result of complex forms.

117

The challenge of today is to understand the problems our technology introduces in the environment – what Aldo van Eyck calls the problems of the architecture of numbers, and what R. M. Schindler was talking about when he said that in architecture one plus one is not two but three. Only an understanding of the issue can reduce the threat. And there is no use rejecting new technology in building; we have no choice, any more than we had a choice in industrializing agriculture. The only choice there, was between famine or plenty: the choice here is between a decent shelter or no shelter. Are we going to have an environment fit for human beings or mass dehumanization of environment leading to a regression of our species?

Habitat tries to show that it is possible to have an environment that is not monotonous, one that has the possibility of identity and of variety, choice and spatial richness, and yet at the same time the use of repetitive mass-produced systems. For me that is where Habitat has been most successful. The fact that the actual components in Habitat were hand-made is irrelevant in the face of the demonstration that a few repetitive components could be assembled to form a variety of houses and community spaces, the kind of environment that people normally associate with the non-industrialized, handcrafted, vernacular village.

People visiting Habitat were reminded of a Mediterranean village. That association was not rooted in formalism; it is generic in nature. The typical Aegean hill villages, the Arab hill towns, or the Indian pueblos are true building systems. They consist of a vocabulary of repetitive components – for example, the Arab village with its cubical room, dome, vault, and court. These components are manipulated by the individual who builds his own house. The houses are grouped along alleys and streets in harmony with the site. Habitat is in the tradition of spontaneous self-made environments, the beginnings of a contemporary vernacular.

Making it work

Once Habitat started breaking the housing industry's rules and conventions, every aspect of the process of building seemed to require rethinking. Some of the products and details we developed were needed to make Habitat work and some were done to demonstrate what we meant by a pre-manufactured factory component.

One of the problems of piling up boxes in a complex three-dimensional pattern is the plumbing. In conventional building each fixture has a vent to the atmosphere to eliminate the vacuum that is created when the water is sucked out of the toilet, tub, or sink. These vents are traditionally carried to the roof, where the odor is dissipated. If we had used this conventional method little pipes would have stuck up in people's gardens and vented the stink of the neighbor below. We asked our mechanical engineers, Huza-Thibault and Nicholas Fodor, to tackle the problem; they suggested Sovent, a system that had been developed in Switzerland. It had never been used but its inventors claimed it could eliminate the need for a vent. It is a funnel-shaped piece of pipe that stirs up the water as it goes down the drain and mixes it with air so that it does not create a vacuum in the trap. We ordered one from Switzerland and, after considerable testing, convinced the City of Montreal that it was worth a try, and they amended the code to permit its use, on condition that we provide reserve systems should Sovent fail. The potential application of Sovent goes beyond Habitat, of course. It would be very attractive even for a vertically stacked apartment building since it would save one complete pipe run. Ironically, the Copper Pipe Manufacturing Institute in the United States recently bought the Sovent patent and now permits its use only in projects where the entire plumbing system is copper.

Another question was the heating-cooling system. My initial thought was that each house should have its own self-contained heating and cooling plant. This would emphasize the feeling of independence. We found a system that appropriately met that principle. It's called Frigistor, a patented system of thermocouples or thermo-electric semi-conductors. It had been used before for heating and cooling nuclear submarines. A Frigistor is a group of sandwiched coated metal plates; if you run a DC current in one direction it heats, if you reverse the current it cools. With a single fan and no other moving part, it air-conditions or heats the whole house. It also acts as a heat pump, absorbing heat from the cold atmosphere and exhausting it into the house, making it efficient in power consumption compared with other electric heating systems. Borg-Warner Corporation of the United States owned the rights, and its Canadian subsidiary built a full-size demonstration mock-up. We were all set to use it when the project was reduced from a thousand units to a hundred and sixty and tooling-cost amortization made it uneconomical.

The alternative we developed was a relatively conventional system. A fan coil unit in each module receives either chilled water or hot water from the central plant. To eliminate the typical radiator or large grille in the ceiling or floor for supplying the hot or chilled air, we devised a very thin half-inch slot as a continuous element around the edge of the room. One section was the air supply and the other was the return. It is flush with the floor and quite inconspicuous in the room.

The other innovation was in the central cooling plant. Normally one circulates water that heats up during the air-conditioning process. This heat has to be dissipated, usually in a cooling tower on the top of the building where water sprays are cooled by a fan. It occurred to me that cooling was potentially a much more attractive thing than just a big slatted box full of water on the roof. It could come to life in the landscape. Children could play in it. We suggested to the mechanical engineers that a series of pools with fountain sprays designed to lose heat through evaporation could replace the cooling tower. They worked pretty hard at it and developed a system that has functioned successfully. We placed the pools under the inclined slope of the building in an area that is shaded all afternoon. It was a pleasure during Expo to see hundreds of visitors cooling their feet in them.

The upper-level pedestrian streets introduced a series of problems, some conceptual and some technical. The first decision we had to make was whether it should be a heated indoor space or open to the weather. The attractions of a heated space in the Canadian climate were obvious but so were the problems. An enclosed street would have to be ventilated thoroughly if we were to avoid accumulating odors from all the different houses. Also, if it were mostly glazed it would become a hot house in summer and would require a tremendous amount of heat in winter. All these factors tended to make it more and more like a corridor and less a street. My own feelings were that we should accept the fact that it was a street and ought to be outdoors, with the proviso that it should not at any time be less comfortable than walking at ground level on a street with, say, two-storey houses on either side.

It was difficult however, to predict air movement around such a complex three-dimensional structure by the river, and I did not feel that we could leave such a critical thing to chance. There are a number of places in Montreal where the mass of a building creates critical wind tunnels: one is next to the Sun Life Building, another is on the plaza of Place Ville-Marie where at one point wind velocity is so high that in winter it is practically impossible to cross. The invisible behavior of air around a building is as critical to the success of the environment as adequate light, but aerodynamic environmental engineers do not seem to exist. In our search, we approached the aerodynamics laboratory at McGill University where one member of the faculty, George Fekete, became interested and was willing to take on a thorough aerodynamic study of the building. I convinced Expo to award him a contract as consultant.

Professor Fekete's study was in three parts. The first was to establish how air would behave around the building generally, in terms of comfort on the plaza, in the individual gardens, in the houses when one opened a window. The second was to find exactly what conditions would occur on the pedestrian streets, to measure the wind velocity on them in relation to some given standard of acceptable comfort, and to develop with us a street shelter design that would deflect and direct the winds so that the street met that comfort standard. The third was to predict through model studies how snow would settle on the building so that we could work backward and provide for built-in snow-melting in public circulation areas.

The first part of the study showed that the inclined structure and the openings within the mass of the building decreased the build up of pressure and made conditions in the gardens and on the plaza relatively comfortable. Through Fekete's studies we discovered that a slot at the bottom of the railings in the gardens greatly decreased turbulence and incidentally reduced the accumulation of snow. (At the end of winter there was hardly one terrace in Habitat that had more than a few inches of snow, as compared with two feet on the roof terrace of my apartment on Pine Avenue.) We made a wood model of the building, three feet square, which was put into the largest wind tunnel at McGill, and a smaller model that could be put in the smoke tunnel, where you could see – not just measure, but see – what was happening to the air.

No standards of acceptable comfort existed, so we had to set our own. We picked a typical residential street with two- and three-storey townhouses in Westmount. Fekete measured the wind velocity and compared it with the wind velocity a hundred feet in the air at Montreal's Dorval Airport, a standard aerodynamic measure. He found that the wind velocity on the street was about twenty per cent of what it was a hundred feet in the air. We then set that as the criterion for comfort. If winds high in the air were blowing at forty miles an hour there would be an eight-mile-an-hour wind along the street; at one hundred it would be twenty. Habitat streets should give equal protection. We kept modifying the shape and location of the plastic street shelters until we achieved the same twenty per cent of wind velocity a hundred feet in the air, along the entire street. Fekete's studies influenced the shape of the shelter, which was designed to deflect the winds in the least turbulent pattern.

Finally, he did a snow-settlement study, sprinkling the model with particles under different wind conditions to find where they would settle. From that information we located our snow-melting system. All public circulation areas within the building were to be automatically cleared of snow by electric heating. After the building was up, the studies proved to have been surprisingly accurate.

Almost always technical problems were the result of a conceptual attitude.

I had always felt that plant life was an integral part of the environment of the streets and the gardens. But to actually achieve that, posed technical problems. Plants within a structure in two feet of earth would dry up very quickly. Three or four days without rain would kill them. Our landscape consultants told us that it wasn't the freezing but the evaporation of moisture from earth that kills plants in the fall and early spring. It appeared that if plant life was to be an integral part of the three-dimensional environment it had to be self-sustaining. You could not rely on people to water the plants, certainly not in the public areas and not even in the private gardens. So the idea of an irrigation system was born, where plant life in the entire building would be automatically irrigated and fertilized.

The resistance to this idea was overwhelming. For some reason it became the symbol of extreme luxury. The whole system cost thirty thousand dollars, about two hundred dollars for each house, and yet every time Expo had a meeting to try and cut things out of Habitat and save money, the irrigation system was inevitably a target. I argued that in the broadest sense plant life is essential to survival; it is the symbol of ecological balance. Hence it has a much deeper significance to us, a deep psychic significance, which must be respected.

The early twentieth century industrial city, which virtually eliminated plant life, is only a temporary nightmare. Even though the nature of plant life in the city is quite different from that in the open country, it has its rightful place. In a typical Mexican town like Taxco, plant life is integrated with the buildings. It gives color and shade and texture to the town. In the industrial city we have eliminated soil by massive paving and construction. Now as the city becomes three-dimensional, as we build it up on many levels, we create a new kind of environment where the plant can exist only if man-made structures make a place for it. A window facing the sun can be shaded with a venetian blind but it can also be shaded with a tree or a vine. The vine very obligingly will shed its leaves in winter to let the sun come in when it's needed and clothe itself with leaves to shade the window in summer. I think that is a superior way of shading a window.

The detailing of a building is an inseparable aspect of design. For the traditional forms of construction, accepted ways of doing things have been developed over the years: a method for terminating a pitched roof on a brick wall, a method for inserting a window in a brick opening, a way of making a sill or mullion in wood. But in Habitat, all these had to be considered from first principles. Each detail – a window, waterproofing and flashing, terrace paving – had to be thought of in terms of its performance, in terms of its logistics in the construction procedure, and in terms of its ability to perpetuate the total concept.

Should the window frames be cast in the concrete? What material should they be made of? How should they operate? I thought the window frame should be invisible. The important thing is that you have an opening in the wall which you want to look out of. The wall surface should stop and the glass should take over. We wanted to embed the frame in the concrete, yet we were designing for great temperature differentials: twenty below zero in winter and ninety above in summer. A regular metal window would sweat, wood required heavy sections. We decided to explore the possibility of using a plastic in combination with metal. With the co-operation of a window manufacturer we developed a whole series of double-hung windows and sliding doors of Geon plastic and aluminum.

The windows appear to be cut into the boxes at random but in fact their location is systematic. We had three or four window sizes, all of which were multiples of the three-foot-six modular unit. As long as they occurred on the grid, they could be anywhere without sacrificing standardization in production. We consciously tried to make the windows face as many directions as possible in every room and in every house. This proved to be extremely significant. The fact that you have windows facing three or four ways makes you feel that you are on your own, in space, that you are not slotted in.

We started the development of the prefabricated partitions and found that we couldn't run electrical wire in them the way you do in a regular wood-stud wall. We couldn't run it in the outside walls which were concrete, either. In anticipation of real modular partitions, I wanted a system that would be totally independent of the walls and accessible for rewiring or any other change in services. We made a baseboard ductway at the point where the partition meets the floor, the door frames themselves being the vertical channel to the light switches. The baseboard was clipped on in modular sections. You could dismount each piece and introduce new plugs anywhere at any time – a new phone or TV outlet, rewiring for a new computer service or a TV dial system that might come in a few years. But then the door frames were too narrow to accommodate a conventional light switch, and a low-voltage system had to be used with a small push button for a switch.

Not always did the results live up to expectations. We had to compromise on conventional partitions, and the baseboard, although installed as a modular component, relied on conventional cable. If we had had enough time to refine the detailing and get code approvals, it could have been a raceway with simple insulated wiring. That would have cut the cost of house wiring by fifty per cent.

I was also concerned with providing a safe environment for children in the gardens and the public places. I felt that if they could not look out, they would inevitably climb the wall railings. The one way to avoid this danger was to provide at least one face of the garden with a kind of window railing, a place where they could sit and look out and still be safe. The top of the railing is two feet wide. When you stand behind it you can't look down into the neighbor's garden. We set a curved, clear acrylic insert below it, from which a child or a seated adult can look out to the view. It curves outward in such a way that the bottom slab becomes a seat for a child.

In the pedestrian streets and public places where I had concrete railings, I introduced three-inch slots every twenty feet that children could look through as they walked along. It was fascinating to watch children once the building was being used. They would go into the garden, immediately sit under the railing, and look out. Walking along the street they automatically looked through the slots. I don't recall ever seeing children climbing on the railings. David Jacobs, the architectural critic who writes for the New York *Times,* came to live in Habitat to write an article about it, and the first observation in his article was how his child reacted to the railings and slots.

Habitat working drawings were completed in June 1965, when the bids were called.

I began to reduce the office staff. Many of the people who had worked for me were then hired by the general contractor or by the precasting contractor to work on their shop drawings and some of their organizational problems, and in fact climbed very fast to positions of considerable responsibility. Others went back home, and some stayed and are part of the office today. But the office was still a substantial size because the operation of checking shop drawings and co-ordinating them on the building site was formidable. Throughout construction we were still calling for tenders on minor items.

In a normal relationship the architect is between the client and the contractor and he is the on-site authority in interpreting the drawings. Here the client was between us and the contractor. He was the authority on the site. He had his own resident engineers, and his own administrative staff, and he would process the payments. We were consultants in the sense that we gave advice, but we didn't have the authority. Al Meyer was the resident architect on the site representing our office, but the Expo administrator was the man who said what was acceptable and what was not. Often we would reject work that was accepted by Expo, or stop payment for something for which payment had already been released. This made life difficult because, by and large, those involved with the project in Expo's construction division were unsympathetic to us and sympathetic to the contractor.

To make things even more difficult Anglin-Norcross, the general contractor, from the beginning displayed an uncommon lack of imagination, an inability to deal imaginatively with any part of the project that was unconventional. Their representatives, particularly in the early days, were playing a political game of writing letters and using job meetings to document testimony that would be useful in claiming extras later, rather than actually getting on with the work. Our weekly job meetings became lengthy and tedious discussions about what should or shouldn't go in the minutes.

I almost lived on the site in those months. I was there three-quarters of my time. If one of the workmen was caulking a window emphasizing the wrong line, I would suggest how I thought it should be done, and our consultants did the same. That created a good relationship with the workmen but it was resented by the contractor.

Right at the beginning one particular event set the pattern for our relationship with Expo and the general contractor. Anglin-Norcross had poured the first foundation wall around the parking area. It was an exposed wall supporting the first level of boxes. The specifications were very clear: this was exposed concrete; it had to be of the highest quality. And yet when the wall was poured and stripped, it was just miserable. I looked at it and said it was totally unacceptable and would have to be demolished and replaced. As this was the first wall I felt this was the place to draw the line. That week I was leaving for India for three weeks; before leaving, I asked that it be demolished, and Churchill agreed. But that same week Churchill collapsed in fatigue and was rushed to the hospital, where he stayed for three or four weeks.

After my departure, the construction manager of Expo, who was second in command and acting for Churchill, reversed the decision and said that the wall should stay. That was a major turning point. The contractor knew that he could get away with murder, and those in Expo who were dealing with him on a daily basis would let him get away with it. After that of course, only in a really bad, critical situation could I get Churchill involved and enforce a decision. On day-to-day workmanship it got to the point that because of scheduling and because of Expo's attitude we couldn't reject work, no matter how bad it was. And this was painful because in some cases things were done very badly.

I'll never forget the day when the first box was cast and everybody – Komendant and the engineers and contractors, and many from my office – went down there. It came out pretty well. We stood there for hours while it was being made. Expo decided that it was time for some good PR and arranged a laying-of-the-first-box ceremony.

This was a big event. Up to that time Habitat was constantly under attack in the press, and there seemed to be a general feeling that it would never be built, couldn't be done. The big Dominion Bridge crane had a capacity of a hundred and fifty tons at the base, but only seventy tons at a distance of a hundred and twenty feet from its edge. We didn't know the exact weight of the boxes when we ordered it. This first box to be lifted weighed eighty tons and was one hundred and twenty feet out – too big for the crane at that distance. We suggested getting another, smaller crane, then we would put the two cranes opposite each other and the box in the middle, connect them both to the cross bar on which the box would be placed. This would give each crane the proportion of the load it could carry, i.e. it would be proportional to the distance from the end of the cross bar to the box.

The contractor insisted that this procedure was absolutely impossible. They delayed the job two weeks arguing that it couldn't be done. Under pressure from Churchill they at last brought in the other crane, put in the cross bar, and lifted the box. The whole thing was done in front of the press in forty-five minutes without one problem. The procedure became so simple that any time the extra crane was required – for about five per cent of the boxes – they just brought it in without question.

I believe it was Commissioner General Dupuy who suggested to Shaw and Churchill that Nina ought to be the one to break a bottle of champagne over the first box. Nina and I were both very moved. It was a bitterly cold and windy day. A group of reporters came down and Nina swung the bottle right against the edge of the box. The stain is still there.

Two months later when the top box was laid, the contractors organized a topping-off ceremony, again in the presence of reporters on a windy day. The box went up with two flags on it – Anglin-Norcross' and Francon's – side-by-side. They stayed there until the end of construction.

They were grand days. There was Habitat, going up! One week you had one box and it had a certain scale, then you had two storeys, then three storeys, then all of a sudden a street was in, and – "My God, I'm walking along the pedestrian street!"

At times too, it seemed the site was swarming with visitors – architects, builders, diplomats – walking all over the building, taking pictures and making notes.

Habitat was not the first attempt to manufacture a house in a factory. The Russians had done considerable work in that direction working with room-size units, in circumstances where the finishes in the house are minimal. But in Habitat we built large units of six hundred square feet, with sophisticated finishes and detailing, meeting high North American standards.

The Habitat boxes are stacked twelve high, each one bearing the accumulated weight of the boxes above. Those at the bottom carry a heavier load than those in the middle, the middle boxes carry more than the top ones. The boxes are not, therefore, completely standardized. Realizing this, people have doubted that Habitat could have been truly mass-produced, no matter how many units were built. But they are wrong. It is easy to standardize four or five types that satisfy closely enough each condition of loading, and then design the mold and prefabricate reinforcing sections to produce variables. In Puerto Rico we are using just eight molds for manufacturing four types of load-bearing boxes, with no sacrifice of standardization from the point of view of production.

127

The immediate problem we faced in Habitat was that we started the structural design from the top down and the scheduling was such that as a drawing was produced (say a unit on the eighth floor) it immediately had to be rushed to the shop drawing department and then to the plant. At that point the fifth floor might not have been completely designed. Because we lacked time we ended up with much more variation in reinforcing and unit design than would otherwise have been the case, and we did not have the opportunity to review the total building and establish the basic standardized types.

The engineers were worried about weight. We had already ordered the crane for lifting the boxes into place and we needed a safety factor. Taking the roof off would reduce the weight by about fifteen tons. That meant we were working with roofless boxes. The components, bathrooms, kitchens, and so on were then installed under a temporary plastic roof. But as a box went up into place, the temporary lid had to be taken off before the next one was placed over it and even then it was not watertight until the proper roofing and drainage were installed. Invariably it would rain or snow at that point and much of the interior would get damaged, particularly the insulation, kitchens, and partitions.

Having made the mistake of casting the roofs separately, I still feel that there were solutions that we could have used to avoid water damage. For example, we could have used a single sheet of polyethylene sloping to a central drain with a hose connection draining through a window. This sheet would have been left in place throughout construction and finally covered with the ceiling plaster board. That would have cost thirty dollars a unit, but none of us thought of it at the time. In the Washington, D.C. and Puerto Rico projects we decided to pour the unit so that the roof was an integral part of the first casting and then pour the floor separately. That meant a complete new design for the form, resulting in a totally enclosed module.

Another mistake was made in planning the plumbing system. Sometimes the plumbing had to extend from one module to and through another before reaching the vertical distribution shaft. As plumbing must be tested after all the connections have been made we could not test it on the ground. To make matters worse, the plumbers, electricians, and carpenters got in one another's way. Each box should have been self-contained, completed, and tested on the ground. The whole sequence of testing the plumbing became such chaos on the site that at one point the contractor just abandoned the basic concept and installed and tested everything in the air.

This was all happening under considerable pressure. Irreversible decisions were made by the hour. The concrete molds were designed very heavy because the contractor expected to pump the concrete from the bottom up. Halfway through the manufacturing of the molds they changed their minds and decided to pour from the top down. By then the molds had twice as much steel in them as was needed.

At one point we had a fairly serious structural failure. One of the long streets had been post-tensioned. The loading of the units began. Early one morning there was a loud bang and the whole end support sheared. Nothing fell, but the structure was broken. Expo officials immediately emptied the building and surrounded it with cars with red flashing lights. All the workmen were sent home. Komendant arrived from New Jersey. Everybody was pointing fingers at everybody else. The general contractor brought in Morden Yolles, a well-known engineer from Toronto, to advise them. It appeared that a welding plate connection had been inadvertently omitted, but there was also a suggestion that the failure would have occurred whether the plate had been there or not. The project was delayed for two weeks while all parties tried to place the blame where it belonged, obviously on someone else. Then Churchill in his usual lifesaving manner came in and said, "I don't give a damn whose fault it is, I want that job going again." That meant reinforcing the whole end and pouring a new wall against it.

The finish of the precast concrete units produced in the beginning wasn't all one could desire. One Sunday I went down to the site and to my horror saw one wall of one of the boxes painted white. An hour later Churchill appeared for a field inspection accompanied by the vice-president of Anglin-Norcross, who had had the sample painting done to show him. The vice-president suggested that we were so strict with the precasters in our demands for a good concrete finish, and the cost of sandblasting the concrete was so high, that if Churchill would agree that everything should be painted Expo would receive a substantial credit – fifty or a hundred thousand dollars, I seem to remember. I countered to Ed Churchill that it would be the wrong thing to do. Once you paint something you have to keep painting it forever. No paint surface is permanent. It will look good for six months but then it will look much worse than the aged concrete surface which looks better with the years rather than worse. And so the exposed concrete remained.

Well, we learned a lot. The Hilton hotel that was recently built with prefabricated boxes in San Antonio, Texas showed that they had learned to avoid some of our errors. They managed to pre-finish the modules completely. Most of the problems could not have been foreseen the first time around at Habitat.

The spirit on the site was amazing. Feeling among the workmen built up as the job went along. They were working round the clock. They kept reading about the building in newspapers – cartoons, write-ups, criticisms – and they cut them all out and stuck them up in different places on the project. Many of our riggers were Indians from the Caughnawaga reserve near Montreal. At six o'clock one morning the project manager of Anglin-Norcross, Bob Hughes, arrived to hear a fantastic sound coming from one of the boxes. He went to the box and saw all the night-shift dancing a sunrise dance on the subfloor before going home.

While there was a great sense of identity with the project among the workmen, at the management level there was an atmosphere of manoeuvring and politicking and letter-writing and blame-hanging, each sub-contractor trying to protect his own interest. It was the inevitable result of awarding a lump sum contract for an experimental project. With half a dozen exceptions I don't feel the job received the kind of ingenuity and imagination that had been part of it in the design stage. Those exceptions I would like to name: Reff Plastics, Francon, Frigidaire, Clerk Windows, and Ishii Brothers who did the carpentry. Among these contractor heroes, I would single out Cipriano Da Re, Francon's chief project engineer; he made the building possible by translating the consultants' designs into concrete reality.

We were working to a critical path, a very exact computer-designed schedule.

We had all-day meetings with Colonel Churchill and his staff to discuss means of meeting deadlines. We had great difficulties because, when it became hard to stick to the schedule, the tendency was to do another schedule. Furthermore, the contractors claimed that they had been delayed by lack of information or lack of drawings, and therefore they wanted extras for overtime, for certain molds and jigs, for extra reinforcing, all of which they expected Expo to pay over and above the fixed contract.

At about that time Mitchell Sharp, who was the federal minister in charge of Expo, became the new Canadian Minister of Finance, and Robert Winters took over the Ministry of Trade and Commerce in Sharp's place. When Winters came in I sensed a total change between Expo and the federal government. He started reexamining Expo's finances and singled out Habitat for special attention.

I started hearing rumors soon after his appointment. Habitat was being questioned from first principles. Tony Peters, Expo's project architect for Habitat, called to say there was talk of abandoning the project completely; he had heard of an investigation into the cost of paying the contractors off at that point and dismantling the building. In fact, he had heard a study was being made somewhere to see, if the building were dismantled, whether the modular boxes could be dropped into the river, and whether the river was deep enough to accommodate them all. Obviously if the project were abandoned it would have to be dismantled before the opening of Expo to avoid embarrassment.

Fantastic as this story sounds now, we were quite nervous and concerned at the time. I was told that Winters was very conscious of his candidacy for leadership of the Liberal Party and that his aim was to come through as the taxpayers' savior – and where could you find a better place than Habitat, which was under considerable criticism in the press for its high cost!

In the end they must have decided that it was not practical to abandon the project – it was half-built at that time – and they started looking at other ways of making dramatic cost savings. Eventually the verdict came down: it was government policy to abandon construction of the north cluster, the third of the three sections that make up the total building. At that point the south and center clusters and the foundation of the northern were completed and we were instructed to see what credits could be negotiated from the contractor.

The situation was too ridiculous for words. The credits we could get from the contractors would obviously be negligible because the costs of the factory, tooling up, and overheads were fixed and would become even more ridiculous when spread over only a hundred and twenty units. Furthermore, many of the north cluster boxes were already cast. But arguing from such facts wouldn't do much good; in Expo, as elsewhere, politics, logic, and economics did not always mix.

I decided that the best way to handle this was to make a big thing of the fact that the building wouldn't be stable structurally unless we built all of it. That was half true, because if we cut the building along the expansion joint that separated the north and central cluster, modifications would be needed to make the structure stable. I met with the structural engineers, and after reviewing the problem, Dr. Komendant and Dr. Monti produced a report showing that the north cluster had to be built in order to balance the structure. This report was happily received by Expo because those concerned with the project felt very much the way we did about the whole issue.

Then came a new threat. It seemed that the minister was determined to swing an ax in some way. He decided that we should not finish the interiors of the north cluster and should negotiate credits with the contractors accordingly. Again this decision had no logic to it whatsoever. The contractor had already bought much of the material and equipment for the houses. We were buying kitchens from Frigidaire that were highly subsidized. If we cancelled the order for forty kitchens we wouldn't get credit for what they were subsidizing. Duct work had been purchased, the windows had been made, and so on and so forth. When you negotiate credits with a contractor for work that has already been awarded you never get full value in the credit. What's more, Expo would lose the rental revenue from forty units for the six months of the exhibition when those rents were considerable.

Once we started negotiating with the contractors we discovered that the most credit to be gotten was approximately half a million dollars, but the cost of completing the work after Expo would be more than twice that. We made a full report, but notwithstanding, we were ordered to change the contract to omit the finishing of the interiors of the north cluster and to accept the very small credit involved.

It was a recklessly illogical decision from the taxpayers' point of view. In 1969 CMHC estimated the cost of completing the north cluster and it was over a million and a quarter dollars.

Then at a formal meeting in the board room at Expo with the minister and other notables, I was summoned and told that additional funds had been made available to cover the contractors' extras agreed upon by Expo, but no further extras would be tolerated. We just had to get to work and make do with the funds that were available. That was in the fall of 1966, six months before opening day.

As the tension mounted, there was constant pressure to change things in the building. Take out the garden irrigation system! Take out some of the lighting fixtures in the public area! Substitute cheaper materials! At one point a memorandum came from somewhere up there saying that the whole elaborate landscape work, the retaining walls and terraces that extended the building's geometry into the grounds, ought to be omitted and the site ought to be sodded.

Each of these directives was the subject of a major battle, but on the whole we got our way. It took considerable manoeuvring and we always had to find technical reasons why things couldn't be changed, because that was the only reasoning that came across.

After the meeting with the minister the pace at the site became indescribable. We were working three shifts. The contractors became increasingly conscious of the fact that they had to finish the building somehow by April 27th. Even though the north cluster interior finishes were omitted a fantastic amount of work had yet to be done. The settlements with the contractors, several million dollars' worth of extras, were conditional on their finishing the building in time. And I must say that at that point all the contractors really got going.

Robert Shaw talked about leaving the factory in place as an exhibit, to show people how Habitat was built. But Expo management decided the factory should be dismantled completely and the area landscaped. But, Shaw and Churchill still felt that the story of how Habitat was built ought to be told even though no budget for an exhibit was available from Expo. Shaw had been a construction man and was fascinated with the building, and it seemed very important to him to do this. He proposed that the contractors, sub-contractors, and consultants get together and mount an exhibit at their own expense. We decided to leave the crane there and, on condition we leave the name "Dominion Bridge" on it, got that company to agree. Francon agreed to cast three extra boxes showing the cross section of the reinforced concrete, and the window manufacturer donated a few extra windows. The structural and mechanical engineers and the quantity surveyors all contributed cash toward the preparation of photographs and panels, all of which went in four modules in the north cluster which were otherwise unfinished. My office put the whole thing together as our part of the contribution.

During the exhibition thousands of people came to Montreal specifically to see Habitat – delegations of planners, architects, contractors, planning authorities from various cities in the U.S., Canada and Europe. We took the tapes of the post-mortem meetings and after some editing played them in one of the units so that people could come in and listen to discussions about the structure, and several students answered questions from the thousands of people who visited the exhibit every day.

The Chatelaine affair

The furnishing of Habitat was a story in itself. To me it was an expression of a deeply rooted problem, the way people set their values and judge their environment. Furniture is so close to people that they react to it very emotionally.

From the beginning I knew we would run into problems when it came time to furnish the exhibit units, and so, in negotiating my contract with Expo I insisted on a clause that gave us design authority over the furnishing of all the areas in the building that were open to the public. At the time Expo didn't give much thought to that requirement, put it in the contract, and signed it, so there it was.

As opening day approached it became clear that nobody in Expo was organizing Habitat as an exhibit. I approached Churchill about it and it was made clear to me that Expo had no budget and was not intending to spend any money furnishing Habitat. Fair enough. We had to get the best we could by begging. We recommended to Expo that an industrial designer who knew the industry be retained as consultant and suggested Jacques Guillon of Montreal, who was doing considerable work for Expo at the time. Guillon thought it would be worth approaching the best designers from several countries participating in Expo to do a few units each. This was going beyond our terms of reference. We were not authorized to negotiate with foreign governments but, ignoring the restriction, we went directly to commercial attachés or ambassadors. Churchill, I suspect, knew what we were doing.

The response was fantastic. Before we knew it, we had Denmark committed to doing eight houses, England wanted to do three, Japan wanted two, and there were others. Everything was going beautifully. We went back to Churchill and gave him a cheerful report saying in effect that we'd got it all solved. The report went from Churchill to Expo management and then things absolutely blew up.

The Canadian Furniture Manufacturers' Association heard that there was voluntary participation from other countries. They couldn't see, they said, how a project that was part of the national effort could be given to foreigners. Robert Winters, as cabinet minister in charge of Expo, seemed to agree with them and instructed Expo to inform the countries that Habitat was a Canadian exhibit, to be done by Canadians. This was very embarrassing, because by that time some of the foreign representatives had met with Shaw and Churchill and been given commitments to proceed. Somehow Expo had to turn round and change it all.

Two weeks later the International Bureau of Exhibitions met in Moscow. Members criticized Pierre Dupuy and Andrew Kniewasser, Expo's general manager, saying that this was no way to run an international exhibition. Kniewasser, who's great at pleading this kind of case, made the point that after all Habitat was an all-Canadian effort, Habitat was a theme exhibit, wouldn't the countries oblige by withdrawing? (That was the first time anybody adopted Habitat as a theme exhibit, incidentally. In the previous two years the theme exhibits department would have nothing to do with it.) There the row subsided: the countries did nothing more about it and Canada was left to handle the furnishings.

Next the Department of Exhibits, which was responsible for going after sponsorship, was given the task of handling the furnishing project. They decided we should have nothing to do with it. When I heard that, I wrote a letter to Churchill reminding him of the design control clause in our contract. Nothing happened. The Department of Exhibits formed a special advisory group of representatives of the furniture industry. At their first meeting I was asked to brief them. I said Habitat was a house that related to contemporary Canadian life. It had to be furnished with regard and respect for the kind of life we lead, for the space we have, for the maintenance we can keep up with. It wasn't just a matter of displaying floor tiles and fabrics, American Colonial versus French Provincial. It had to have some meaning in terms of contemporary Canadian life.

Realizing that the committee was going to use Habitat as a catalogue, we tried another approach. Guillon and I lunched with the chairman of the furniture manufacturers' committee. We asked if he would be willing to have half the units done by Canadian manufacturers and the other half by the designers from various countries. He said he would consider the suggestion, but right after the meeting, he put pressure on to kill the idea. In subsequent meetings of the committee, from which I was barred, there was a good deal of indignation that Guillon and I should consider we had any right to say how Habitat should be furnished. Most of the members of that association manufacture for the mass department store market. Most of the manufacturers of, let's call it, "consciously designed furniture" are not members.

Then the committee offered to furnish all twenty-six exhibit units free on condition that *Chatelaine* magazine be given the sole responsibility for designing them. *Chatelaine* is a Canadian women's fashion and household magazine. The Department of Exhibits was delighted: "We've solved the problem of Habitat!" The commitment was made. The industry was delighted: the design responsibility was to be in the hands of a magazine they all advertise in.

I was sending registered letters and telegrams to Shaw and Churchill and at one point I got sufficiently upset to send a telegram to the chairman of the National Design Council, John C. Parkin. I wrote: "I request the Council's assistance and help in trying to get Habitat furnished in a way that is compatible with the standards of the National Design Council." (In the end the Council failed to make a single firm resolution on the subject.) When Expo management heard of that, they hit the roof. How dare I consult a federal agency over their head! I answered that design control was in my contract and if *Chatelaine* were given the design of the units I would try to stop it by court injunction. This was very painful for me because I was in effect attacking Churchill and Shaw, people who were close to me and to whom I was indebted. Expo's exhibits department argued that we surely couldn't get Habitat furnished the way I wanted free and consequently they'd rather have bad furniture than no furniture. I said I'd rather have no furniture than bad furniture. Let people look at the units empty!

I was quite convinced, however, that we could get the best designers in the country, and the manufacturers they worked with, to furnish the units in Habitat free. Guillon and I made a list of some of Canada's finest designers and manufacturers: Dudas Kuypers Rowan, Bob Kaiser, Christen Sorensen, Guillon himself, and others. We approached them on our own and asked if they would do one or two units each, free, working with their usual manufacturers. We hoped they would be able to custom-design prototypical furniture for the project as an exhibit. We got positive response from enough to do twenty-two units.

When we returned to Expo with that proposal the battle went wild, for now Expo was in an even more embarrassing position. We had managed to sign up the best designers in the country, most of whom were already doing work for Expo: Dudas Kuypers Rowan were designing the whole Man the Producer pavilion, for instance.

Meanwhile *Chatelaine* made its first presentation. It was the most vulgar, ugly, bargain-basement stuff, pettily concocted. I just couldn't believe my eyes. I couldn't believe that what I saw there was being seriously proposed for an international exhibition. We said, "Either they are dismissed or we'll have a press conference and say exactly what we think." Expo was nervous about the damaging effect. They suspected I might leak the whole thing to the press and talk about going to court. They could just see the press picking it up, the headlines, a lot of editorial criticism, little programs on CBC, and so on. Things were getting too hot to bear.

Churchill then called in *Chatelaine's* man in charge, a representative of the committee, and me one Saturday morning and said, "We're not leaving this room until we settle this matter." At the end of a long day, I was offered a compromise. *Chatelaine* was to do half and we were to have a free hand with the other half. It was two or three months before the opening of Expo. I concluded that if half was done by *Chatelaine* and half by the designers we selected, at least people would have a basis for comparison and that in itself might be interesting. So I agreed, and that's the way it was done. In the end when people came to Habitat they knew the difference.

The politics of the *Chatelaine* affair are really an expression of a fundamental cultural issue – an expression of the thought processes and the considerations that individuals apply in planning their house, their furnishings, and the nature of their shelter.

Many of those who understood very well why the building shouldn't be painted, or why we should not compromise in the construction process, or why each house should have a garden, did not understand as clearly or as simply why we should not have pseudo-American Colonial furniture, or why there was more to furnishing the Habitat exhibit than a furniture advertising campaign. Instead they put the issue in terms of contemporary versus traditional, not the quality of the environment that could be made.

In fact, when the first *Chatelaine* submission was made I was asked to make comments on it. I was told not to put it on the basis of "don't like" or "do like," not to put it on the basis of contemporary and non-contemporary, and I accepted that. This was an opportunity to try and state where a design submission did or didn't meet what I felt were the needs of a workable house. I wrote things like: "This chair is too big for this room." "This chest does not make sense in relationship to the space available." "This particular object blocks the view." "This color scheme breaks up the continuity of the house and makes the rooms appear smaller." "Wallpaper over beams and pilasters destroys the clarity of expression of the structural system of the building, which one wants to comprehend when one is in one's house." It had nothing to do with whether they were contemporary or non-contemporary.

Why do people design their own environment so badly, so devoid of anything that has to do with the way they live? Why should a middle-income Canadian family living in Habitat choose furniture that is an imitation of something that was designed for a totally different set of circumstances, for a room that may have been eighteen feet high, or made during a time when furniture was hand-carved wood? Today it's mass-produced by machine. We have a wealth of materials that can give us good furniture.

The whole furniture affair was an expression of how arbitrary the design of our houses is, how much our decisions are shaped not by how we use and live in a house, but by secondary associations: associations with what we consider to represent "belonging," success, status, impressing our friends. Style and fashion are directly proportional to the degree of arbitrariness in the design,

138

and they increase as the object becomes more irrational or as it is increasingly motivated by considerations that are not the primary reasons for the existence of that object.

I've been asked a hundred times: "What style do you furnish your house in?" or "Do you like Modern?" The trouble with the question is that it expresses the idea that there are a number of equally valid alternatives and therefore it is a matter of personal choice which you select: French Provincial or Cape Cod Colonial; Spanish-American or Modern – Modern being an equal partner with the others, just another stylistic vocabulary. That assumption is fundamentally wrong. There are not that many equally valid choices. Style, which is a formalized vocabulary, has very little to do with the question, "What is a house all about?" When I think about furnishing a house, many questions come to my mind:

What is the family's style of life?
Is the furniture comfortable to sit on or lie on or eat at in terms of their living habits?
Are the materials cold, such as metal or stone? Are they warm to touch, such as wool or wood? What is the climate?
Is the furniture related to the size of the space?
Is the quality of the material such that it absorbs dirt or is it easily cleanable? Does it lend itself to easy maintenance, or does it consume much energy to clean and keep tidy?
Is the maintenance of the house related to the style of life?
Is the furniture flexible enough, in terms of the way certain rooms are used during different times of the day and night?
If the family moves frequently, is the furniture light and easy to transport?

Process comes into it too:

Is the furniture made with the kind of processes and materials that would make it economical and therefore easily available to the family?
What materials lend themselves to such processes?

All the above is concerned primarily with physical aspects but there are many psychological considerations too:

What is the emotional import of the colors of all surfaces?
What do the colors and textures of the walls and floors do to the perceiving of the space; do they make it feel smaller or bigger?
Do the textures and colors of the walls reflect light from the outside; do they create brightness and less dependency on artificial light?

All these questions come to mind when somebody asks me, "Do you like Modern?" I don't know how to answer that question. I don't know if my house is Modern. I've designed furniture for my own house, selected things to put in it, but nevertheless the question of Modern or not Modern has never entered my mind. When people ask what style of furniture one likes, they are ignoring most of the questions that I raised.

"Do *you* like modern furniture?" Much so-called modern furniture does not respond to the hundreds of demands which we make on furniture. Many people say, "I don't like Modern because it is cold."

Such an irrelevant approach is responsible for ridiculous situations. Often it is a negation of the nature of the object. For example, if a man living in Bombay puts down a thick wool carpet which is going to get moldy with the humidity and which is going to be uncomfortable in the heat, it's a negation of the nature of the floor in his house. A man living in Montreal or in Scotland who puts in a marble or stone floor which absorbs a great deal of heat and therefore feels very cold is equally doing something that contradicts the nature of the object. What makes an Indian in Bombay carpet his house with thick wool carpets? I suppose he's seen it in *Life* magazine, he has feelings of admiration for a style of life that isn't his. By carpeting his house he's able to feel he has upgraded himself, and he's prepared to suffer the carpet's moldy heat.

The same is true of our clothes. Women's fashions are quite unrelated to climate or to comfort. If you watch a woman walking on a really pointy high heel, as they did not long ago, it's the most inorganic thing you can think of. The whole thing is shaking and about to collapse at any moment. Half the woman's weight is concentrated on one little heel one-quarter of an inch square, which penetrates practically every flooring material we know. Four years later the same woman couldn't consider in her worst dreams wearing the same shoe, because it's out of fashion. Men are no better. We wear wool suits and ties in a hot climate and it becomes so unbearable that we have to create micro-climates inside buildings with air conditioning.

Fashion is a diversionary tactic because it makes it possible to concentrate energy on something which is not the environmental issue. In other cultures this has not always been true. Arab dress is very much related to the climate. It hasn't changed for thousands of years. It's comfortable in that climate, comfortable for walking, easily washable. The Indian sari also hasn't changed for thousands of years and I think it evolved for organic, environmental reasons.

As a matter of personal taste we select things that please us. The choice is not logical but they obviously have a place in our house. If they didn't, many houses would be identical. A house should be unique, as unique as one's face or personality, it should not be irrational. It is paradoxical when people make decisions for reasons that are in contradiction to rational environment.

I was prepared to choose any number of designers in the country and give them a free hand in furnishing Habitat. But the ideal would be real tenants doing their own places rather than having them "decorated." Habitat was not supposed to be an expression of my personal way of life, but an expression of certain values, one of which is, that the way we make things and do things in our own culture is meaningful. Today we consider as objets d'art what past cultures simply made for daily life. Utensils, clothes, buildings, music – they were part of a ritual of life and the process of life. The Greeks made things for use in daily life and the art in them is the art of the people expressed in making them, not art for art's sake. Today we have a whole world of manufactured things that make up our environment, lamps, tables, carpets, cars, clothes, airplanes, suitcases. There – as the Bauhaus taught us – is the root of art. Most of what comes under the heading *art* today, painting, sculpture, means very little to me. Objects I use mean so much more.

There is a pretentiousness in our culture. We ignore or degrade the things that should give art to our life, and create a subculture of so-called art that is irrelevant. If we put our energies into thinking about the things that we really use in our lives we would be producing what we admire so much in other cultures.

That was the real conflict with *Chatelaine,* a conflict between two basically different attitudes to life.

After the meeting in Churchill's office I had no further contact with them. One day a few weeks later I arrived at the site and there was an enormous eight-foot sphere made out of papier-mâché with funny holes in it, pink and lime in color. It looked like the cut-up kidneys of a Martian. I asked what it was and was told *Chatelaine* had just delivered it. It was a play sculpture for the playground. A manufacturer had donated it. I said, "Over my dead body!" That same day I tried to get Churchill to have them remove it, but he was away. So Nina and I went down that night. There was that enormous thing sitting on the moonlit plaza. The only thing to do was roll it out of the building. I started pushing it and it made a big racket. Suddenly, four security guards jumped out from one of the houses and one of them grabbed me as if I were trying to steal the thing. He said, "What are you doing?" I said, "I'm the architect of this building, I'm moving this thing out of the place." They asked for identification and called the chief of security for Expo, who soon arrived with siren wailing. They were sure they had caught a thief. In the end, they didn't lock me up. But it took two weeks of continuous phone calls and pleading to get Expo to instruct *Chatelaine* to take it off the site.

Almost every journalist who has interviewed me has asked: "When did you first think of Habitat?"

Most people think of design as styling. You style a building: you *stylize* it. And because styling is related to a single pictorial flash, people think that in the process of design you walk around waiting for that flash to hit you, then you put it down on a paper, and that's how it happens. Ayn Rand's novel *The Fountain-head* romanticized the creation of the moment. In *The Fountainhead* the creative process, if I have to choose one word to describe it, was a *formalizing* process, whereas I feel that design as I experience it, is a *synthesizing* process. The word *design* doesn't exist at all in many languages. In French, *dessiner* is "to draw" rather than "to design." In Hebrew we have *tichnun,* which is "to plan" or *itzuv,* which is "to give form," literally, physically to make form. You make a pot, you shape it with your hand. You are not putting it down on paper to translate it later.

The reason I cannot answer the journalists' question is that I have experienced design as process.

It is easier to talk about the politics of a building and the administrative process of getting it built, of the confrontations, than of the inner workings of the design process. And while it is probably true that for every line drawn a thousand words are spoken and written, and that for every hour spent conceiving a building many hours are spent in the process of realizing it, it is nevertheless also true that in the final analysis most of the energy is spent on conception. Two aspects of this process seem to be significant: one has to do with the formulating of the program of what the building *ought* to be; the other has to do with the genesis of ideas, and the process that leads to what the building actually ends up being.

A moment of genesis for me was the time that I first thought about the idea of identifiable houses floating in space. Almost every project has those moments of realization that have to do with the program and the echoes of this realization in physical images, but it would be an error to think of them as "flashes of inspiration." Le Corbusier gave to one of his most beautiful books the title *Creation is a Patient Search.* These moments are not possible unless they are part of a prolonged process of analysis, of a bombardment of images in response to a search.

But what is even more significant is that these moments in themselves are really quite meaningless. The thought of houses floating in space is only a part of a jigsaw puzzle. That the houses are to be made in a factory and assembled in a particular pattern in space; the geometry in which they interlock; the methods by which they are connected; the system of circulation leading to them – these too are all parts of the puzzle.

Even detailing of the building is part of this inseparable process. Habitat's door-knobs and doors, the way they fit into the wall, light switches and partitions, floors and windows, bathrooms and kitchens, railings and roof-decks, street shelters and elevator cabs, planters and the lighting of the public areas, had all to be conceived in the context of the whole, in the context of the environment they make.

I have found this difficult to talk about because separating so-called conception or design from realization is in itself quite artificial. If there was something unique in the experience of Habitat, it was the way these two were integrated into a single alternating and pulsating process. (It was probably this unity that allowed the building to become a reality.)

How do you talk about it, anyhow? How do you communicate those moments of torture, search, and frustration and those other moments of excitement and fulfilment, orgasmic moments – that kind of growth from blurred images, ideas and thoughts, almost independent images which slowly become clearer and start clicking with each other, and then generating realities you would have never thought of in the first place?

And so I could never answer the journalists' question without taking half an hour to do so. I used to say, "Oh well, you know, it takes a long time, it's the whole evolution of things, you don't think of something in a moment." If I try to answer the question more carefully with reference to Habitat, I must start with some moments in the years when I was a student, when I first saw Le Corbusier's early books and his 1920 sketches of apartment buildings with gardens. Then there was that moment later in my fifth year at university, when I tackled the housing design problem. I had started off drawing townhouses and slabs and then I thought, "I can't do that." And I took a block of wood and cut it up into individual pieces to represent houses. Then I grouped them, not thinking of them as a building but as houses, in a simple checkerboard pattern.

There must be places and towns and houses and gardens that I don't even remember now that helped form Habitat. One of the most powerful images in my childhood was of the hanging gardens of Babylon. For me, they were the Garden of Eden and I had many fantasies about them. The fact that no one knew how they looked, that they were a mystery, that there were no drawings of them whatsoever, made them even more attractive to me. I'm sure those childhood fantasies have something to do with my feelings about the city that are expressed in Habitat.

The corollary of *synthesis* is *process.* In my thesis the simple idea of a house and a garden began to have a physical being, a spiral formation with the mechanical services and circulation penetrating it, houses grouped like a tent enclosing a public space, and all the engineering logistics of a membrane that supports itself in gravity.

Another very important period in my life was that year I spent in Philadelphia. I had much more time to myself. I had acquired new friends, and this was a time when a lot of more or less floating ideas about design were articulated, were tied into a more workable mosaic of ideas, almost a theory. An attitude, anyway.

In Philadelphia Anne Tyng introduced me to a book she called her bible, D'Arcy Thompson's *On Growth and Form,* the great classical work of the turn of the century about the science of morphology. I consumed it. It was through D'Arcy Thompson that I started understanding the nature of form.

Thompson talks about the shell:

"In the growth of a shell, we can conceive no simpler law than this, namely, that it shall widen and lengthen in the same unvarying proportions: and this simplest of laws is that which Nature tends to follow: The shell, like the creature within it, grows in size but does not change its shape; and the existence of this constant relativity of growth, or constant similarity of form, is of the essence, and may be made the basis of a definition, of the equiangular spiral."

Thompson conceptualized the evolution of living form. Still talking about the shell he says:

"But God hath bestowed upon this humble architect the practical skill of a learned geometrician, and he makes this provision with admirable precision in that curvature of the logarithmic spiral which he gives to the section of the shell . . . *The same architecture which builds the house constructs the door.* Moreover, not only are house and door governed by the same law of growth, but, growing together, door and doorway adapt themselves to one another."

For me this was more important than any work on architecture that I had read. It had to do with the essence of form. Still talking about the shell:

"It exemplifies very beautifully what Bacon meant in saying that *the forms or differences of things are simple and few, and the degrees and coordinations of these make all their variety.* And after such a fashion as this John Goodsir imagined that the naturalist of the future would determine and classify his shells, so that conchology should presently become, like mineralogy, a mathematical science."

Thompson also talks of achieving infinite variety within repetitive systems. This touched the core of what for me is a central issue of architecture today – being able to create variation and permutations of dissimilar objects within repetitive systems. He was discussing the raison d'être of a single living organism, and I was extending this thought to the organism of environment.

Nature makes form; form is a by-product of evolution. The science of morphology deals with the reasons for the evolution of particular forms. One can study plant and animal life, rock and crystal formations, and discover the reasons for their particular form. That helps us to understand what man's form-making process could and should be.

The nautilus has evolved so that when its shell grows its head will not get stuck in the opening. This growth pattern in morphology is known as gnomonic growth; it results in the spiral formation. It is, mathematically, the only way it can grow.

The same is true of achieving strength with a particular material. Look at the wings of a vulture, at its bone formation. A most intricate three-dimensional geometric pattern has evolved, a kind of space frame, with very thin bones that get thicker at the ends. The main survival problem for the vulture is to develop strength in the wing (which is under tremendous bending moment when the bird is flying) without building up weight as that would limit its mobility. Through evolution the vulture has the most efficient structure one can imagine, a space frame in bone.

For each aspect of life there are responses of form. Consider the relationship of a maple or an elm to sun. These trees are in a temperate climate and need to absorb a great deal of sun. They have wide leaves arranged in a spiral grouping that exposes the maximum area of leaf. In contrast the olive tree has a thin leaf. One side is light, one dark. The leaf rotates so that the light side always faces the sun, because it is essential to its survival that heat not be absorbed and that moisture be preserved. The same is true of many cacti, which turn themselves perpendicular to light. In the forest we find plants that usually grow in shade under trees develop larger and broader leaf forms and spread themselves. Each plant develops a form that responds directly to its survival needs.

One of the bees' problems of survival is to store honey and so through evolution they produced a space pattern that stores a maximum of honey using the least possible wax. Their three-dimensional system of space packing is a very efficient way of storing fluid.

146

Economy and survival are the two key words in nature. Examined out of context, the neck of the giraffe seems uneconomically long but it is economical in view of the fact that most of the giraffe's food is high on the tree. If the absorption of light is essential to survival, then large, seemingly uneconomical leaves are developed to absorb it. Economy and survival are interacting forces. Beauty as we understand it, and as we admire it in nature, is never arbitrary. It is a by-product of this complex interaction: the color and shape of flowers directly relate to their ability to attract insects; the color and formation of insects relate to their ability to camouflage themselves against the background of flowers. Form and pattern are constantly related to the needs of survival.

Thinking of architecture in terms of the morphology of living organisms was an important step. As soon as you compare the design process of an environment to the morphology of an organism you become aware of the crudeness and the arbitrariness of the man-made forms. Because of the limitations of our understanding and primarily because of the limitations of our means of building, our environment is a caricature of the perfection that man might achieve. It is the imperfection, the gap between the complex life-function of environment and the forms and structures we have made, that creates the duality between the urban, and the organic and natural.

We experience this every day. We have two kinds of distinct feelings in the environment, one which we associate with being in the city, the other with being in the open country – the sensations of walking in the forest under branches and leaves swaying in the breeze. The contrast is recognized whenever we feel the need to withdraw from the urban environment and go back to nature, which restores in us a certain peace and stability. This difference between walking in the urban street, in man-made structures and being amongst the trees, rocks, and water has to do with the difference between being in an environment which approaches perfection in its natural response to the demands of function and survival, and the one made by man which is an imperfect solution to equally complex demands. I believe that as the man-made environment approaches the perfection of the form fulfilment of natural organisms, this separation between the man-made and the natural will disappear, that we as men will be equally fulfilled in either man-made or natural environments.

Let me illustrate this in terms of a building problem. The eye is a complex mechanism; it changes with light conditions, the pupil expanding or shrinking, the eye rotating in different directions, or focusing to different distances. Compare this to a window in a structure; a fixed pane of transparent material in a wall. Yet what we ideally require of a window is not unlike what the eye provides. The window should shrink or expand according to the quality of light and the time of the day and the season. It should move in and out of the wall in response to the sun's penetration and the direction in which we are looking through it. Its transparency should vary, sometimes allowing all light through, sometimes very little. It should have the quality of becoming instantly opaque. It should expand and shrink like the shutter of a camera.

Think for example, of a roof structure with straight beams and columns, and compare it to the intricate three-dimensional fabric of fanning and folded cantilevering in the leaf of the palm tree, a perfection of accommodating stresses with the minimum materials in the most intricate but ordered pattern. Columns and slabs and beams can be geometrically more accurate, but expand this to walls and spaces, and to movement of air and climate, and to the subtle needs of man's psyche, and you have an architecture infinitely more simple yet apparently more complex.

Thus it has become fundamental to my whole attitude to architecture that we must consciously live this kind of process in understanding the nature of our environment and of the materials and processes that produce it. This will progressively result in a better environment. It is complex because the forces that shape human environment are both physical and psychic. The primitive American Indian, who feared nature, expressed this in his spirits, made masks of their images, and hung them in his doorway to protect him. He was satisfying a psychic need; so it was not arbitrary.

Once the environment is thought of in terms of morphology, then it is easy to see and say that the environment is made up of a multitude of *structures* and that the understanding of these structures is essential to the understanding of the design process. This use of the word "structure," to mean the many facets of the morphology of environment, challenges the conventional architectural use, i.e. that which holds the building up. By challenging this limited meaning of the word we expose a serious shortcoming in our attitude towards design.

When I was a student at McGill, the work of Mies van der Rohe was admired because it was said to express structure. If a building had a frame of steel beams and columns then, instead of hiding it, Mies came right out and put it on the surface. Peter Collins, who taught us history of architecture, used to say, "This is rational design because it expresses structure." He would talk of "rational architecture." "The work of Le Corbusier is totally irrational," he would say. "It does not express structure." As a student I suspected this view because intuitively I felt I would rather be in an environment made by Le Corbusier than one by Mies van der Rohe. Where had the argument gone wrong? It gradually became clear to me that we were misusing the word "structure." We were using it merely to describe the skeleton that holds a building up.

Now as the word "structure" is used in morphology its synonyms are: *organization, complex,* and *arrangement.* Each aspect of form is an aspect of structure. The structure of a building is not just what holds it up; it is also the structure of light, the structure of air, the structure of the distribution of services through it, the structure of movement, the psychic structure of human

148

response to location, identity, and privacy. All these are *structure.* While Le Corbusier did not exaggerate the expression of what held his building up, he did respond in a more organic way to light, say, or to movement, whereas Mies, while expressing the fact that his building was made of columns and beams, denied most of the other aspects of structure. The sun moves in the sky. It is weak and low in winter, strong and high in summer. Our relationship with the sun varies with the time of day and the time of year. A tower with identical glass walls facing in four directions is ignoring the structure of light.

Even the argument that Mies' buildings express what holds them up is misleading. If you consider the fact that a tall structure is not only affected by the force of gravity but by horizontal forces of wind and earthquake which are almost equal in magnitude, then the arrangement of vertical and horizontal columns and beams is the most inefficient structure you could have. Like a house of cards it tends to want to collapse. The entire strength is dependent on the stiffness of the joints, because it lacks any form of triangulation to make it rigid. In contrast, Buckminster Fuller's geodesic dome is an organic structural response to these forces, a geometric arrangement which is self-stiffening.

Environment is made up of a multitude of structures. Some of these structures or functions are physical and some are psychological. It's important to put this in historical perspective. It was Louis Sullivan who said: "Form follows function." It was the CIAM architects, who, in the twenties and thirties, responded to it. The whole problem of arbitrariness in design was being questioned. This was a fresh open-ended development, yet it was over-simplified. For example, CIAM's charts would show that the height of a building should be related to its distance from the next one in such a way that the sun would hit each building. From this chart they would generate a scheme of ten rows of town houses equally spaced and this, they said, was a response to function.

By the fifties, many architects were saying, "Functionalism is dead. It's monotonous, it's boring, we have to have 'a rich environment,' we have to have 'delight'." So, they started playing stylistic games with grilles, ornaments, and decoration. But the ten rows of town houses, equally spaced, are a gross over-simplication of function. The sun doesn't stand still, it goes round in an arc, and the angle of the arc changes every moment of the day and from one day to the next. If one were to make an arrangement of houses that took this fact into account then, through the same response to function, one would arrive at the most complex and visually rich arrangement in space.

This reaction of the fifties occurred not because the basis of functionalism was wrong but because it didn't go far enough. Rather than reacting in such a retrograde way and going to a world that is arbitrary and stylistic, the dominating approach in the architect-designed environment in North America – what little of it that is left – we must explore the fundamental nature of living form. When we talk about structures, the infinity of structures, it's important to avoid the danger of isolating and exaggerating any particular aspects of them. I am making a movie with the National Film Board of Canada. In it, a man designs a tree. He's never seen a tree before. He writes down all that is important: fluid must flow upwards; sun has to come downwards; cells reproduce in a particular way, and so on. But, alas, he forgets about wind. He makes a beautiful efficient tree, except that it has no trunk. It's a dome of leaves with a network of branches. As he finishes, a storm comes and blows the whole thing away. Now he designs another tree. He takes all the leaves, puts them in a little box and hangs them on the trunk, thus eliminating all the branches. It is a much more economical tree, but it won't survive because it needs a certain area of exposure to the sun to produce its food. Moral: economy is directly related to survival.

I've been in dozens of meetings with housing officials who would sit back and say: "That's uneconomical, we don't want a garden, we don't want open space, we don't want this, we don't want that, we are perfectly happy with the standards we have." Architects have said, "Habitat is uneconomical because it is an open structure. If you had put the houses in a closed pattern and reduced the area of outdoor spaces, roofs, and exterior walls, it would have cost much less." That is absolutely true. But it is my belief that having an outdoor space by your house, and daylight, and the ability to identify your dwelling, are essential to survival. I conclude that it is a moral obligation to make, with the least possible material and labor, an environment that satisfies the requirements of survival; that is, among other things, an environment that expands man's life and aids his spiritual growth.

It is much easier to comprehend the physical aspects of structure than the psychological ones; we have enough common precedence in natural organisms. Psychic structures are particular to the environment of man. Their fulfilment is equally as important as any of the physical; they are the pivots of man's well being.

I became aware of the depth of this concept when working on a joint paper for an Aspen Design Conference with Christopher Alexander. Irritated by the conference's theme, "Order and Disorder," which was inspired by Ben Shahn's call for the value of disorder, we decided to analyze some basic psychic structures, those usually associated with disorder – identity, the need for variety, and how an individual can affect his own dwelling, the need for change. Essentially, this is what we said:

"People want to feel that they can shape their own personal environment, they can change it, they can modify it, they can choose it, that it's not imposed on them, and they like to feel that it's not the same as everybody else's, because they are not the same as other people. In fact, the ideal would be dwellings that are as different from each other as human faces and personalities are different from each other. This seems to be true of most societies. There are very few where conformity of the individual to the overall group is so strong that he does not have that need for identification. But there are certain societies where the identification isn't to the individual but more to the immediate group, such as the Indian pueblo. The individual felt so much part of his tribe that he was satisfied with that kind of identity, and so the physical environment expressed it. The pueblo was the identity of a tribe."

The need for identity in the dwelling appears to be a basic human need that goes back to even simpler forms of animal life, as Desmond Morris in his book *The Naked Ape* suggests:

"One of the important features of the family territory is that it must be easily distinguished in some way from all the others. Its separate location gives it a uniqueness, of course, but this is not enough. Its shape and general appearance must make it stand out as an easily identifiable entity, so that it can become the 'personalized' property of the family that lives there . . . Endless rows of uniformly repeated, identical houses have been erected in cities and towns all over the world. In the case of blocks of flats the situation is even more acute. The psychological damage done to the territorialism of the families forced by architects, planners and builders to live under these conditions is incalculable."

The degree of individual and community identity varies from culture to culture. You could draw a graph showing the shift from more community and less individual identity to the opposite, and you could place cultures at various points along it.

At the conference both Alexander and I proceeded to demonstrate the possibility of physical systems that could respond to this one aspect of psychic structure. Each of us independently suggested ways in which an individual could differentiate, change, and identify his own environment, thereby producing certain qualities which Ben Shahn may have associated with the term *disorder.* Just as this psychic structure of the environment generates the need for formal response, so each other aspect of the psychic structure – whether it has to do with our perception of space, the qualities of environment conducive to learning or working, or the relationship between individuals living together – must be part of the total design fabric.

Morphology is the key to understanding the physical organism of environment and this understanding is a key to better design. But understanding is not methodology and it is this methodology of design which still remains a deep mystery.

Building as system

Hermann Hesse says, through *Siddhartha:*

"I can love a stone, Govinda, and a tree or a piece of bark. These are things and one can love things. But one cannot love words."

It is easier to say what should be than make it so. It is easier to understand what a building or city should be like than to develop a methodology that makes it so. When we study the morphology of natural organisms, we are conscious that evolution by a process partially mysterious has brought about the object we are studying. But we cannot rely on evolution to create the man-made environment.

The more involved I became in the development of building systems the more conscious I was of the multitude of structures that had to be accommodated and the difficulty of achieving a solution that satisfied all these structures perfectly. On one hand, I am convinced of the validity of a rational process by which we must design, on the other, paradoxically, I find that the process is neither rational in the simplistic sense nor linear. That is to say, it does not follow predetermined and set procedure. But, if we are to improve our cities, if we are to design better environments, then unless we are prepared to rely on the mystical quality of design talent that so few apparently possess, it becomes necessary to evolve methodologies which, by their very nature, result in an improved environment.

This should not appear as an over-optimistic goal, considering the fact that by contemporary standards the men who built the vernacular villages of the Mediterranean and the American plain, environments that we admire, managed to do so without intricate training.

Soon after the Philadelphia sessions with Anne Tyng and Dave Rinehart, and the development of the concept that environment is made of a multitude of structures, I attempted in an organized way to itemize what these structures were for a particular environment. In these attempts I was overwhelmed by two facts: one, it appeared that these structures were very numerous, and two, the process of synthesizing them into a workable organism, a lived-in form, was a highly complex, almost formidable, challenge.

It was at this time (well before I met him) that I came across the writings of Christopher Alexander, particularly his book *Notes on the Synthesis of Form,* which was the first comprehensive attempt to deal with the design process as a logical system. Alexander's insistence on logic and a rational process, and his reference to design through evolution in the past, clearly articulated some of the theories which we were involved with. His theories deal with, ''the process of inventing physical things which display new physical order, organization, form, in response to function.''

In *Notes on the Synthesis of Form,* Alexander selects a simple object and illustrates the various parameters relevant to its design. From the simple example of the choice of materials to be used in the mass production of a vacuum cleaner he builds up to the problem of the total environment, saying:

''Consider the task of designing a complete environment for a million people. The ecological balance of human and animal and plant life must be correctly adjusted both internally and to the given physical conditions. People must be able to lead the individual lives they wish for . . .

''the intuitive resolution of contemporary design problems simply is beyond a single individual's integrative grasp.'' Alexander proceeds to propose ''the use of logical structures to represent design problems.''

Alexander selects the example of a village in India, and outlines the relationships and parameters that must be considered in the design of this village. He goes on to suggest a methodology utilizing a mathematical process that can be programmed for computer processing. What fascinated me about *Notes on the Synthesis of Form* was that it acknowledged the complexity of the multitude of structures that constitute the environment and attempted to resolve them into a workable methodology.

It was in 1967 that I first met Alexander. The occasion was an American Institute of Planners Conference in Portland, Oregon, where we had both been invited to deliver papers. It was an unforgettable event; each of us had heard of the other and we were pleased to meet. That was the beginning of an intense exchange, one which has been of significance to the development of my own thought and work.

Chris has come to be one of my very closest friends and it is difficult to speak of the qualities of a friend without extending beyond his work, which is what I want to discuss here. He has certain qualities that are relevant to an understanding of his thought. He came to architecture through mathematics, and this is significant. He had obtained his Ph.D. in mathematics at Oxford before coming to the U.S. and doing another doctorate, in architecture, at Harvard. He brings to architecture a heritage of logical thought, the very foundation of western thinking. He is also, profoundly, a humanist in the full and old-fashioned sense of the word. The depth of his honesty and humanity are expressed in something he once read to me. I was staying in his house at Berkeley, as I always do when out west. I was on my way to a difficult meeting with the representatives of the California state college system and the college students. I was uneasy about my response to the situation. Chris pulled Lao Tzu from the shelf:

"Truthful words are not beautiful; beautiful words are not truthful. Good words are not persuasive; persuasive words are not good. He who knows has no wide learning; he who has wide learning does not know."

Alexander's concepts evolve from a basic respect and trust for people. He refuses to rely on rare talent as the quality necessary to make a better city or a better environment. He insists in his search on discovering those ways in which all men, thinking honestly, make the environment. Though we come from different backgrounds, we share two important interests: one is faith in a rational process; the other is our interest in the environment that has been the product of evolution. We both believe, for example, that one of the most significant books to be published in recent years on architecture is Bernard Rudofsky's *Architecture without Architects,* page after page of small and large-scale environments made by men for themselves.

Since *Notes on the Synthesis of Form,* Alexander has gone on to develop these thoughts. He has articulated the term *patterns.* Patterns of the environment, he says, are "a system of generating principles, which can be richly transformed according to local circumstances but which never fail to convey their essentials."

He suggests that with a language of patterns, one can make the environment just as one makes sentences with words. There is an affinity between his term *patterns* and the term *structures,* as evolved in our discussions in Philadelphia. Neither are parameters or requirements; what is significant about them is that they are statements of the generic qualities of a particular environment.

But this concept of pattern also highlights a most serious problem in any attempt to develop a rational design methodology. I will try to illustrate with a specific example. In 1968 Alexander and his Center for Environmental Structure were commissioned to participate in the design of a multi-service center. Rather than use the conventional approach, they decided first to develop a series of patterns to describe the generic qualities of the environment which make such a center. Such a pattern language, Alexander suggests, could then be used as a tool for the development of any multi-service center on any site in any city. The book of patterns published by the Center is a very comprehensive program for that particular environment. It encompasses many of the generic qualities of this kind of place. Alexander went on to demonstrate the application of these patterns in evolving several specific buildings applicable to different sites in different cities.

In discussing it, I was particularly concerned with two aspects of the process. One had to do with the completeness of the document. I was aware, as of course was Alexander, that there were many additional patterns that had not been documented, that it would take considerable time to compile, or rather discover, all the relevant patterns. Of even greater concern was the question whether this set of patterns, if given to any architect, would produce a good multi-service center. Would, for example, a group of students of unequal abilities as architects produce equally valid and perfect solutions to the problem of this building, or would there be a great degree of variation in the fulfilment of the problem depending on the capability of the individual? Indeed if there was, wasn't the pattern just another way of making comprehensive programs? To put it differently, is the key the discovery of the patterns, or is it the synthesis of patterns into a whole environment? Does the rational statement of patterns lend itself to a continuing rational process of *synthesis* or is that process of synthesis still dependent on an intuitive process in the human mind which, at the present time, does not lend itself to rational analysis or understanding?

I was to be confronted with a similar but more down-to-earth question later in our work on the Fort Lincoln project in Washington, D.C. Soon after the work on the Fort Lincoln project began, a meeting was called in Washington by Tom Rogers, director of research and technology of the Department of Housing and Urban Development (HUD). Rogers is a physicist who was with the Department of Defense for many years and was brought to HUD in the belief that a scientist who knew how to get things done through research and development programs and a scientific methodology could apply these methods to housing.

Those concerned with the design of the Fort Lincoln project, Paul Rudolph, Harry Weese and myself, were called in, together with many HUD officials. Rogers said, "Look, I'm a physicist, I'm not an architect. I'm in a position here where I have to review various proposals you will be making to us and I have to assess them and say that one is more or less successful than another. How can I assess them?"

He went on to say that he had begun to think about all this because a month earlier I had come into his office and told him that his department was constantly comparing apples with potatoes, talking about construction costs without relating them to what was being provided in terms of amenities. I told him that his people were comparing costs of nine dollars and twelve dollars a square foot, but ignoring the fact that in one case, for example, sound separation between dwellings might be provided while in the other the neighbor could hear every cough and whisper. Unless one assessed what one was getting in environment quality, talk about construction costs was meaningless.

Rogers was disturbed by the word *amenity.* He looked it up in the dictionary and found it meant "pleasantness." He though the word was dangerous. He said, "How can one assess these things?" I said I felt that they could be assessed. I felt that there were many things one could put down as needs or requirements. It might be better not to use the word *amenity* but to replace it by *needs* and *requirements.* There was no cult or mystique to evaluating different solutions.

Paul Rudolph said nothing at the meeting, but we flew to New York together that evening and he said, "You know, I totally disagree with you. I don't think it's possible to measure architecture in this way." I went back to Montreal and began to write down the various things which I knew I could put down on paper, the kinds of things Rogers should have in mind when he was assessing these projects, or any housing project, or any environmental solution. I knew it was going to be full of value judgments, but at least I'd put them down and see what the implications were.

I started with the house itself. I put a statement: "Any family should have a private outdoor space, open and exposed to the elements, of about the same size as its indoor living space." Then I wrote: "Conclusions: All forms of apartment houses as we know them today are unacceptable as they do not conform with this requirement."

I wrote: "It is mandatory that a family in its dwelling should be able to lead a normal life, which includes children playing loudly, music, parties, and the occasional fight, without being heard by its neighbors." This is a clear and simple statement, one which relates to the pattern of life most people prefer. Few politicians would disagree with it publicly. But, practically all forms of multi-storey housing fail to conform to this requirement.

Some statements referred to the overall community: "In any form of grouped dwellings children between the age of three and six should be able to leave their house unattended, wander to a distance of say a hundred or a hundred and fifty feet, and meet a few children of their own age." The implications of such statements are far reaching. It suggests that a certain minimum of families should live along each circulation line. It also means that the area ought to be safe for children. That doesn't work on a busy city street, and it's difficult to achieve on the twentieth floor of an apartment building. Yet, it must be, if it is a valid requirement, true of any form of housing. Accepting such a requirement immediately throws out many forms of housing we build today.

Here is a partial table of requirements I prepared:

Condition	Criterion	Comment
The family cell, space to live	Sufficient space for family day-time activities, entertaining and meeting with friends (assume ten).	Larger families will require larger living space or additional separate spaces. If the figure of friends entertained is changed to fifteen or seven, it would greatly affect size of space.
Outdoor space	Every family or individual must be provided with an outdoor space equal to or greater than its interior living space. This is essential to proper functioning of the family. The nature of the spaces themselves would vary from climate to climate.	This criterion makes unacceptable ninety-nine per cent of all apartments constructed for family living, and most of what would be classified as garden apartments or maisonnettes. If satisfied within a high density environment, it would invariably result in new housing forms.
	The outdoor space must be continuous with the indoor spaces for family functions.	Houses or row houses where court yards are independent of the living space are not satisfactory.
Sleeping	Sleeping facilities for young children should be close to those of their parents. Teenage or older children should have separate sleeping accommodations. Families with children of different ages should have two children's sleeping areas.	The typical apartment or row house plan repeated indefinitely without variation does not fulfill this requirement. This criterion would make it mandatory to have sufficient variety of plans to meet different family requirements.
Children	Every child should have a private sleeping space (a North American criterion; other cultures may be different). Children should have work and play space of sufficient size for these functions.	Separate bedrooms for children are by necessity too small for play and work. Convertible space must give privacy for sleeping but open up for activities requiring more space during the day.

Condition	Criterion	Comment
Individual adaptation and flexibility.	House design must allow the individual to adapt and change the dwelling.	This criterion suggests various technical accommodations to permit changes or modifications to spaces and facilities.

Outer shell	Criterion	Comment
Privacy - acoustic	A family should be able to function normally without hearing or being heard by its neighbors. "Normal" functioning includes occasional fights, playing loud music or instruments, children playing and running around. A decibel rating similar to that of single family house walls with a six-foot air space should be considered minimal.	This criterion would cost more to satisfy in high density housing than in low density forms. It renders unacceptable all forms of conventional multi-storey housing, including flat slab construction and thin block partitions between dwellings, to say nothing of steel studs and other less sound-proof systems. It inherently means the separation of walls and ceilings, the introduction of air spaces, etc.
Privacy - visual The outdoor space	The family should be able to carry on normal functions without being observed by others.	
Privacy - visual Windows	The living and dining spaces should not be observable from another dwelling closer than one hundred feet.	Maybe it's seventy or maybe it's a hundred and fifty feet, but whatever it is it affects the design.
Orientation	In the Florida climate, glass area should not face south or west unless adequately protected. In the Quebec climate, some openings and living spaces should receive sun. A dwelling should receive at least three (four, six) hours of sunshine per day.	

Outer shell	Criterion	Comment
Orientation cont'd.	In hot climates, openings should be arranged to capture any prevailing winds and make dwellings less dependent on mechanical air-conditioning.	A major re-orientation in housing design, which now tends to depend on mechanical devices.
Identity	North America is traditionally a single-family-house culture. It is mandatory that the dwelling unit must be recognizable and definable from the outside by the occupant when he is in its immediate vicinity.	Most current forms of multi-family housing, including row housing, where individual unit identity is suppressed, or single family houses identically repeated, fail to meet this criterion. It suggests a greater variety (not an arbitrary one of a change in material or color to increase recognizability and physical definition of increase identity.

Communication	Criterion	Comment
Access to house	Access to the house should be through pleasant space in which there is daylight. It should be possible to sit or talk to people. No accumulation of odors. Provision for children similar to the experience of a residential street.	Double-loaded corridor apartments, access gallery apartments, walk-up apartments with stair towers do not conform to this requirement.
Access to house, children 3-6	A child of this age should be able to leave his family dwelling on his own and wander to a minimum distance of one hundred and fifty feet, meet at least six to ten children of his age, and find some play areas.	As above; but even typical row houses with their entrances on a trafficked street would not conform. The number of units sharing access and play areas should be determined from this criterion.
Children 6-10	Access to play areas and play fields within an area of five acres.	Complete separation of cars and pedestrians within the inner community mandatory.

Communication	Criterion	Comment
Children 10-17	Access on their own to cultural and recreational facilities such as movies houses, libraries, parks, sport centers, etc.	Necessity of mixing non-residential functions within the community mandatory. Typical suburban subdivision does not conform to this requirement as it is dependent on cars.
Adults, places to meet	Within the community there must be spaces where adults can spontaneously meet or just sit around.	The typical suburban sub-division or row house arrangement ignores this requirement.
Relation of dwelling to car	The ideal arrangement for the North American family of any income group is to be able to drive into the kitchen.	One must investigate the extent to which this is possible within multi-storey housing. Where it is not possible, carts which can be loaded with parcels can be kept by the parking space and at the entrance of the house. They should not have to be taken up or down steps (a lesson from Habitat).
Relationship of vehicular and pedestrian traffic	Within the inner community of 5,000, pedestrians and vehicles should never cross.	
Public transportation	Public transportation is mandatory so that the family will not be dependent on one (or two) cars.	The typical suburban sub-division, which is too low in density to permit public transportation, does not conform.
Family relationships	Entrance to houses should be shared by about four families, to permit social inter-dependency. This assumption may be wrong in number or even in its basic form, but something of the sort must be established. It is certainly true in the self-built *favellas* of Latin America.	The typical arrangement of corridors with entrances spaced at equal distances does not conform. The court or small city square does.

Communication	Criterion	Comment
Communal identity	People need to be able to identify with a larger community unit. This can be observed in most vernacular village architecture.	The inner community must have physical expression or be capable of being identified within the city (hierarchy).
Mixture	The ideal community is a mixture of various individuals and families of different size and make up. Older people, families with young or older children, single people.	The community must include a sufficient variety of dwelling types to insure this mixture.
	The community must also have within it a mixture of families of varying professions and racial origin (this of course is a value judgment that can be challenged, but writing it down forces one to face it).	The mixture of dwelling types should include high and low cost housing. If there are subsidies, as in public housing programs, they must be to units within the community rather than to an entire project.
Common facilities	Facilities beyond the reach of individual low income families, such as work shops, car shop facilities, furniture making shops, greenhouses and plant supplies, should be provided by the community.	

The intermediate community	Criterion	Comment
On foot	Within fifteen minutes' walking distance the family should find a medium-size park, shopping facilities of a minimum of 100,000 square feet, a variety of cultural and recreational facilities, elementary school, and some employment opportunities.	Paul Goodman's "A community is the integration of work, love, and knowledge." Dependency on the car must be decreased, particularly for families who own only one car. Typical suburban subdivision and public row housing projects could not conform as presently built.

The intermediate community	Criterion	Comment
By mass transit and cars	Within ten minutes by mass transportation or car must be major employment opportunities of varying types, regional shopping facilities of a minimum of 500,000 square feet, high schools and trade schools, a major regional park.	This criterion primarily affects the design of a city. Many of the requirements for mixed land uses within a dense development are a by-product of this criterion.
General considerations	The community must be designed so as to take full advantage of natural amenities, existing treed areas, natural topography, views.	
	New construction in an existing city must achieve physical and social continuity with existing construction.	Most urban renewal and public housing developments of the past twenty years have ignored this criterion.

There are many assumptions in this list that can be questioned, but if one assumption does not apply, another assumption replaces it. Requirements differ from culture to culture. Some requirements may be perfectly true in India and absolutely untrue in New York.

As I was completing the list, I realized that what I had drafted was *an environmental code.* Just as there is a building code for fire and other safety matters, we can make one which protects the individual by giving him a sound basic environment. Like any code, it cannot be static; it must accommodate change as standards and life styles change, but as a document related to the quality of environment in its broadest sense, it is or can become "An Environmental Bill of Rights."

I must grant Paul Rudolph that probably one could take this environmental code, which is in a sense a program, and develop a project which fulfills it to the letter, and at the end one would look at it and say, "My God, I'd hate to live there." Rudolph is probably right when he says one cannot measure architecture. I think he means one cannot measure environment, and I suppose the reason is that we could never document all the requirements.

There is a similarity between the question that this problem raises and the multi-service center developed by Alexander. If the list of patterns or requirements of the environmental code were foolproof, it would guarantee the results. It was with this in mind that I suggested to Alexander that a group of students should be given the problem of the multi-service center using the pattern language, to see to what extent this tool would uniformly improve the results. I did not see the results but was told that the experiment showed there was considerable difference in the solutions to the problem. In my opinion, this difference must have been directly related to the design capability of each student. To my dismay this result put me in the same position as Paul Rudolph when he stated that one could not guarantee the results, a statement I had reacted against.

This paradox can be attributed to the incompleteness of any given group of patterns; even if we listed several hundred patterns, there would be several that we failed to include. We may fail to state the desired nature of light in the space or the importance of the texture of walls. Since the number of patterns is almost infinite, such an omission is very likely. I know that Chris deeply believes that it is possible to accumulate a treasury of patterns sufficiently complete to guarantee the results, that is, to get a good environment which is not dependent on the mystique of the design talent of the individual using them. I wish I could think this is so, for it is an appealing resolution, but even granted the existence of a complete list of patterns, an even more complex question arises: By what process do we synthesize this great number of often contradictory patterns into an organism which is the whole environment? Can we synthesize it without relying on good old-fashioned intuition, which is very variable from one individual to the other? Will a synthesizing process not have the danger of exaggerating one aspect of a structure of environment over another, just as the dome shaped tree designed by the man who forgot that the tree must withstand winds was a caricature of what a tree really ought to be?

Some of these questions are critical, I believe. In a program I undertook with a group of students at McGill in 1970, the students became obsessed with accumulating information and expanding the program for the project which they were to develop – a transportation master plan with terminal facilities for Montreal. There was a strong reluctance to deal with any aspects of the study in physical terms, a reluctance to make physical plans, and a directing of all energies toward statements of what it ought to be. But statements of intent, no matter how inspiring, are not physical reality. Any creative and clearminded person could make a good program. A school principal could make a very good program for a school; with the insight he has into school life he could state many relevant patterns, but he could not design a school. Alexander suggests that just as it was possible for the peasants of an Aegean island to make their own village using a pattern language, so it must be possible for the school principal to make his own school. In this overall perspective the conventional role of the architect is unimportant, made obsolete. He points out that if anyone can design, and if architects are all joining forces to accumulate a treasury of patterns, then the role of design fundamentally changes. This view has in it a key to the unanswered question: the design process is one of synthesis and integration. Words can only be program. Physical elements can be generic, can *condense* design, can become *building systems.*

It is fascinating how from two opposite springboards, from my physical involvement with building systems and Alexander's theoretical structuring of environment, we have both converged on a similar conclusion. Alexander says patterns are not programs, they are generic in nature. He further states that "real patterns state a geometry." I have come to realize, working with building as systems (particularly the San Francisco State College Union), that a physical system can embody certain generic qualities of the environment. A building system, not in the sense that it is a technical assembly of repetitive parts, but a building system that consists of elements which are *space-makers,* elements which have inherent in them the environmental characteristics synthesized from generic requirements. In the case of the San Francisco Union this environmental system could then be applied to a specific site and specific program by the students themselves; the qualities of the environment would be fundamentally the same.

Let me explain how *space-maker* differs from program. In 1969 I was commissioned to design a school in Montreal in which many progressive methods of education were being experimented with. Before designing the building I had extensive discussions with the teachers and students. The teachers explained that the typical classroom did not lend itself to the way they wanted to use it. Some of them wanted to sit in a circle and talk, others had the students working at tables, others showed slides or had illustrated discussions. In some cases the students sat in rows; in other classes they danced. The students had similar observations. They did not feel, for example, that the teacher should always be behind a desk. When they sat in a circle, they said, it would be nice to have a pit which would bring them closer together; when they were watching slides, it would be nice to have a raked or terraced floor to give everyone a clear view of the screen. All these different uses had to be interchangeable at any given time. This much was program, possibly what Alexander would call a pattern, inasmuch as it is true of all schools, of all classrooms in which different activities take place.

When it came to designing the buildings we tried to find ways to implement this. Was there some way the rooms could be instantly changed from a pit to terraced seating to flat floor? And from these thoughts emerged a physical solution: the room floor was arranged as three layers of cubes above the fixed floor. Each of these cubes opened up to become a chair and a table. By taking the cubes from the center of the room and arranging them at the periphery, you could make a sunken pit. By arranging them in rows you could make a terraced room. By filling the center of the room with the cubes you could make a flat floor. This was one aspect of a space-maker: a physical solution to a generic problem. There are similar generic qualities to the physical solution of other problems: the quality of lighting, for example, and the ability to change classroom sizes so that they can equally comfortably accommodate three, ten, or fifty. Each pattern must be translated to a physical space-maker. I think Alexander has come to the same conclusion after developing the multi-service center patterns – that requirements at the literal level have to be translated to solutions at the physical level.

I think this attitude has in it the potential that Alexander refers to when he says that the peasant making his village did not need an architect. Time and evolution had evolved particular space-makers, the court, the dome, the vault, a wall with a particular way of making a window; or in other cultures a thatched roof on a wood frame. Each of these was a space-maker that had built into it the generic qualities of the environment it made. Whereas in the past, evolution and time evolved these space-makers, today in the context of our own cities we must compress time by making a contemporary vernacular. Many space-makers can then be related to each other by an overall structure – a kind of DNA of the city. Design is transformed to a process at two levels: one where systems are evolved for anyone to use, and design at the community level in which systems are adapted by the people who will live there. The role of translating the generic qualities of environment to space-makers, the structuring of a DNA of the city, is a highly creative act demanding perception, and compressing evolution of time.

When I was doing Habitat, I was bombarded by painters and sculptors who wanted the opportunity to do a mural here, a sculpture there. At first I just avoided them without really knowing why. And then I realized that most often when so-called fine art was put in architecture, it was like make-up, compensating for the inability of the architecture to respond to life in such a way that it satisfied our emotions. Think of the enormous new plazas in the middle of an American city, with glass towers all around. The scale of the buildings ignores human beings, their form ignores our climate, plant life has not been made an integral part of it, or has at best come into existence in little pots, the plaza is exposed to light and heat in summer, to snow and wind in winter, a threatening barrenness – and we hope that a mural or a great big sculpture in the middle will correct all this.

In Habitat, because the building is air-conditioned and this requires water-cooling, we were able to have fountains in the landscape that the kids could play in. The cooling of the building and the playing of children were integrated with terraced pools and sprays of water. In the same way the grouping of the houses in space created complex and changing patterns of sunlight. The public responds by saying Habitat is like a sculpture! But no, Habitat is environment, not sculpture.

A total and comprehensive design will result in a place that does not need to be saved by art. Conversely, objects and places conceived in an integrated and unarbitrary way have the makings of what we sometimes call art.

Airplanes are excellent examples of man-made objects that result from an evolutionary process of design rather than from fashion. The forms of aircraft have evolved over sixty or seventy years. More perfect solutions to the problems have been achieved at each stage. I don't believe any airplane designer has ever stopped and said, "I'd rather do this because it's more beautiful than that." He is concerned with weight and speed and aerodynamic behavior and hundreds of other things, and yet I think most people will agree that airplanes are among the most beautiful man-made objects in our environment.

The aircraft is a kind of vernacular design of our time. When we studied the history of architecture at McGill, we started with the pyramids (very briefly, half a day) and then jumped to Greece and studied the Parthenon and the temples of Olympus. It never occurred to me then that these were probably two per cent of all the buildings built by the Greeks and that Athens probably looked like the island of Mikonos today. We didn't regard that as architecture, we didn't even study it. As a student, I really thought of Athenian houses as being little Parthenons. Then we jumped to Roman temples, a little Romanesque, then Gothic Churches, and then for one year, the Renaissance. By and large our tradition of the architect-designer today is the Renaissance concept: the man who is an "artist" – and with *artist* there is implied a certain liberty to be arbitrary. I don't think that's been true of vernacular art.

So, parallel to the history of architecture that we studied was another kind of history of architecture that we didn't study: man beginning to make shelter, man making villages and towns that were really building systems – vernacular building systems, evolved in an organic, morphological way. He was very influenced by the materials. If he had mud he used it in a way that was true to the nature of mud, if he had stone he used it according to the nature of stone. He didn't try to make the stone look like mud or like wood. (Only when he was making temples did he do that – not when he was making shelter.)

A variety of vernacular non-architected architectures evolved in different cultures, and these were similar in form and vocabulary even though they were developed in different parts of the world. This architecture was not designed in our sense, nor was it a work of art in the eyes of its builders. The people who built it did not think of it as art at all, they thought of making themselves shelter in a way that pleased them and in a way that responded to the forces that affected their survival. In the same way the Greeks made utensils of metal and pottery to cook in and to store water and now we treasure them as works of art. The Greeks never thought of them as art. They were just making useful things the best way they knew. They chose materials and processed them and decorated them in a way that responded to their own images but never in contradiction to usefulness.

We have, evolving through centuries, a tradition of non-art, vernacular architecture, and then at one point in contemporary life disappearing. What is lacking today is a vernacular, our own vernacular. We need to create one which is an expression of our life and technologies. The people who built their villages, the man who designed his own house and built it himself, worked in a simple situation. Today we have great factories and industries and organizations producing the environment. Can we recreate the situation where the man who lives in a house is part of the design process, in some way affecting the end-product? That would totally change the role of the designer. He would not be an artist with license to express himself, he would be an instrument of expression (though in that he would of course also be expressing himself).

I believe that an essential part of form-making is to be truthful to the nature of the solution in terms of material and process. The Greeks carved vertical grooves in the columns of their temples to emphasize and express the fact that there was a vertical element of support. They emphasized natural behavior. But the baroque architect made spirals around his column to pretend it wasn't really acting as a column, or he painted a scene over it to make it disappear, to make it look as if it wasn't there. It was a stage set, a make-believe world. I believe that the expression of truth, calling an arch an arch, makes an architecture of growth, one that is open-ended; the architecture of pretense, of defiance of physical truth, is an architecture that is retrograde because it is dead-ended and arbitrary.

I find myself quite apart from the architects who believe in the cult of architecture as an instrument of expression *per se.* I feel the wrong emphasis is made when Lou Kahn speaking at the International Congress of Architects and Engineers in Tel Aviv in 1967, said, "Expression is all that architecture is about." Buckminster Fuller talked about humanity, about its capacities and capabilities and the materials and the resources it has and how it uses them. The peasants who built a village on a Mediterranean hillside thought of shelter and their community and the relationships between them and the mud and wood they had for building and the sun they lived with and the water they had to collect, from which emerged their environment. They didn't think of it as expression, although it obviously was. They didn't think they were artists, though they obviously were.

So, I basically disagree with Philip Johnson, who says everything is possible in architecture today: "There are no rules, surely no certainties in any of the arts. There is only the feeling of a wonderful freedom."

I absolutely disagree with him. We have very few alternatives to the right solution. Only by being totally arbitrary is it possible to have no rules and complete freedom. In terms of the forces and realities of life today, a solution is a process of moving toward the truth, which is the complete opposite of freedom from rules.

I feel that most dramatically in my relationship to the world of painting and sculpture today. It is not significant to my development. What saddens me is that I feel I am living in a society that has diverted much of its creative energies to the world of visual art at the expense of the art of life. (I'm waiting for somebody to get up and cry, "The Emperor is naked!") I respond more to micro-photographs of rock crystals or animal cells than to most of the painting of today.

To quote Piet Hein:

There is
one art,
no more,
no less:
to do
all things
with art-
lessness.

There is a visual stimulus in our lives that did not exist two or three generations ago. Our visual exploration of nature, the optical devices that surround us, add something to our experience. Just look in the microscope!

I have a cloth picture from northern India on the wall of my office. It is a montage of embroidered fabrics of different colors in the shapes of various animals. It was made by peasants in the State of Gujarat, who use such pictures as pillow cases and as part of their clothing. It is art, but to them it is something they use in their daily lives, an object of daily life. This life object expresses the whole world of animals and nature around them. I'm sure the woman who made it did not think of herself as an artist. In less sophisticated cultures people made things to use in their daily lives, shaped them in their own hands, in their own image. They made pottery to cook in. They wove things to lie on. They made clothes to wear, they decorated the clothes for different occasions, they used color and patterns and everything was integrated into the process of living. The act of making something was linked to the act of living. Art was part of life. Worshipping was part of life. Objects were made for worshipping in the images of man and the symbols of God, not the making of works of art. Today we cherish these objects of life gone by as art; but what about the objects of life today?

Even the presence of this cloth picture on my wall is artificial, for it is not part of my own life.

When I said that to a friend one day, she said, "How can you say that, after all such a significant part of our culture is in the visual arts." I tried to explain that what I meant was not that the act of making a painting or sculpture was artificial, but that the artificiality lay in the way it related to daily life and to the environment. I asked her to imagine that she was going to Mars, she was in a space ship built and designed in the best tradition of space ships. It had elaborate controls and dials and watches and warning lights, and it had TV screens, and it had apertures focusing on the sun and the moon and the planets, and it had sleeping compartments molded out of the wall in which you were suspended weightless and other areas molded out of the surface and the floor, for eating and preparing food, it was all one continuous womb of an environment; and I asked her, "Could you imagine a painting hanging on the

170

wall of this space ship?" After thinking for a while she said, "No, I couldn't."
I said, "Could you think of a Mondrian on the wall?" and she said, "No, it would
not be right there." She went on to say, "You wouldn't need it because the
entire space ship, the dials and the controls and the screens and the panels,
they would all form kind of a Mondrian." This was, of course, precisely what I
had meant: that the integrated environment generates the kind of intensity of
experience which is complete, and to which every activity of life contributes.
That does not mean that one should not make a painting or design a record
cover or illustrate a box, but that the environment as an experience must be
integrated.

It is not the question of art in our culture, it is more a question of the total
cultural bias that we live with – a split or duality in the culture so profound that it
has penetrated the basic expressions in language. To say "it is functional but
not beautiful", or conversely "it is not enough to be functional, it should also be
beautiful," is a negation of the unity of nature, of the beauty inherent in the
expression of truth and order – an order based in the fulfilment of function in its
broadest context.

It is inconceivable that something which is not functional should be beautiful.
This schizophrenia is so deeply rooted that even our most profound thinkers fall
into the trap. To paraphrase John Kenneth Galbraith speaking of the city, "We
must now realize that it is not enough to have functional cities, we must be
prepared to pay the price for aesthetics and beauty." Only the total debasing of
the word *function* to express the most obvious and simplistic aspects of
function could result in a city which is functional but "not beautiful" and it is
this schizophrenia that makes us regard the utilitarian objects we use in our
daily life as apart from other objects we collect as so-called art.

I am not saying that all art in our lives must be the by-product of utilitarian
needs. But, there is a question of cultural emphasis. The fact is, that our life is
full of opportunities for the art within us to influence our environment. Instead
we ignore them. We uncritically delegate the making of them to others. As a
matter of cultural pattern we do not look to the total environment as something
that gives us satisfaction in life. The energy that would have gone to that is then
replaced in creating a make-believe world that has nothing to do with our life
process. Think of some of the garbage hanging in our galleries and relate it to
the possibility of art in our life unrealized in the cars we drive, the cups we drink
from, the dishes we eat from, the vacuum cleaners we sweep the room with, the
clothes we wear. As we enter an era of greater integration of human thought, a
return to unitary thinking and yet a new evolution of it, the concept of the
artist – the man who, as a professional, makes objects of art for others – must
become much less important in our life. Our furniture, our cars, made so that
they are more meaningful in our lives, will become our art.

These thoughts are very much inspired by those of Sir Lancelot Whyte. For the
first time since the Renaissance, and probably under the influence of Eastern

thinking, we are coming to believe that there isn't a dual world of so-called science and so-called art and humanities. We recognize a certain unity in nature and in human energy. Whyte's concept of unitary thinking is important and suggestive. In his *Aspects of Form,* twelve different people, an astronomer, a chemist, and a physicist among them, talk about form in their own disciplines, and discover that there is a unity to it all. In *The Next Development in Man,* Whyte's central theme is that Western man has been trained to think in terms of dualities: Good and evil, cold and hot – always dualities. But dualities don't exist, he says. Everything in life is process and a mixture of both. There are no absolutes. No absolute light or dark, no absolute good or evil. The understanding of process leads to unitary thinking.

I think that this will be the most important coming change in our culture. The people running to New York art galleries and paying sixty or a hundred thousand dollars for a couple of red circles on a white background are part of an illusionary world and have not yet experienced that change which we are now living. The whole scene would appear incredible to a visiting Martian. As Buckminster Fuller puts it in *Nine Chains to the Moon:*

"When there is time perspective on [Henry] Ford equivalent to the 400 year interval between ourselves and Leonardo da Vinci, which enables us to appraise da Vinci as the greatest artist of the Middle Ages, Ford will undoubtedly be acclaimed by the people of that later day as certainly the greatest artist of the 20th century."

17   . . . Happily ever after

Back in Habitat, D-Day was coming very close, and it was very difficult to believe that the building would ever be ready in time.

It's amazing how unfinished a building can look five days before completion. One week before the opening of Expo, while tenants were moving into some of the units and furniture was arriving, the building was covered with construction garbage and debris. The site was still full of equipment, the area surrounding the building was terraced but piled up with dirt. You couldn't believe it would be ready in time. The last four days were a transformation. Garbage was removed by the ton, the equipment got hauled out – twenty-four-hour shifts, people coming in and out. Two days before opening an army of gardeners arrived with truckloads of sod and right in front of our eyes the whole thing changed in forty-eight hours. By the opening the grass was all green, the planting was all in, the streets were swept clean, the building was finished. It was just incredible. There were hundreds of deficiencies, little things that had to be done, but you didn't see them. You saw the finished building.

On D-Day – April 27, 1967 – the building opened. No one, including myself, had believed that Habitat would be ready in time. The fact that it looked so unfinished up to the last moment was responsible for a lot of hysteria and concern.

Nina and I moved to Habitat one day after the opening. I was personally so busy with the completion that the whole business of moving and getting furniture designed or bought was very much neglected. We lived for a month with hardly any furniture.

In the first place, we had not intended to move into Habitat. Our first thought was that the rent was too high and it just didn't make sense for us to move. We were living then in a duplex on Pine Avenue in downtown Montreal. At one point Expo decided that Mr. Dupuy ought to have two apartments combined into a sort of a royal residence made up of four boxes on the eleventh and twelfth floors looking out in four directions. So the unit that had been originally reserved for him became vacant. That was only a few months before the opening. At that point we decided to take advantage of the available unit and that we would indeed move in. For one thing, the rent during Expo would be a business expense, and the other factor was that, by that time, Expo had received a report recommending that post-Expo rents be forty per cent below rents during Expo. We felt we could afford those rents after Expo, so we could rationalize the higher rent for our apartment during the exhibition period itself.

Two months before the opening I received a call from Ottawa saying that Prime Minister Lester Pearson had decided to have an apartment in Habitat and would I make mine available. We had by then ordered our furniture, most of which was to be built in. I was nevertheless inclined to say, "Yes," but then another suitable unit was found for him on the third floor. The Prime Minister always stayed in Habitat when he was in Montreal during Expo.

There was not much of a ceremony when the building was finished except an informal party given by the general contractor, for the people who actually worked on the building. But, finishing Habitat was really part of finishing Expo and, on opening night, there was a big party in the main hall of Place Bonaventure with several rock bands, light shows and thousands of people. It was a real swinging party.

From the first, Habitat was a great public success. The newspapers raved about it. The flow of people through the building averaged something like thirty thousand people a day, in the six months of Expo a total of seven million. There was a constant stream of dignitaries and officials, many of whom I saw, some of whom I didn't.

I continually got calls from the Expo visitors' service: "Governor Rockefeller of New York is here, will you please take him through the building . . . The U.S. Secretary of Housing is here," etc. I took Rockefeller through, I took Secretary of Housing Weaver through, but eventually I decided that work had to go on and I just couldn't continue doing it, except for very special cases. Among the professional writers I saw were Wolf Von Eckardt, writing for the Washington *Post,* Ada Louise Huxtable of the New York *Times,* David Jacobs who wrote for the New York *Times* magazine and for *Horizon,* and novelist Penelope Mortimer who was writing for the *Sunday Times* in London.

Tony Peters, in his new capacity as exhibit director, took over the hosting of notables through the building: a list that included Earl Mountbatten, Princess Margaret, General de Gaulle, Lady Bird Johnson, and Mayor Lindsay of New York. Some of them made public comments or held press conferences, mostly saying very positive things about Habitat. Lady Bird Johnson said she wouldn't like to live there. Then the articles started appearing: the *Sunday Times,* and the New York *Times,* the Washington *Post, Time* and *Life* magazines, most of which were very sympathetic. In contrast there were some very critical articles. I recall one by Edgar Kaufmann in *The republic,* in which he said Habitat was a monstrous stage set for a Frankenstein film. That made me sad, because Kaufmann happened to have been responsible for getting Frank Lloyd Wright to design Fallingwater for his father, and that is the most exciting house I've ever seen.

We were constantly under pressure to let our own house be photographed and published. But we felt that the privacy of our home was very important to us. We wanted our friends there, but we didn't want to make it into a public place. Once however, a whole group of young kids wandered in, not realizing that this was not an exhibit unit; they opened our door, and walked right through the house. They were surprised to see us there, when they reached the bedroom.

When the President of the U.S.S.R., Nikolai Podgorny, came to visit Dupuy, the whole building was covered with trench-coated NKVD people. They came in the lobby to go up to the Dupuy apartment on the twelfth floor. Podgorny and Dupuy went up in one elevator, the bodyguards went up in the other, which got stuck halfway and trapped them for an hour, to the panic and dismay of the RCMP and the other NKVD.

There were always secret agents in the building because either Pearson was there or some other head of state was visiting. Nina was taking the children for a walk one day when she saw de Gaulle walking up the stair above us.

The day U Thant stayed in Habitat there was a knock on our door about eight o'clock in the evening and a pale-faced secret agent said, "Please take your family and leave the building immediately." The first thing that came to my mind was, "My God, a structural failure, a crack somewhere." I said, "What is it?" He said, "I can't tell you. Just get out of the building." I said, "You've got to tell me. I have a responsibility for this building and I just have to know what's happened." And he said, "We just got a note that there's a bomb in the building." I said, "Oh, is that all," feeling absolutely relieved.

We all got out of the building, leaving, to our children's dismay, the goldfish behind. The note said the bomb would explode at nine o'clock, and I thought, if I were going to destroy Habitat there would be half a dozen places where I would place the bomb, half a dozen places that are very critical to the structure, where a strategically placed bomb would be very damaging, just as putting a bomb under the anchorage of a suspension bridge would easily destroy the bridge. I rounded up a group of RCMP and Navy bomb experts who had arrived and we started running through the building to all the places I felt we ought to look. Nine o'clock came and no bomb went off. U Thant left next morning.

They were a very lively six months. Every night there would be a party on some terrace and you would hear the music as if it were coming over a distant mountain. Some of the visiting ships docked right in front of us had bands and the sound would carry over the river.

Of course we had our own party, but not until three months after the opening because only then did the last of the furniture arrive. We covered our part of the building with colored lights and had a twenty-man steel band, playing loud enough to be heard in downtown Montreal. They were on one terrace while people were dancing on the other terraces.

We had a pretty good idea that the public response to Habitat was positive, but in the last days of Expo we became aware that we ought to have some kind of documentation of it. I was also encouraged to get that documentation by the U.S. government, who felt it would be useful in our programs there. I suggested to Central Mortgage that with thirty thousand people a day going through the building, there was a unique opportunity to sample their feelings about the environment. The U.S. government would have shared the cost, but Central Mortgage turned it down, so I decided we would do it on our own. We made up a questionnaire and hired a number of McGill students to give them out on the site. We got twenty-thousand-odd questionnaires filled out. In response to the question, "Would you like to live in Habitat and would you raise your children there?" eighty per cent were favorable.

The questionnaires were taken over, processed, and indexed by Cornell University for a comprehensive study of Habitat, *Anatomy of a Prototype.* The Cornell architecture students also interviewed the permanent tenants of Habitat after Expo. Preliminary results from the survey showed that ninety per cent of the tenants felt there was adequate privacy both within the dwelling and on the terraces. Ninety-five per cent felt that the open walkway system and the relationship of the car to the house in terms of climate were good. Ninety per cent said they expected to live there more than five years. Of course these are people who chose to move in, and it's foreseeable that they would be sympathetic. You might well get negative responses from others.

One of our first steps after the completion of Habitat had been a thorough post-mortem. Where, because of lack of time or knowledge, had we gone wrong? Where should the system be changed? I invited the superintendents and field foremen of all the contractors who were on the job and all our engineers, the mechanical, electrical, and structural engineers, and the senior people on my own staff, and we had something like ten evening sessions, with enough cheese and wine to loosen everybody's tongue. The mechanical engineer said what he felt he did wrong, for instance, and then he had to listen to the plumbing foreman who told him what he felt was wrong, and so we got the two experiences, the theoretical designer and the man who had to do it.

These post-mortems extended over a broad range of topics. There were discussions on the nature of concrete and the system of casting and the pros and cons of load-bearing systems. We talked about the nature of an assembly line and the shortcomings that we experienced in Habitat in terms of actually achieving one. We heard about the day-to-day problems and conflicts of the

176

plumbing superintendent and the electrical superintendent, and about the very real field problems of fitting the pieces together.

We had a long list of construction deficiencies that had to be corrected, but we got very little support from the Expo bureaucrats in forcing the contractor to fix the faults. A lot of the work had been done in extreme haste and done improperly. The topping in the streets, the flashing, the roofing, were all wrong. It was only after insistence on our part that sufficient monies were held back to assure that the work would be done.

But at that point Anglin-Norcross, the general contractor, went bankrupt. (That had nothing to do with us. They had, in fact, made some money on Habitat as a result of the settlement, which was very generous to them, but they had lost money on other projects.) This really made things complicated because, while Expo had a hold-back to do some of the deficiency work, the whole problem of guarantees and settling with the trustees and the sub-contractors became an absolute maze of legal complexities. As a result, many deficiencies never got corrected. When Central Mortgage eventually took the building over, Expo turned part of that money over to them but not all of it, and so Central Mortgage fixed some of the deficiencies but not all of them. Some of them are still there today, to my dismay.

Toward the end of Expo I became concerned about the lack of plans for the future of the building. The Canadian Corporation for the 1967 World Exhibition would cease to exist as a corporation, and there seemed to be no decision as to who would own the building or what would be done with it. The matter came to a head because many of the tenants wanted to renew their leases, and there was no one to renew them with. I felt it personally because I wanted to negotiate a lease to stay there and give up our apartment on Pine Avenue, which I had kept through the summer. I tried to get some kind of action but could get nowhere.

I foresaw that if there was no landlord, the building would sit empty, and even if it sat empty for only a short period, it would be very damaging: not damaging physically, but a building that is empty acquires a certain stigma.

The only statement that I had from Expo, from G. D. Rediker, the comptroller of the corporation, was that I could stay on a monthly basis for the same exorbitant rent. The whole attitude was pretty ridiculous, and so we moved back to Pine Avenue and everybody else left the building, some of them people who also wanted to say.

Several months of uncertainty followed. It was said that the National Harbours Board might take over the building, then that Central Mortgage might take it over, later that it might be sold as condominiums. No one knew what would happen. One reason was that the three governments were sitting down and bargaining, and the dividing of the assets took several months. While that was happening the building sat there empty, and was being run on a haphazard basis. The irrigation system wasn't drained and was damaged, conversion to winter conditions didn't take place, causing some serious damage that had to be repaired later. Finally an announcement was made – I think it was February 1968 – that Central Mortgage was taking charge of MacKay Pier, including Habitat, for a limited period of time.

One might expect that they would then have started a vigorous rental program to get the building filled as fast as possible. But they didn't. For a long time they held onto the property without knowing what to do about it. When I inquired about rents they said the new rent scale had been established; a twenty per cent reduction from Expo rents, roughly. The study made by Bud Andrews and Eric Bell of Community Development in consultation with the Montreal Trust, which recommended a forty per cent reduction after Expo, had been ignored. The rent for our apartment had been seven hundred dollars a month and CMHC reduced it to five hundred and ninety dollars, compared with the four hundred dollars that Andrews and Bell had recommended. I felt the building wouldn't fill up at those rents. They had to acknowledge that they had a handicap, that because only part of the project was built there weren't community facilities on the site, there weren't schools, there weren't shops, and those inconveniences had to be made up by reducing the rents. Besides, the rent should be related to rents in other parts of the city. A good place to compare it with was Nun's Island, a development a mile upstream from Expo, where a three- or four-bedroom townhouse was renting for between three and four hundred dollars a month. Many people thought the high rents were related to the cost of the building; that was not so. The building had been written off as an exhibit and was transferred to Central Mortgage at reduced book value, so they could have established any rents they thought fit. They could even have filled it up with public housing tenants and set rents just to cover the maintenance costs.

Eventually we moved back in on a month-to-month lease, paying the high rent and hoping that things would change.

Central Mortgage's ideas about Habitat were quite different from ours. They felt the building was not a place for families. Their initial approach towards renting was that it was for single people or for corporations who would use it as an entertainment center. Hector St. Pierre, executive director of Central Mortgage, was quoted in *Time* magazine as saying: "I just don't believe that this building is the type of construction for people with young children; and I've nothing against children. I have seven of them." That, of course, influenced CMHC's attitude toward renting the building.

They were getting nowhere. The building was empty and the papers, particularly the Montreal papers, were having a ball. Habitat was empty because "people have rejected the concept," because "they don't like the idea," because it is "a white elephant." I couldn't keep my feelings within me any more and when *Time* called and asked me how I felt about it, I said it was empty because of a ridiculously high rental structure and because the building was misunderstood and mismanaged by the Central Mortgage and Housing Corporation.

Time made a big story out of it and that seems to have had a positive effect because two weeks later CMHC reduced the rents. They were still not down to the Andrews and Bell recommendations but within a short time thirty units were rented, mostly the small units to single people who could afford to pay those rents. But the big units were still not moving.

I continued my criticism. It led to a meeting with Ian Maclennan of CMHC, who asked, "Why are you criticizing us?" After this conversation, things started to improve. Central Mortgage opened a grocery store. They produced a limousine service to take tenants to and from the city. They reduced the rents a second time, this time bringing them very close to the Andrews and Bell recommendations, and several families moved in.

The tenants in Habitat now are a heterogeneous group of people: McGill professors, musicians from the symphony orchestra, executives, artists, businessmen, older people, students, bachelors. They range from two or three young designers, who share the rent and have no furniture in the place except for a few wall hangings, to wealthy executives in the hundred-thousand-dollar bracket. They all appear to feel strongly about the building as a place to live. I know about twenty of the tenants and I learned about some of the others in a very revealing article in the Toronto *Globe and Mail* called "Habitat Lives". Characteristically, this appeared in Toronto while the Montreal papers were writing about Habitat being deserted and sending their photographers to take tricky shots of the building through a fringe of weeds.

There's an interesting difference between the professional criticism the building has received and people's response to it. You get a man like Reyner Banham, a renowned architectural critic, saying, I suppose after considerable thought: "Privacy was totally ignored in Habitat." And you get the people living there saying that they are very satisfied and happy with the privacy they have there. You get critics saying, "Habitat was built without regard to the Montreal climate." Yet the people living in it say, "We love its relationship to the elements, in all seasons."

Another problem was Central Mortgage's reluctance to commit themselves publicly to future plans for the building and the area round Habitat, whereas Nun's Island in their rental program didn't hesitate to say what a wonderful place it was going to be, with golf courses and shops, and people responded to that and moved in. Central Mortgage kept saying, "We don't know what will happen to the area." For all people knew, it would become harbor warehouses a year later. This reluctance to communicate a more imaginative plan to the public was, I think, responsible for the public feeling that Habitat was far away, even though it is only two minutes from downtown. There was a feeling it was distant, isolated. People stopped me in the street in the winter of 1968-69 to say, "It must be very cold living in Habitat." My response was: "Well, when it's cold on Sherbrooke Street, it's cold in Habitat." But there was this mental image of the snow blowing through this building behind barbed wire in the middle of the harbor. I think that has been overcome now because people are living there, and they are very happy and vocal about it.

After the second rent reduction things started moving fast. By May 1969 the building was full and we were instructed to proceed with studies for the completion of the north cluster interiors, some of which were already reserved.

Nina and I, meanwhile, had become desperate. On one hand we felt the rent was too high for us to keep up with and, on the other hand, there was our landlord actively discouraging families with children from moving into the building. At that time, ours were the only two children in the building. We felt it was irresponsible to stay if our children were to be isolated in this way, and we decided to move out. Just after we had made our decision, ironically, rents were reduced and several families with children moved in.

There were other factors, of course. I was constantly getting involved with the administration of the building. I would come in and see vulgar gold anodized aluminum ashtrays in the lobby and I would get all upset about it and try to get them changed. This became quite a burden for both of us. It was taking an increasing amount of my energies and attention, which in turn irritated Nina who felt I was possessive of the building to the point where it was not healthy. I think she felt the need to move, so that I could "cut the umbilical cord", as she put it.

Leaving was made a bit more difficult for me when the press wrote it up in such a way as to suggest that I was abandoning the building and that made me feel quite guilty. But it was one of those painful things one has to do sometimes. I hope we will go back there eventually.

18

Washington, D.C.:
An abortive attempt

My flirtation with the U.S. government goes back to the days when Expo was still operating.

I was invited to give a talk about industrialized housing in Washington. Wolf Von Eckardt, the architectural critic of the Washington *Post,* was to be a speaker too. He had earlier interviewed me in Montreal and written about Habitat. He suggested that I meet Robert Weaver, the Secretary of the Department of Housing and Urban Development (HUD) while I was in Washington and told me he had spoken to Under-Secretary Robert C. Wood, who had expressed interest in meeting me. So when I went to give my lecture, a meeting was arranged with Weaver, Wood, Commissioner of the FHA, Philip N. Brownstein, and Mr. Weaver's executive assistant. We met in Weaver's office and I showed them drawings and photographs of Habitat and some of the studies I had been doing since then. The next day, at Weaver's suggestion, I had a meeting with about twenty high-ranking FHA and HUD officials.

One of the people at that meeting was Jim Simpson, who was head of the technical research department. After my presentation, he told me he felt my work was closely related technically to the work of Ed Rice and his firm Conrad Engineers, who had been doing modular housing construction studies and precast work using Chemstress concrete and also had been doing the Instant Rehab project for HUD. In this project bathrooms and kitchens were prefabricated and dropped into the core of old tenement housing in New York in a forty-eight-hour renovation. He felt that we would make a good team and that we ought to get together.

Right then and there, he got Ed Rice on the phone, told him how he felt about it, and suggested that Rice and I meet as soon as possible. The following week I was in San Francisco. I flew down to Los Angeles where Rice lives and met him and his staff. This was the beginning of an important relationship. They are the structural engineers for most of my present work.

Rice was in the midst of building a precast apartment building of three-dimensional modular box units using two-inch walls. It was a conventional design, a regular twenty-four-unit six-storey apartment building, built with box modules. I was amazed to find out during our first phone conversation that Rice knew everything about what we were doing. He knew about the size of our units, our bathrooms, the thickness of our walls, and some of our problems; obviously, he had been keeping in very close touch with our progress. Instant Rehab had just been completed at that time.

A few weeks later I was invited to make a presentation to the President's science and technology advisory committee in the White House annex. Shortly thereafter, Ed Rice and I were called to Washington and told that HUD would like us to join forces on a specific project. We were to make a study for public housing in Washington, D.C. using Habitat environmental design with Conrad engineering technology. The District of Columbia housing agency would be the immediate client. Our task would be to select a suitable demonstration site, make cost studies and designs to prove feasibility, and then build a public housing project.

I went ahead with a detailed design study for each of four sites we thought most promising, including development of a system incorporating all the Habitat lessons in an attempt to reduce costs. We still had no contract, but we were regularly told that it would be signed "next week", or "very soon." I was encouraged to think that this was just a technicality, and was advised not to worry about it. Four months and thirty thousand dollars later some major changes took place in HUD and suddenly I was told to stop work. The project was abandoned, the contract would not be signed, no funds would be forthcoming. I had assumed that, as in Canada, if the government told you to go ahead a contract was a technicality. In the U.S. if you've done work without a contract, it's considered to be "promotion" and you just don't get paid.

The studies had included a detailed design for one particular site in the suburb of Anacostia, and one at Fort Lincoln. The density would have been about double that of Habitat Phase 1. Yet there were economic advantages to restricting the building to six storeys with the concrete box system.

The problem was to establish such a density with a box system without going over ten storeys and keeping most of it within five or six floors. Very encouragingly, we achieved a density of about forty houses per acre, gross. These were large houses, so that we are talking about a population density in excess of two hundred people per acre, gross.

This was our first opportunity to change and modify the system after our Habitat post-mortems. First, the mechanical system was greatly simplified. Instead of running services through the pedestrian streets, we took them directly to the ground in vertical shafts. The structural system was also simplified by eliminating the street as a load-bearing element and introducing vertical supports along the inclined plane to reduce the cantilevering or arch action. We reduced the variations in connections and openings in the boxes. Conrad Engineers planned for the use of expanding concrete that pre-stresses the casting chemically and allows a reduction in the weight of concrete in each unit.

In this phase, I still stuck to the sixteen-foot wide module, but I changed the entire module in such a way that most of the partitions were on a module line rather than at random as at Habitat. That meant it would be possible to pour each of the partitions in concrete with the rest of the box when it was being poured, at a cost substantially less than a partition built with studs and panelboard. We also planned to cast the electrical wiring in conduits in the concrete to eliminate the mechanical sub-floor. The theoretical costing at the time came in around sixteen dollars a square foot about one-seventh the square foot cost of Habitat Phase 1. This first post-Habitat application could be described as Habitat without major geometrical changes but with all the technical lessons applied.

A few months later, while I was on a trip to Puerto Rico I heard that I was urgently needed in Washington the following day. I called Ed Rice and found out that the Fort Lincoln project, one of the sites we had made proposals for, had progressed. Architects and planners had been commissioned to do a master plan for it. We were not being considered for the whole Fort Lincoln site, but HUD convinced the land agency that a little corner of the site ought to be appropriated for technological experimentation, for which HUD would make some funds available.

The entire "who's who" of building technology was invited to Washington that day: Neal Mitchell from Cambridge, Mass. who presented his systems, various universities that had done system studies, Carl Koch and Sepp Firnkass from Boston, the whole gamut of innovators in housing. Rice and I presented the scheme we had already done for Washington. A few days later, the decision was made to use this corner of the site which could accommodate about four hundred units, split it in three, and invite Harry Weese, Paul Rudolph, and myself to do a third each.

I was pleased with the appointment, but extremely disappointed with the scope of the project. One of the things I had said in my initial presentation was that any project of less than four hundred units ought not to be done unless very substantial R&D funds were available. As it was set up, the parameters of the project guaranteed failure from an accounting standpoint. It was so small that you just couldn't justify any tooling-up costs. You couldn't even afford to design it if you were on a regular fee. The feasibility study funds amounted to twenty-two thousand dollars for each of us, and I had already spent thirty thousand dollars in the initial study and still had to fund the engineering studies. But, after a lot of soul-searching, I decided to accept the invitation and proceed with the work.

Working with housing authorities on the development of the project was in a sense a new experience. Unlike Habitat where we were dealing with exhibition officials, here we were dealing with professional "housers." These individuals had been dealing for many years with a particular sector of the housing market, that is, low and moderate income housing financed or insured under the various FHA programs. For that type of project, over the years, a particular procedural formula had evolved, a particular housing vocabulary you could call it. Naturally then, in the many meetings we had with various individuals within HUD, a profound confrontation took place between our proposals which challenged established practice and their comfort in doing things in the familiar way.

There was a kind of subtle undertone in all the meetings. In the pre-Fort Lincoln days, when we were dealing strictly with public housing authorities, I always got the unspoken message that the project ought not to look too good, it ought not to appear luxurious. A garden or pedestrian walkway or anything like that made everybody nervous. A young FHA architect in one of the meetings said, "It just looks too good. It's not a matter of the cost even, it's just that it's going to be a problem." The other attitude was: "We didn't ask you to improve housing standards, we want you to cut costs." But, on the Forth Lincoln project there was the conscious effort to do something good. The only difficulty was that it had to be done for the same cost as run-of-the-mill public housing, and be better, and all this as a one-shot hundred-and-twenty-unit project.

After several months of painstaking effort, the contractors, George Fuller Construction Company and Stressed Structures Inc., came in with a guaranteed bid for $17.44 a square foot, approximately ten per cent above the cost of the standard low income projects, and that was based on the production of a hundred and twenty units only. The contractors said they would go down to about fifteen dollars a square foot if a thousand units were ordered.

There were in addition, serious problems with the District of Columbia building code. For example, after working for a long time to get all the south windows under cantilevers so they would be shaded, we discovered that according to the code windows under a cantilever were not permissible. Neither did the code permit open walkways or open stairs.

To demonstrate the shortcomings of the code, I brought down the working drawings of Habitat and had a meeting with the code officials in which we demonstrated that each and every one of the code restrictions that were problematic at Fort Lincoln would have made Habitat impossible too. And yet I was there because of Habitat! I made a strong case that the code was restrictive and illogical, and a special task force was formed with representatives of FHA and HUD and the District of Columbia building department. Eventually they recommended that the code be changed. Since it would take years to change the code, we suggested it ought to be treated as a prototype. But there was resistance to making a special category for experimental construction that could circumvent the code without creating a precedent, which was the way we did it in Habitat.

We were pressed to continue our efforts to bring the cost down, but without budging on the size of the project. The choice became one of reducing the standards, like eliminating the terraces, omitting the covered parking, etc. I wanted very badly, to build the project but there comes the moment of truth: build at what 'price'? at what compromise? and compromise for what reason?

The issues became clear and that course of action unacceptable. Since we were only ten per cent over budget, with an experimental project of a hundred and twenty units and a guaranteed bid, it seemed only logical that HUD should go ahead. It would also have been logical to make some R&D money available to cover that ten per cent. After all, the project was too small to justify tooling up or design investment by the participating industries, and once in full production it would obviously be within HUD's cost parameters. I felt that $17.44 was an excellent price for what we were offering. I finally stated that we wouldn't change the basic scheme: wouldn't change the design, wouldn't take the gardens out, wouldn't take the covered parking out. I took a kind of "take it or leave it" attitude. In the same meeting Paul Rudolph said that with more time he could cut his costs down. His costs were about the same as ours. Harry Weese's project, conventional townhouses of lower density, using panel construction, had costs comparable to HUD's standards.

A little while later I read in the papers that my project was abandoned. By that time we had spent twenty-eight thousand dollars in addition to the initial thirty thousand dollars, all for a fee of twenty-two thousand dollars. I wrote Tom Appleby, the head of the Redevelopment Land Agency, that I felt the RLA ought to be honest and state publicly that the project was feasible had they been prepared to build a thousand units, rather than say simply that it was not feasible on the basis of cost. My letter was never answered.

At the conclusion of the Fort Lincoln contract we submitted a comprehensive report in which we assessed in detail the prerequisites for making prototype projects successful. One point was that either there should be a minimum of a thousand units (ideally five thousand) to justify the investment on the part of contractors, or it should be done on a small scale with R&D money to make up the difference. Another point: don't try to change the whole building code for one project. Take it out of the code by saying that it's research, to be handled separately without setting precedents. A third point: tell the participants from the beginning exactly what they have to provide by way of physical and environmental requirements, and exactly what costs they are aiming for.

A pleasant footnote to the Fort Lincoln story can be found in the terms of reference for Operation Breakthrough, announced by HUD in mid-1969. Breakthrough was HUD's (and Romney's) first large-scale thrust into industrialized housing and it was interesting to see that almost every one of our recommendations in the final Fort Lincoln report was adopted. The first phase was to be done on a cost-plus R&D basis in which a limited size prototype would be constructed. Ultimately, full production of five thousand units would take place for each of the systems awarded a contract. The Breakthrough call for proposals also went to some length to describe the quality of environment or standards expected in the dwelling units. It unfortunately did not extend these standards to the overall community. Nonetheless, even in the area of handling codes and unions the Breakthrough project seemed to have gained much from the Fort Lincoln experience.

19

New York:
On the waterfront

A number of visitors to Expo were important to the continuation of my work. One was Carol W. Haussamen of New York. She heard of me from Wolf Von Eckardt, who met her when he wrote a story about Instant Rehab, which she had sponsored.

Carol owns considerable real estate in New York. For many years she has been active in sponsoring and initiating projects which she felt were of value to the community. The best known project is Instant Rehab. She also sponsored the beautification of 58th Street, including the design of street furniture, lighting, etc. A sense of rare elegance surrounds Carol and all that she does. Our job meetings, for example, always took place in the library of her vast penthouse apartment overlooking Central Park. Her interest in Habitat and her wish to sponsor a project which would extend these ideas to the circumstances of New York were a natural continuation of her work in the city.

Carol came to Expo 67 toward the end and I took her through Habitat. Her parting words were, "We must make one in New York, sweetie." A few weeks later she called to say she had met with Mayor John Lindsay of New York who had also seen Habitat, and that he was most enthusiastic about the prospect of a New York Habitat and suggested some city land could be made available for such an experiment. Soon I was in New York, and together with representatives of the city planning commission, the city housing authority, and Carol, looked at a number of sites, all waterfront or over-water.

Carol's idea was that the project should be privately financed as luxury housing. It would be easier to initiate experimental concepts in luxury housing and let the ideas filter down than start them off in low-income housing. And I think she was looking at it as a commercial venture, too.

The two most attractive sites were both on the East River: one around 95th Street just north of Gracie Mansion, the mayor's residence, the other between

187

the Fulton Street fish market and Wall Street. I favored the downtown site, but Carol and her real estate advisers felt that uptown was less risky because it was accepted as a luxury residential area. My design for the uptown site was in considerable detail and well advanced into the estimating stage when the real estate advisors and Carol changed their minds and decided that downtown was the place to go. The progress of the Lower Manhattan urban renewal plans were partially responsible for this change. There was also a considerable reservoir of Wall Street people as potential tenants for a project within walking distance of their work and many of the financial houses and corporations were likely to rent apartments as well.

To justify paying the price of prime Manhattan land we had to achieve unusually high densities. In addition the project was to encompass a mixture of housing and commercial uses. The density of the uptown site was two hundred units per acre but the density recommended by the city for the downtown site was three hundred units per acre. It meant I had to build very high, close to fifty storeys. In these circumstances I became aware of the shortcomings of the box shape and rectangular geometry. I had been aware of these limitations in Habitat and even in my thesis, but the difficulty of finding a better answer and the fact that one could get away with rectangles in lower structures made me stick to the simplest solution. But with Habitat New York it became obvious that one had to find a modular unit that could be grouped to form a structure that carried its forces to the ground and resisted the horizontal forces of wind and earthquake in an extremely efficient way.

The obvious direction to explore was self-stiffening rigid geometrics; the ideal would be a module related to a tetrahedron or an octahedron, because of the strength inherent in their forms. The tetrahedron is the most stable form in nature, but I became aware in various experiments and studies that the spaces it produces are restricting, and furthermore you can't completely fill space with tetrahedrons; about a third is left over when you've packed in all the tetrahedrons possible. I wanted a plan generated by right angles for the sake of internal organization and because such spaces could most easily lend themselves to furnishing by the future tenant. The problem then was to find a triangulated space structure, a structure which is inherently stiff and efficient in transmitting forces, which nevertheless produced rectangular rooms. The solution I evolved was an octahedral modular unit measuring thirty-two feet across and high, sustaining within it a two-storey cube. When grouped in space, as they were for the uptown site, octahedrons form a triangulated space structure such that the housing modules touch only at the edges and at the end points. Each house, therefore, would be truly suspended in space – never the face of one against another.

But when it came to the downtown site, the octahedral geometry I developed for the first project seemed inefficient for a fifty-storey building. Furthermore, the cost estimates indicated some serious inefficiencies in the utilization of space and the distribution of mechanical services.

188

It was at this point that I decided to tackle once more the possibility of building a structure which is primarily in suspension. From a conceptual point of view it is obvious that in a multi-storey structure considerably less material would be required for structure in which the major stresses are carried in tension. A high-tensile steel cable with a cross sectional area of one square inch can carry in tension two hundred thousand pounds; the equivalent area in a column in compression, assuming an efficient shape that would prevent buckling, would carry only twenty thousand pounds. It is obvious that in any structure which acts in tension there must be some complementary elements that act in compression, but as Fuller has shown in his tensegrity truss structures, when these can be separated and the elements of compression concentrated and reduced in number, a very efficient structure results. I had attempted on several occasions in the past to evolve a total system in which the module itself is in suspension. My exploration of such systems in my thesis and later on in the Habitat plans all bogged down either in conceptual problems, or in unresolved technical problems inherent in a tensile structure, but the New York project seemed to have all the right parameters for such a system to be economically realistic and buildable.

The most obvious solution is to build vertical cores which contain the circulation and services, and then to suspend the floors or modules off cantilevered trusses on top. But this has two obvious shortcomings. First, the loads of all the units must go up to the top of the building then be brought down through the core. This is acceptable in itself if the total system results in material reduction, but the vertical compression tower itself is acting as a mast fixed only on the ground and subject to enormous horizontal wind and earthquake loads. It must, therefore, be made exceedingly stiff unless it is to be braced at various levels to other towers to stabilize it. Second, the loads of the houses carried by the cables to the top of the structure are transmitted to the tower via trusses which are elements in bending moment and quite inefficient. My main efforts were directed to eliminating these two weak elements, the truss and the tall unsupported mast, by introducing a major catenary system radiating from the compression tower in three directions – a most stable arrangement, somewhat like a suspension bridge going in three directions – off which were suspended, in turn, the housing modules. The catenaries, stabilized by being fixed to the ground, gave stability to the compression tower, and carried themselves in tension.

There were a number of additional advantages to this arrangement. The lower levels of the project were to contain an extensive commercial center, and the space requirements for such activities are different from those of the dwelling units. These areas would be free of the structural supports of the residences above. In this suspension scheme the lower levels of the building were totally free from the structure above. This also responded to the city planning commission's wishes that the lower levels of the structure be substantially open so that people behind the complex in the Lower Manhattan area would not have the river view blocked off. Thus evolved a structure which I could best describe in this way: three fifty-storey-high masts off which in three directions are suspended enormous sails of housing units connected to the ground at the extreme edges and to each other at the center, and sheltering under them several acres of public facilities and spaces.

This concept generated a whole new set of characteristics. The foundations became simpler and were reduced in number (they had to penetrate a hundred feet below the river to bedrock). The modules could be identical in structural design since all they supported was themselves. The thickness of the cable even at the fiftieth floor, including the fireproofing, was three inches, so that the efficiency in terms of the materials and useable interior space was almost incredible.

Considering the many years I had hoped to develop a tension system, this was a very exciting development. Habitat New York is not a plug-in, but the units are nevertheless standardized. We have avoided the redundancy of a frame superstructure with plugged-in modules where, in the case of a compression building, structurally both are doing the same thing. The modules are designed to be only strong enough to support themselves, and they are hung from the suspension structure, which is in tension.

To determine feasibility and cost estimates we all had to do considerable detail work in the area of structural analysis, particularly Conrad and T.Y. Lin, our engineers. T.Y. Lin himself participated in working out the tensile system with its multitude of problems, deflections, and construction and erection procedures. The George Fuller Construction Company, who joined forces with Carol W. Haussamen and participated in the development of the project, assigned some of their senior personnel to analyze each and every aspect of the building – the problem of building foundations and parking below water level, pouring the service towers in concrete with slip forms, and so on. We developed a method by which the modules could be lifted into position by a hoist located on top of the tower, with an extension running along the catenary cables, thus avoiding the need for a crane. This was particularly critical in view of the fact that no known crane was available that could lift the modules within the reaches and height required.

By mid-1969 we had completed the preliminary plans and the first run at construction feasibility and estimates, both of which had positive conclusions. Because of the great number of unprecedented procedures, however, it became apparent that considerably more detailed plans would have to be made. These could only be financially justified once the real estate and financing aspects of the project had been resolved.

We had numerous meetings with various city departments co-ordinating our efforts with their total master plan. As the plans progressed some external problems emerged. Other developers were very keen to put office buildings on the prime lands that had been designated to us. The board of directors of the

New York Stock Exchange and their architect, Gordon Bunshaft, of Skidmore, Owings & Merrill, who were planning a structure right next to us, were unhappy about their prospective neighbors. A residential community did not appear to them to be compatible with America's highest financial institution; they could envisage mothers with baby carriages strolling in the stock exchange plaza at lunch time.

20   Puerto Rico: Breakthrough

Fred Epstein and Haim Eliachar were two others who visited Habitat during Expo 67, but I had not met them then. Epstein spent two whole days in the construction exhibit, studying in detail the plans and sketches. He is chairman of the board and Eliachar was then president of Development International Corporation and its subsidiary, Development Corporation of Puerto Rico, a builder-developer company that each year puts up about a thousand units of conventional housing in the public and private sectors in Puerto Rico and the continental U.S.A. They had also built projects through the AID program in Peru and Mexico, among other places.

It is not exactly an everyday happening when a developer putting up conventional housing in the public and private sector comes to an architect who is doing, certainly from the developer's point of view, extremely experimental work, and commissions him to develop a building system. Some background on Epstein and Development Corporation is therefore relevant.

Epstein, a relaxed, friendly New Yorker who graduated as an aeronautical engineer (he flies his own plane), started as a builder of single family houses on Long Island. In 1957 he moved to Puerto Rico and within a few years became one of the most successful and largest developer-builders on the island. He built houses, public housing units, apartment buildings. Eliachar, who was then his partner, also had considerable building background, including prefabricated wood structures. Epstein had done very well and at the time we met was becoming very conscious of the more subtle set of values that must confront a builder on this continent. He had a genuine and strong desire to do something good, and the security of one who had done well and could afford it.

There was a mixture of personal and business considerations motivating him. On one hand he liked Habitat, was really excited about it. He has told me that when he first saw it he became determined to do the same thing on a successful commercial basis, to prove that it could be done in the context of business. With his keen builder's eye he immediately saw the critical technical difficulties of Habitat and realized that in Puerto Rico he would not be confronted with most of them. As he recalled later, Puerto Rico was obviously the right place: concrete technology was advanced; concrete construction for housing was accepted; the climate eliminated most of the problems of insulation, heating, and protection of mechanical systems. If the system was to go, it would be best to start there.

Epstein also has a total view of the business he is in, something you discover as you get to know him. This total view suggested to him that industrialized building was the coming thing, that modular space cells were something he was reading about in all the trade journals, and that his company ought to explore its potentials. At the beginning of our association Epstein was negotiating an expansion of his company by including some prominent Wall Street bankers as partners; they, too, had responded to the idea of the company's involvement in modular housing and had encouraged investment in it.

It was just after the closing of Expo that I received a call from Haim Eliachar. He and Epstein were interested in Habitat, he said, and they felt they could build it in Puerto Rico successfully. Would I like to come down there and discuss it? At that time I was getting at least a couple of calls like that a week and wasn't taking them very seriously. My test was to say, "Are you prepared to cover all my expenses?" Eliachar said, "Of course we will." That eased enough of my scepticism for me to accept the invitation. I met him in New York two days later and we flew down to Puerto Rico. Epstein had arranged for a number of meetings with Puerto Rico government officials: the head of CRUV, the public housing authority; the head of Fomento Cooperativo, the Commonwealth government co-operative agency which sets up co-operatives for housing or industry; and FHA officials.

The chief administrator of Fomento told Epstein that they would consider having Development Corporation build a Habitat in Puerto Rico, which they would buy on a turn-key basis and make into a co-operative, providing the costs were within the prevailing limits of the 221 (d) (3) housing program (a U.S. federal program of low-interest loans for moderate-income housing). This closely related Habitat Puerto Rico to my efforts in Washington, which were also for the 221 (d) (3) housing program. Fomento offered to make a site available and agreed that if for any reason Fomento caused the project to be abandoned, they would cover the cost of design and feasibility studies up to a hundred thousand dollars. Development Corporation signed a contract with Fomento to proceed with design and feasibility studies and I, in turn, signed a contract with Development Corporation. I called Ed Rice and asked him to join me in Puerto Rico to assess the problem and discuss the production facilities with Development Corporation's management.

At Habitat in Montreal, the plant was on the site. At Habitat in Washington, it would have been very close to it. But it couldn't be close in Puerto Rico. In fact,

Development Corporation envisaged shipping modules to all parts of Puerto Rico and by barge to the Virgin Islands and, eventually, to islands farther away. So it became essential to develop a module that could be shipped on the highways and by barge, which meant that it had to be restricted to twelve feet in width; you couldn't ship the Montreal module, which was seventeen feet wide.

This constraint and the requirement of meeting the 221 (d) (3) cost limitations posed a tough problem. As soon as you reduce the width of the unit you discover that a stair running from one floor to the next one above can't make it in one run unless the boxes are always set parallel to each other. Even then, if you had one box on top of another and two rooms in the top one, you would need space for a stair run and a corridor side by side, so that the space needed for circulation in the house would still be enormous. Also, two-storey houses didn't make much sense in a tropical climate and yet a single-storey house required extensive corridor space and made it very difficult to achieve privacy between, say, sleeping areas and living areas.

These considerations led me to strive for a split-level module. I jogged the module half its height at the center line, with an incline that corresponds to the angle of the stair, producing a sort of elongated honey-comb effect. The smallest house was one unit, a number of units in combination could make a one, one-and-a-half, two, or two-and-a-half level house. It was even more versatile than Habitat. The angle of the incline and stair was repeated at the end faces of the module, so that there was a projection in the shape of a sideways V. This projection became a window with its top half solidly louvred against the sun and the bottom half of glass which, because it was inclined inwards, was shaded so that one could look out even at high noon without the sun penetrating the house. Storage units, kitchen, bathroom, and even some built-in furnishings fit well into these V-shaped spaces, and even though the volume contained was similar to that of a rectangular room five feet shorter, the feeling of the space was much greater because the room extended five feet farther at eye level, which is the level critical to perception. The overall efficiency of the space was at least equal to the same space in a box with vertical walls, and the circulation was better. Compared with the full stair run and extensive corridors of Habitat Montreal, there was just the half stair run on the incline itself and the landings; no corridors whatsoever.

Many of these design developments were generated by visits to both traditional and newly-constructed Puerto Rican communities. Most public housing projects had windows made with solid aluminum louvre jalousies and because of the very severe heat and sun penetration, the louvres were shut for the entire day. Since the people were unable to open the louvres for fear of overheating the house, they were living in virtual darkness.

In San Juan I visited old Spanish houses with their central courts open to the sky, around which were all the rooms. So, when the cluster was designed, rather than form exposed roof gardens as in Habitat Montreal, we developed a plan in which the garden was a court with dwellings cantilevered overhead to shade it.

By far the most important conceptual development of the Puerto Rico project was the great reduction in the number of pieces that make up the system. In Montreal the modular boxed units formed approximately half of the total number of precast pieces; in addition, elevator cores, street sections, access stairs, and other pieces had to be manufactured. A substantial percentage of the Habitat costs was in these additional pieces. Dramatic savings could be achieved if, in some way, these units could be reduced in number. It was from this that we evolved the idea that the module, by virtue of its shape, could accommodate some of the functions that had been provided for by the additional pieces in Habitat. If the shape of the roof of the module made it possible for it to act as a stair, one could eliminate the access stairs. If the roofs of some of the modules could form a pedestrian street, one could eliminate separate street sections. The module that was eventually designed formed houses, created the internal circulation, created the system of passages, exterior stairs, and pedestrian streets on its exterior surfaces, and practically eliminated the need for any additional pieces.

We also made use of the hilly site and were able to plan at relatively high densities, without the use of elevators, a structure that was in fact five or six storeys high. We thus had an overall gross density of forty units per acre (including the park), without the use of mechanical conveyance.

Not everything went smoothly. The feasibility study had shown that the costs were within the FHA limitations, in other words the project was feasible. The hill site we had chosen in the center of San Juan was made available by the Navy to the Redevelopment Land Agency of Puerto Rico. As soon as the project was publicized pressure from the residents around the site started to build up. They didn't want any construction going on around them, particularly not a moderate income project. Then, we ran into difficulties with the local FHA office, which for some reason – perhaps as a kind of backlash from the Fort Lincoln project – became very hedgy and expressed doubts about many aspects of the project. But here we were within the budget. We were generally within the code. There was nothing that could be questioned. We had a reasonable answer for everything.

As always with projects of this magnitude, the maze of authorities and the communications between, gave the frustrating feeling of trying to shake hands with an octopus. A letter approving the project was issued by the Washington office of FHA, only to be ignored by the local office, who claimed that since the project was not in any way experimental, it was within their own jurisdiction. Negotiations between the various Commonwealth government authorities sponsoring the project and owning the land and the planning board were difficult to co-ordinate. Epstein and his staff found out that breaking new ground in this business was certainly different from building conventional housing. In one year Development Corporation had spent over two hundred thousand dollars on the development of the system. I think a less determined person would have exhausted both energy and patience and abandoned the project.

To the hedging we encountered, Epstein's response was: "I'll go as high as I have to. I'm not going to take 'No' for an answer, particularly when it's not substantiated. If you have any objections you are going to put them down on paper and you are going to have to back them up."

Nor was my own profession any kinder. As soon as I had started working on the project I checked the procedures for performing architectural services in Puerto Rico. I was first told that as this was a government project, local licensing was not required; nevertheless it was advisable. Two separate bodies had jurisdiction over licensing: the Commonwealth Government board and the *collegio* of the architects and engineers. I contacted the president of the *collegio* who received me very nicely and organized a luncheon at which I made a presentation of the concept of Habitat to the *collegio's* board of directors. There was enthusiastic response at the meeting and the president stated that for special projects of an experimental nature, a temporary license could be issued to foreigners. This friendly beginning deteriorated once the project was nearing reality. A license was denied by the board and my attempt to make a joint venture with local firms, a standard practice under such circumstances, were, to put it mildly, discouraged by the *collegio.* At one point I was asked to sign a waiver of my rights to the design and its authorship, and was told that my firm's name could not appear in any way on the drawings. What made me sad about these events was not so much the administrative difficulties that had to be overcome, but finding national boundaries in an area where professional co-operation and exchange of experiences are so essential.

Eventually things started falling into place. It was subtly suggested that the site ought to be changed, and once we had done that and chosen a smaller hill further east in the city, the approvals started coming. First FHA sent a letter declaring the project feasible. Eventually the planning board also approved. The new site was much less visible, which seemed to make many people more comfortable. Perhaps they were right. This was the first run of an experimental building system. Notwithstanding all the difficulties, many individuals in the public agencies were enthusiastic about the project from the outset and, once communications had been established with the FHA officials and their doubts relieved, we also had general co-operation from them. But to me it proved the fallacy of my hope that "after Habitat it would be easy." Once it departs from accepted practice, a project that confronts the system requires considerable energy to realize and the experience is not transferable from one community to another.

Simultaneously with the beginning of the work on Habitat Puerto Rico, Fred Epstein finalized negotiations leading to a major part of Development International Corporation being purchased by two of the most prominent Wall Street

197

investment bankers, Wertheim & Company and Unterberg Towbin Co. They, too, proved to be strong believers in modular housing generally and the Habitat system specifically.

In 1969, a year after we began work, Development International Corporation went public through the issue of stock on the New York Stock Exchange, with the Habitat Puerto Rico factory being financed with part of the proceeds.

Because of my involvement with the company as its architect for modular construction and since the company's going public was undertaken in part because of its intentions to specialize in modular construction, I was invited to become a member of the Board of Directors of DIC. The implications of accepting such an appointment were numerous. Certainly everything about the traditional role of the architect would be incompatible with it. In a sense, it was a moment of truth; I had been saying design and construction had to be integrated, and here was a chance. After some weeks of serious reflection I decided to accept.

For almost a full year we struggled uphill like an ant with an overweight burden, slowly obtaining one approval after another, resolving the many administrative problems, and at the same time going ahead with the working drawings. Harouzi Wainshal, DIC's Executive Vice-President – Operations, led the company's efforts in organizing the factory operation, selecting and ordering equipment, and setting up an organization capable of mass production housing. Conrad Engineers, the firm which earlier worked on the Fort Lincoln, the New York, and the San Francisco projects, broke new grounds in an unprecedented structural engineering analysis designed to minimize the material content within the structure, notwithstanding its considerable geometric complexity. As they put it, "We could not have considered it with the tools available to us a year earlier." But with new computer programs they had developed recently, the analysis was possible. There were three trunkloads of computer work sheets to impress the building departments that had to approve the structural design.

At the beginning of April 1970, all had been finalized and the project at last was offered for sale as a co-operative through the organization of Fomento Cooperativo. Two weeks after the first ad appeared in the San Juan papers the project was sold out. In June 1970, the equipment started arriving in the factory, the molds had been ordered, and construction work commenced on the site.

I am constantly confronted in meetings with the comparative costs of traditional construction, ranging from single family houses to high rise apartments. The comparison between one form of housing and another, between the economics of Fort Lincoln at thirty units to the acre, Puerto Rico at forty, and New York at three hundred, made me aware that density had far-reaching implications on all aspects of housing. Density was one variable, with others on the other side of the equation, namely cost of construction and the quality of the environment. Neither density nor its economic implications could be taken for granted.

It is commonly assumed that the need for higher density in the cities is the by-product of the population explosion. A corollary is that countries with a lot of open space do not really need high urban densities. I think both assumptions are wrong.

Density is not related to population growth, nor to the availability of open space elsewhere. I do not think the density problem of Montreal or Toronto is substantially different from the density problem of, say, Tel Aviv, even though Canada has more open space than Israel. Density is a by-product of the evolution of metropolitan cities, and metropolitan cities are the by-product of fundamental social and economic forces. These forces have created the need for concentration of people and, as a result, high density: more people wanting to be together, to have more amenities and more variety and choice, and business and corporations wanting to be together because they depend on each other for services and pools of skilled people. This concentration, leading to unprecedented growth, has created a kind of new super city. Its size and complexity have made our methods of planning the city two-dimensionally obsolete. Streets, lots, and buildings on them are too restricting, it is like trying to plan a direct-dial telephone system with mechanical means. If we could plan in three dimensions, if we could think in terms of continuous buildings rather than individual buildings, of networks of movement rather than individual transportation facilities, if we could subdivide space instead of land, we could create a better environment notwithstanding the density. But, the implications of density on the building processes are so great that one must first ask whether increasing densities are inevitable.

I had always assumed that the cost of building housing at different densities would be more or less the same: an apartment in a multi-storey structure would cost more or less the same as a house of the equivalent area. To my surprise, a comparative analysis showed that unit for unit, assuming equal amenities, high density cost much more to build than low density housing. The term *equal amenities* must be emphasized, for in assessing housing standards we usually consider only those aspects affecting the interior of the dwelling and not the total environment, a practice that has evolved from extending standards set for single family housing to all other forms of housing. It is generally accepted that the small single family detached house constitutes accepted minimum housing standards on the North American continent. Let us examine what this minimum is.

Our suburban house has a little garden. It has a fair amount of privacy and, being a separate entity, considerable identity. But, as we have proceeded to build higher density developments, it has become more expensive to provide these taken-for-granted amenities of the single family house. When land cost a dollar a square foot, a garden measuring twenty by thirty cost six hundred dollars. In a multi-storey structure open space costs six or seven dollars a square foot or four thousand dollars for the same garden. Six or ten feet of air separating the wood-stud and brick walls of two adjacent houses is enough to give good sound privacy to a detached house; but it is a major technical problem which costs considerably more to overcome in two dwellings touching each other or on top of each other, as in an apartment. The denser the environment, the more complex and costly it is to achieve these standards.

Many planners have spoken about dispersal as an alternative to density. The most articulate is Jean Gottmann of the University of Pennsylvania, who first used the term *Megalopolis*. He has suggested that the tendency of the city is toward extreme dispersal, which would mean low density. The suggestion is that cities would be evenly dispersed over vast areas, a view that relates closely to Frank Lloyd Wright's Broadacre City concept.

I agree that dispersal is inevitable. Everything that is happening in the field of transportation will lead to greater and greater dispersal. But I believe that the form of dispersal will be much more structured than Gottmann suggests, because of the nature of the transportation systems and because of people's apparent natural preference for concentration. Rather than disperse limitlessly and evenly, we would be dispersing concentrations. It is the difference between an unharvested field of wheat and the dispersed piles of straw bricks left by the combine harvester.

The fact that we are strait-jacketed into a two-dimensional planning pattern and lack the facility to rethink the city in three dimensions, is making the city quite absurd. Pedestrians get in the way of cars, and cars crawl from one red light to the next. Two-dimensional planning results in irrational situations. We put up enormous office buildings and then put up apartment buildings and town houses in their shadow. We want sunlight in a house and don't particularly care if we have sunlight in an office, in fact we may prefer northern light. We build great parking garages in prime space and then build shopping concourses – in which daylight would be a great asset – underground. Because we're dealing with a two-dimensional pattern of individual buildings on the ground, we have to dig to provide services and pedestrian links underground, the least appropriate space for the concentration of human beings.

Suppose we could take the downtown of a city, separate all buildings into cubes, and rearrange them. You could for example, have houses arranged in space where they would have sunlight and a view and they could create membranes – you could say, umbrellas of leaves – below which would lie a continuous public space with shops and recreational facilities protected from the elements. These in turn could serve areas of offices and light industry and below that could be a network of transportation and parking and terminuses. The three-dimensional network would make it possible to walk through the whole complex without ever crossing the path of a car, or drive without ever stopping at a red light. Instead of always having to come down to ground level to go from one high building to another, one could move horizontally at many levels.

Brasilia, the new capital of Brazil, is a striking example of a new city made obsolete by its two-dimensional structure before it was off the drawing board. While you can drive in that city without ever stopping you absolutely can't walk there. Nor are its urban functions related to the way the people use them; instead there is government in one place, housing in another, major shopping in another. Nor is it possible to improve much on this unless the city is considered from the outset as subdivided space with all its functions integrated and three-dimensionally arranged.

Brasilia is a city divided into separate neighborhoods, and each neighborhood has its little bit of shopping and a little school. But people want variety, they're not willing to limit themselves to that token shopping in the neighborhood, to one butcher or clothing store. Stratifying the whole city into separate neighborhoods connected by highways doesn't work. The same problem occurs in Le Corbusier's great apartment slabs, each of which had a shopping street in its middle level. My feeling was that unless all these shopping streets were linked to each other to become one continuous shopping street in the air, they would never work.

Three-dimensional organization and planning make it possible to achieve complete micro-climates—to respond to the elements in a positive way. Living beside the sea we get breezes because air heats faster over land than it does over water and convection currents are created. In mountain country one kind of vegetation is found on northern slopes and a totally different vegetation on the southern slopes. These phenomena of micro-climate can become part of the design of the city. In a hot climate it's possible to group building elements three-dimensionally so that all houses face north and shade each other, or to group houses in such a way that convection currents of air are created in shaded areas, penetrating the houses and creating breezes. In a cold northern climate it's possible to group houses so that they enclose and shelter public spaces and, packed closely and bubble-like, capture sun and light.

21

San Francisco:
The space-maker

One morning, while Habitat was still under construction, I received a letter from the Associated Students of San Francisco State College. They were writing fifty selected architects to inquire whether they would be interested in designing their students' union building, which was to be built with students' funds. The letter said in part: "We want a building or buildings which are about what students are about – generous, exorbitant, energetic, anxious, frivolous, raw, shy, with some secret spaces and some intricate spaces. We would like to design and build our own building and pay ourselves the architect's fee and the laborers' wages. Since we cannot, we wish to do the next best thing and that is to find an architect who will watch and listen and interpret us and let us learn from him as he learns from us."

I was very moved. I sat down immediately and wrote back. A month later I received a phone call. Eight architects, including myself, had been selected to be interviewed for the job. Among the others were Paolo Soleri, Bertrand Goldberg from Chicago, Victor Lundy of New York, Hirshen & Van der Ryn and Marquis & Stoller, both of San Francisco. I flew to San Francisco and at ten o'clock one sunny morning arrived at the campus. The college grounds are either brilliantly bright, blue sky and sun, or covered with fog. They are right in the area where fog rolls up from the sea like a bunch of giant sheep walking over the campus buildings. Often the campus is foggy while downtown San Francisco is sunny.

Something immediately resonated in me when I arrived on the campus. Seeing the students lying on the grass, on the campus green, the men with large moustaches and the women with long hair and informally dressed, I felt I was back in Israel. I met with the college union council, seven students and seven members of the faculty and administration. I spent several hours talking with them about my work.

I spoke of morphology, of the design process, of the need to be unarbitrary, of spaces that could be randomly changed to meet changing needs, and I spoke of the vernacular, of the idea of a village made with discipline yet infinite variety. As we sat around the table speaking, I felt as one of them. We were more or less the same age; there was much affinity in our political and social views, in our values, even in our tastes. I said I would design the building with them, that I would be their instrument, but that at the same time I had strong feelings about the environment; it would be an intense exchange.

After the meeting some of us went out and sat on the campus green. We talked of many things, not of the building. In parting I said that I very much wanted to do the building but that my desire to do it was equal to my fear of being unable to live up to it.

I had already heard something about San Francisco State College before they wrote me. The year before, the students had initiated an experimental college with classes run by students for students in subjects that are normally not taught academically. Several members of the council, Margaret Nixon (its chairman), Albert Duro, Dona Michelson, Karen Duncan, had been active in the experimental college and in other radical student activities. The program had been nationally publicized and recognized. Generally speaking. San Francisco State had the reputation of being one of the most radical and active campuses in the U.S., more radical in many ways, I feel, than Berkeley. The students were a complete mixture: long and short hair, left and right, radical and content. The campus grounds at lunch time looked like a biblical pasture. I felt very much at home, very comfortable. I have often flown from meetings on that campus direct to Washington for meetings with HUD officials, and the contrast was almost too much to bear. It was like flying from one country to another.

Several weeks passed and I put the whole thing out of mind. Then came a phone call from Margaret Nixon. She said, "We would like you to design our building." I was thrilled, and frightened to death. Could I really live up to what they deserved? Could I live up to Habitat? I immediately flew down and met them all again, heard with some pleasure about all the deliberations and discussions that went on before the selection was made.

The students had prepared a program two or three years earlier; it was a neutral program, just the space requirements for different rooms, dining area, that kind of thing. I thought it was essential to have a very live program of what the building was all about; that we should make a program together before I designed the building. Because I wasn't registered to practice architecture in California, I would have to delay entering into formal contracts while I got local associates. But we decided to sign a programming contract immediately and then go on to the contract for the design of the building. So, I spent many many days on the campus talking to students and administrators, and looking and listening. On one occasion the students invited Paolo Soleri, the runner-up – an architect I very much admire – to come to the campus and have a joint series of informal talks about architecture in the presence of the students and with their participation. They were exciting and rewarding sessions.

The seeds of the images that later emerged in the union were planted in the development of the building program. Each activity was discussed thoroughly before conclusions were fixed. The students felt that the activity of eating should not be institutionalized, that you should not eat in a vast cafeteria. We walked around Telegraph Avenue in Berkeley and other areas where there was good food at reasonable prices and tried to discover why this was. We found they were usually small kitchens run by one man serving a specialized food. So, we decided to break up the dining hall into seven areas, each with a separate kitchen where individuals would have concessions, which they would run just as they ran their own little restaurants. That way the students would get good cheap food. New facilities were explored: we felt that students with children should be able to bring them on the campus, even if they were coming for only one lecture, so there should be a nursery where they could leave them. We felt that the building should be extremely flexible, particularly in such areas as the offices. There should be spaces where half a dozen people could work together one day, and the next they could be broken up into little cells for individuals, then opened up again for larger groups.

We talked a great deal about the relationship of the building to the rest of the campus. The campus has several parts and the crossroads of the circulation connecting them is exactly the site chosen for the building. Having the union at the crossroads was ideal, but how do you make a structure which has rivers of people passing through it?

Should it be raised on columns, or should it have a tunnel or passages through it? It was this question that generated the feeling that the building ought to be like a hollow hill, light and translucent, arching over the crossroads. You would not go under it or round it; you would experience it fully with all its activities as you walked through it.

Of even greater significance was the question of the relationship of the building to the people coming into it. Watching the students at lunch time as they approached the existing cafeteria gave me an indication of what would happen once the union replaced it. Literally thousands of students approached the building from all directions simultaneously. Three or four thousand students could reach the union within ten minutes. It was obvious that a building with one entrance was inappropriate, it would be a caricature of the kind of entrance that this structure should have. Then, one day, as I digested these observations, there emerged the concept that the building should allow people approaching it from any direction to just walk up the walls. You should come toward it and simply climb up or down its exterior surface until you reached the restaurants, meeting rooms, or offices. You should be able to move from one area to another outside as well as inside the building. Thus the building evolved with an outside surface that was a series of steps, terraces, and inclined planes covered with planting.

We tried to determine the facilities that would be required to accommodate the student government. Every student society had a pretty clear idea of the number of offices it needed and the number of meetings it held every week or month. But it became apparent that these changed continually, that there was no way of predetermining the number of offices, or whether they should be for groups or individuals, or even whether it would be better to have ten meeting rooms accommodating fifty people each or two rooms accommodating three hundred. Nor could the students afford to duplicate the facilities. We decided that the ideal solution would be one in which the office work spaces could be quickly redivided into private spaces or opened up to accommodate groups and that this conversion should not be something that involved technicians or carpenters but rather that the students should be able to move walls themselves and redivide the space. Similarly, the meeting rooms should accommodate several hundred people, but be subdividable. When someone pushed a button, a series of walls could come down and sub-divide a large room into five workable rooms, an instant space changer.

The trustees of the state colleges specifically required the union building to be compatible with the buildings surrounding it. The campus buildings are nondescript, thirties pseudo-modern, pink and pastel green concrete buildings with horizontal strip windows, mostly designed by the California State architectural office in Sacramento. They aren't even bad buildings, just non-buildings. Right now the campus green is the existing meeting place. The union building would be the new meeting place. It must be completely part of the park and, from the point of view of the students, apart from the academic buildings around it.

You could not ignore the environment, you could not turn your back on the existing campus, you could not build a structure that would ridicule it, and yet it was the expression of another culture, of another life style and another set of values. As Doug Shadbolt put it, when I told him of this: "When there is social change you must expect that there will be a change in architectural expression."

As we discussed it a particular image emerged: the academic buildings surrounding the campus green forming a wall and the union integrated with the green, an extension of the grass and the plant life. This relationship would make the union sit peacefully and harmoniously with the surrounding buildings – as part of the campus green surrounded by the academic buildings. From this first image emerged the concept that the union must become a three-dimensional park, as if the grass had parted to form several levels – the building covered with and penetrated by the plant life of the green, the terraces and stairs and inclined planes becoming places to sit and climb on, the rest being covered with earth and planting.

All this was determined in the programming stage which extended through several months before the building was physically designed.

The uniqueness of the situation was that the building was being constructed with student funds. The students committed themselves and future students to pay twenty dollars a year each and with these funds they have the capacity to sell forty-year bonds. With that capital, plus about half a million dollars they have accumulated in past years, they intend to build the building.

Even though this is a student building, it has to tie in with the administrative procedures for state-college structures. The chancellor's office's campus planning division is responsible for implementation. The board of trustees, who run all eighteen state colleges in California, have to approve the selection of architects and the schematic design. On a day-to-day basis we dealt with the chancellor's chief architect (formally, Vice-Chancellor – planning) Harry Harmon.

The students met some opposition to the way they had hired their architect. It was felt that they should have worked from a list of California architects. When I was selected, I detected a certain feeling of uneasiness in the chancellor's office.

I decided to associate my office with a San Francisco firm and chose, after considerable discussion, the firm of Burger & Coplans. Shortly thereafter both my appointment and that of Burger & Coplans was approved by the trustees, and the contract was signed. Several months later the design was completed. I arrived in San Francisco with a great big box which had a model and a set of drawings in it. I slowly unscrewed the box and took the model out, and then they all started jumping around it. One of the faculty members made a little paper flag and wrote *Moshe Swings* and pinned it on the model. They felt this was what they wanted, and I felt I had lived up to their expectations. That evening there was a party with many students and members of the council at Margaret Nixon's place.

As designed, it is a complex building with an intricate variety of spaces, small rooms, medium-sized rooms, and very big rooms. There are offices that measure ten by fifteen, private work areas, bookstore, dining halls, a theater, meeting rooms to seat twenty, fifty, a hundred, or seven hundred people. The biggest room is a hundred by a hundred feet of column-free-space – a hundred times bigger than the smallest room.

Each space is generated by combinations of a repetitive open structural element, a kind of basic "space-maker." It is a three-dimensional bent that makes a small room or, grouped with further units, acts as a dome to make bigger and bigger rooms. The units are to be precast off the site, shipped to the site, and assembled. They are not space cells; the finishes, electrical, mechanical, and other components are done in place, conventionally; but the fact that the structure is formed by a repetitive "space-maker" means that every other part of it – windows, stairs, pipe runs, heating units – can be organized into repetitive and simple components. I think the union is an example of the potential organization of more complex buildings, schools, libraries, theaters into a systematic building methodology even though they are an assembly of unlike functions and spaces.

What I found fascinating about the "space-maker" was that, by virtue of its form, it created a particular quality in all the spaces it made. As the rooms became larger, they grew taller. It was not just extending a space by moving a partition to increase the area as we do in an office structure, adding some more space sausages, but an enlarging of space in a three-dimensional way, with proportionately more height, more light, and more air. With a more perfect form, this generation of varied spaces could become more and more versatile. This quality of setting the generic qualities through the "space-maker" extended itself to every aspect of the building: its form made a stair and terraces on the outside surface; it made a place for planting; in combination it formed not only efficient space structures but also a network for the distribution of mechanical services and a repetitive heating-cooling system; it formed continuous hollow vertical spaces for shafts containing escape stairs, elevators, and other services.

But it also raised an interesting question of scale. If one was building a total campus, would it not be almost like a forest of leaves without trunks and branches? I think the answer is "No." As the scale of construction increased to encompass the total campus – a small city – so would the number of elements or space-makers, major walkways, services, transportation, horizontal and vertical elevators. Great open meeting places would form a hierarchy, the branches and the stems and leaves all working together, a structure that could be added to, changed, extended.

We all looked forward to seeing the building go up. But then we started to run into problems with the chancellor's office. They resented the decision to include a new dining facility and demolish the existing cafeteria. They questioned our decision to incorporate the book store. They asked how such a design could be accurately priced. They considered the building too "far out." I met the chief architect, Harry Harmon, and went over the plans with him. He himself was amiable, but I had the feeling that there was some nervousness about the building. The trustees had to approve the schematic design, but for months we couldn't get it on their agenda. Finally, we were told that we could make an off-the-record "pre-schematic" presentation to the trustees, which would be followed a month later by an official meeting for a decision.

Traditionally, buildings are not presented to the board by the architect who designed them but by the campus architect who is retained to co-ordinate the entire campus. And in the case of San Francisco State, it happened to be the state architect from Sacramento. I objected to that and insisted on presenting the building. One of the trustees happened to be an architect, Charles Luckman, the principal of one of the largest firms in the U.S. and formerly president of Lever Bros., and he started off by cross-examining me on a number of detailed questions: "How do you clean the windows? How do you waterproof the joints? How do you take the irrigation pipe through the slabs? How do you seal the windows? How do you do this? How do you do that?" He indicated they would need a great deal more detailed information before they could make a decision about such a building. The state architect would not support the building, which he felt was incompatible with his campus, and Harry Harmon, the architect of the chancellor's office, responded negatively too. Although this was just a schematic design, we were clearly being asked questions that normally would be asked in the working drawing phase.

The next presentation didn't take place for two or three months. By then I had decided to advance beyond the schematic phase and had many more detailed drawings, and estimates. The students had prepared their own brochure which they submitted to the trustees. In concluding their report they stated: "By virtue of its setting, by virtue of its uses, and by virtue of the ideals to which we are committed, the building should be designed in an idiom distinctly its own. Such an idiom should be a confident, even powerful language of form, and a language which would translate easily back and forth with the present buildings on the campus. We see the design as an intelligible architectural concept. The architecture is based upon a conviction about methodology and process, and within its own parameters of forms, of engineering, and of visible and articulate harmonies this design will be judged."

In introducing the building they stated: "Other things being equal, we wanted a building which would be composed of various and energetic forms, which would stimulate the most creative uses of it, which would be enhanced by the play of natural light upon it and through it, which would transcend the question of luxury versus utility, which would integrate part to whole, inside to outside, which would be an expression of comprehensive anticipatory design science, that is, a building flexible, adaptable, generating new uses as new generations of students come to use it."

The formal presentation to the trustees took place in Los Angeles on one of the state college campuses. I presented the building, again only after insisting that I should, but this time there were formal presentations against the building by the chief architect of the chancellor's office and the state architect from Sacramento. They felt the design was incompatible, technically unresolved, etc. The college president, Robert Smith, made an emotional plea for the building, and the president of the associated students also presented his case. Some amazing comments were heard around the room that day. One trustee commented: "How are you going to get the snipers out of that building?"

All this was happening simultaneously with other conflicts on the campus. Another confrontation was taking place between the college and students on one hand and the trustees on the other. George Murray, a part-time teacher who was also a member of the Black Panthers, was giving militant speeches around San Francisco. The agenda that day included the Murray issue together with the building issue. I think the building was viewed by many as an expression of the independent spirit of San Francisco State. I don't think the building was being judged just as a building, or as a design; it became, as the magazine *Revolution* later stated, "an important symbol."

The building was rejected five to two. But the college was encouraged to return with more technical information and more detailed cost estimates. I came to the conclusion that the only way to deal with this situation was to get a contractor to make a guaranteed bid on the basis of more detailed drawings. We decided to go ahead with part of the working drawings, at least those which were necessary for obtaining a bid, or of areas about which the trustees expressed concern, such as window details, connections, heating and ventilating, etc. We did some of the preliminary working drawings, then chose two contractors and asked them to look at the job, not just to make estimates, but actually to be prepared to sign a negotiated contract. H. C. Beck, one of the larger U.S. contractors, came up with a price that was within the budget, just over five million dollars, and were willing to sign a contract immediately. We got formal letters from many of the sub-trades: from window manufacturers to the maintenance people who clean windows; from waterproofing people to mechanical suppliers, each saying something to the effect: "Yes, we have examined the drawings and it is technically all right."

Of course there was not much we could do about the question of compatibility. How do you deal with such a subjective question? But we did move the building by about thirty feet to overcome one of the criticisms, that it was too close to the existing library. Meanwhile, the whole campus had become extremely involved with the building and by the time we went back to the trustees, six thousand student signatures had been collected, requesting that the building be approved. The faculty senate unanimously voted support of the building. San Francisco State College has an advisory committee of distinguished members of the community and it unanimously voted support for the building and asked that it should be approved. Mayor Alioto sent a telegram saying the building was good for San Francisco State and good for San Francisco. To my great delight, the architectural profession turned out in support of the building. Telegrams were sent by over twenty members of the faculty of the Berkeley department of architecture and planning, urging that it be approved. The American Institute of Architects, San Francisco chapter, circulated a petition and obtained many signatures including that of the president of the chapter. The San Francisco Museum of Fine Arts held an exhibit of the building. There was overwhelming public support. And we had that estimate from the contractor who was prepared to sign a contract, and we had a very comprehensive technical report.

Meanwhile, our relations with Mr. Harmon's department in the chancellor's office were getting more and more complicated. They would ask a question and we would respond by sending material; it would not be acknowledged, and months later the same questions would be asked all over again. When we presented the letter from the contractor who was prepared to sign a contract, they said: "Well, he does not really mean what he says, he's just trying to get his foot in the door for a negotiated contract."

The crucial trustees' meeting took place in Fresno this time. It would have made a good movie. The committee that had to approve buildings consisted of eight members of the board of trustees. The chancellor's chief architect and the state architect opened an attack on the building. This time there were (surprise!) new objections. The chancellor's chief architect had measured the areas of the building. Since the structure consisted of bents with inclined walls, there were areas which had no headroom. We had considered this fact by omitting these areas in the effective cost tabulations. But, by playing around with these numbers Harmon tried to show that this was really a very expensive building. I corrected the record and showed that his figures were distorted, and that turned into a lengthy discussion which became quite heated at times. Charles Luckman honestly summed it up that day. Pleading against the building, he said, "We are against extremes. Any extremes. Good or bad, we are against extremes." Other trustees also attacked it bitterly, while still others supported it strongly. It came time to vote. The motion was that building should be rejected. Four members said "No," it ought not to be rejected; three members said "Yes," it ought to be rejected. The chairman added his vote to the "Yeas," making it a tie.

It was then transferred for decision to the entire board of trustees. Sixteen of them were present at that meeting in the afternoon. (Governor Reagan, who is a member of the board, was absent.) There was only a short discussion. Two trustees made pleas for rejection. The chancellor himself, who is a voting member of the board, said he felt it was an ugly building, but the union was needed and if San Francisco students wanted to live with that ugliness, let them have it. Two members of the board made pleas in support, and the final word came from President Smith, who said he couldn't function on the campus without that building; a rejection would be a slap in the face to the entire community. A score of supporting telegrams were read by the chairman, and then the motion: that the building be approved. The vote was eight in favor, seven against. The chairman then exercised his prerogative and cast his vote: no, to make it a tie. For the second time that day the building was not approved.

Still later that day the trustees ordered President Smith to fire Murray, the Black Panther lecturer. There was complete insurrection on the campus, a strike of the students followed by a strike of the faculty. Rejection of the building was a factor in it. Shortly thereafter Smith resigned. All of this took place in November 1968.

For several months the campus was totally disabled, hardly functioning. Dr. S. I. Hayakawa was appointed acting president, but had little if any contact with the students. At one last meeting Hayakawa expressed support for the building, but at that time the students refused to attend any meetings with him.

During my trips to the west coast, two events gave me insight into the dynamics between the students and the authorities there.

The first was on the occasion of a demonstration in Berkeley. Students had asked that Telegraph Avenue be closed to traffic so there could be more room for pedestrians. The request had been turned down, and, following demonstrations, a curfew was declared.

I arrived in San Francisco that afternoon and drove directly to Chris Alexander's house in Berkeley, where I was staying. In the evening, Chris, two of his associates and I were driving down University Avenue. The curfew was on, but there was considerable traffic on the streets. We stopped for a red light, and found ourselves suddenly surrounded by three police cruisers. Before we realized what was happening we were all pulled out of the car, our hands placed on the hood, our pockets emptied and their contents thrown on the sidewalk. A large van arrived, and out of it jumped several policemen who fingerprinted and photographed us right there, and wrote details. I stated that I had just that day arrived from Montreal and was not a resident of Berkeley.

We had a dog in the car with us, so the police wagon brought us first to the pound to deposit the dog. We were then taken to the Berkeley prison, picking up several students on the way. Scores of cars passed us uninterrupted.

Four hours later we were informed that two hundred dollars bail was set for each of us and that we would have to report in the Court House the following day. I had a hundred and eighty dollars on me, and Chris had about twenty-five dollars. That was enough for one bail, so Chris went out and contacted a bondsman who raised the bond to free the rest of us. It was four o'clock in the morning by the time we got out.

During those hours we sat with the students and chatted, sharing the experiences surrounding our arrests. Men and women, black and white, we all had one thing in common; we were dressed informally, we all looked under thirty. Some had long hair and some wore the Black Panther uniform. It was obvious that each of us had been arrested because of his appearance and what this aroused in the minds of the policemen, for all of us had noticed large numbers of other people in the streets, driving and walking, who were not similarly stopped.

The following morning I arrived for my meeting at the San Francisco State College and told the students and faculty the story. They came to the conclusion that I was obviously due for a haircut.

What impressed me most vividly about that night was the polarization between students and establishment, a polarization between two groups in the same community so intense that one associates it only with civil war.

212

I relived some of these experiences again several weeks after the trustees ordered President Smith to fire Murray and rejected the Union design. At that time the campus erupted with demonstrations and strikes. On this occasion I arrived to find thousands of students on the campus green, marching with placards and chanting. There was, so far as I could see, no violence. The famous San Francisco riot police surrounded the campus, and suddenly there was silence. From four different directions approached, at double pace, phalanxes of riot police, ten abreast, blue uniformed, helmeted with acrylic guards across their faces, arms holding riot sticks horizontally across their chests. Each phalanx was led by two officers carrying what looked like a laser machine gun; actually, it was a weapon for tear gas. Beating and fighting began. A group of us stood by the site for the College Union and watched until waves of fear-filled students, withdrawing before the police, forced us to move away.

Looking back I find it incredible that fifteen thousand students who were prepared to pay for their own building, and who had support from the president, the faculty senate, the advisory committee, and some of the most respected members of the architectural profession in San Francisco, could be frustrated by sixteen trustees who meet once a month to run eighteen colleges. And that in a state where Reagan was elected on a platform of "conservatism," which we are told supports decentralization and community control of community functions. This was a project that surged on the constructive energies of students over a period of five years – a campus effort to get a building built with their own money. If the building had gone ahead at that point, it would have involved the whole campus, had everyone working together creatively. We were going to buy looms and all the textiles in the building were to be woven by the students. Students were going to become involved in planting the building in collaboration with the department of botany. Students were going to make the furniture, and make the graphics, all kinds of things. So what do the trustees do? They say "No." And then they're surprised when the campus blows up.

Most disappointed of all by the rejection of the Union design were the individuals on the Union Council who had devoted years to it. Most of them left the campus in disillusionment. Albert Duro had been one of the most active Council members. Six months later he wrote me the following note from Italy: "Though San Francisco and the College Union affair are very, very distant for me now, the legacy of love for architecture and the friendships that are the only tangible results of that experience will never be forgotten."

Epilogue

In June of 1969 the board of directors of the Associated Students was dissolved. In one of their last meetings, they unanimously moved a resolution that Moshe Safdie, Burger & Coplans were to remain the architects of the Associated Students and that the future student government was to make an effort to realize the building." In September 1969, I met with the newly elected student government. It reaffirmed support for the building and the wish to realize it. At that time, San Francisco State College students' funds were in receivership, frozen and under the control of the Attorney General of California. Until the receivership is lifted the students are unable to act.

22

Israel: A return

I went to Israel in December 1967 to give a paper at the International Congress of Architects and Engineers. It was my first return since 1954 and it was therefore a great event. At the Congress, I met the Minister of Housing, Mordechai Bentov. We had a long chat in which I briefed him on the progress of Habitat, and the project then underway in Puerto Rico.

It was just six months after the Six-Day War. I told him of my ideas for a new town for the Arab refugees and suggested that now, since many of the refugees were in areas within Israeli control, such a project could be initiated. He responded with much interest, suggested I write him a brief on the subject.

I summarized my thoughts in a report entitled "For and By the Refugees." It suggested selecting one or two locations in which a new community could be built; it could be part of an existing city or a totally new town. New industries would be established, housing factories would be built, training centers in which refugees would be trained in new skills would be organized, and the refugees would build their own town, which could also supply housing components to Israel. The program could begin immediately. In the first stage, a comprehensive design and feasibility study would be made, a site would be selected, and the leaders of the Palestinian community would be contacted and invited to take part.

It is not possible to discuss this proposal without dwelling on the political thoughts, shared by many Israelis, that motivate it: that the future of Israel is in a life of harmony and federation with the Arab world generally and the Palestinian Arabs specifically. Many, if not all, Israelis feel badly about the existence of the Arab refugees, but fewer see the solution to it in the context of Israeli action. Such action is only logical in the context of a reorientation of Israel's emphasis on its future in the Middle East. Its logical expression is a common market and a Middle East federation. The consequences to Israel as a state, with its close ties with world Jewry, are fundamental. The price for such a federation is to acknowledge a dual allegiance: to world Jewry as well as to the region. Israeli law cannot suggest, for example, that sixteen million Jews may be permitted to come to live in a region one day at the expense of those already living there, even if this is only a theoretical possibility. This does not mean stopping immigration; it means that the responsibility of Israel is dual – to world Jewry and to its neighbors.

For me, this issue always came alive at the cultural level. Israel is an integral part of the Middle East. Over half of the Jewish population of Israel originated in the Middle East. My ancestors, in addition to Hebrew, spoke Arabic and Spanish, enjoyed Arabic music, built in the traditions of the region, and made Middle-Eastern jewellery, carpets, and textiles. Nowhere has this fact been so clear as in the architecture of Israel. As you approach Jerusalem from the valley, the road ascends to a crest overlooking the western hills of the city. Down the slopes, a deserted Arab village hugs the hill, small and larger cubes made of the stone of the mountain: domes, arches, vaults, the mosque's tower, shaded passages, all in harmony with the landscape and the sun. At the summit of the hill is a series of long four-storey apartment structures built in the late fifties. They are scaleless, inhuman. They do violence to the mountain. They are foreign, as if imported from some rainy, cool European suburb. Driving from Jerusalem to Nablus and Yonder in the hills of Shomron, you go through fields and terraced vineyards and little villages, all of which are in unity with the land. Driving from Haifa to Nazareth in the hills of Galilee, passing by the new towns and developments, you are constantly confronted by the brutality of new housing projects that rape the hills and the landscape.

I once gave a lift to a young soldier. He was on leave. We were driving toward the mountains of Galilee. He spoke critically of the Arabs; all he could think of was what sort of soldiers they were. I was impressed by the fact that though he was only a few years younger than me, he did not remember the time when Israel was founded – he had not known the Arabs, except as a minority in Israel or as subjects in occupied territory. He did not hate them, nor did he respect them. They were, he said, bad soldiers. I said to him, "That may be, but they build so much better than we do and their towns are so much more wholesome than ours. Their art, their pottery, their clothes, their jewellery, their music is the soul of this land; there is so much we can learn from them."

I have always hoped that Israeli and Arab would build together and learn from each other. Such building and working together, planning together, would mean more than negotiations and agreements.

I sent my proposal to the minister and it was discussed by the cabinet and considered seriously. The minister had a press conference and released the contents of the report. It was said that some action of this kind was being considered, but many months passed by with nothing happening. There was no question that Bentov was solidly behind some such proposal, but the cabinet, as a whole, was not in a position to act.

Several months later, the government of Israel was approached by Baron Edmund de Rothschild, of England, with a proposal that something should be done for the refugees, and immediately. Minister Bentov told the baron of my proposal and suggested we meet. Some correspondence ensued and shortly thereafter we met in Montreal. The baron had for many months been very active in discussing the possibility of a large scale program: new industries, agricultural aid, the possibility of a giant desalination plant combined with agricultural industry in the northern Sinai. Through our discussions, we concluded that future development had to be industrial in nature, and that new industries had to be complemented by the building of new communities. A program could not be imposed, it had to grow from the people. It had to be done with their participation.

During this period, I met Stewart Udall, Secretary of the Interior under President Lyndon Johnson, and was invited to join his Overview group, which he had formed to undertake large-scale environmental projects. I suggested Udall and Overview act as co-ordinators of the feasibility study. Udall and Rothschild met and agreed to join forces. On several subsequent trips to Israel, I met with many individuals, Israelis who would undoubtedly be involved in such a program. I also travelled in the occupied areas. I went into some of the refugee camps and we sat in the central coffee house with the muchtar and the elders, and chatted about employment and housing and how they would react to such a program, and it became apparent that at the level of subsistence and livelihood, of employment and housing, the politics of power groups and of rigid alignments did not exist.

In the winter of 1969, Housing Minister Bentov came to see Habitat in Montreal. He arrived during the worst snow storm of the season. We walked through Habitat, the winds blowing, the snow coming down in large pieces, the place looking right out of an illustrated book of fairy tales. The minister told me of the growing volume of immigration, of the need for housing of higher standards, and of the need for new technologies to cope with Israel's severe manpower shortage. We talked of the possibility of Habitat and its feasibility in Israel. Shortly thereafter, the ministry invited me to come for a series of consultations to assess the building of the Habitat system in Israel. I spent ten days discussing each and every aspect of the project. At the end, we signed a contract commissioning me to undertake full preliminary plans, cost estimates, and feasibility studies for a Habitat building system for the Israeli Ministry of Housing. Three months later, the completed report indicated technical and economic feasibility, and delineated in a preliminary design the first community to be built in the hills of Jerusalem.

Many aspects of the program for Israel are like Habitat Puerto Rico: room sizes, apartment sizes, and densities are similar. There are some fundamental differences: a shortage of certain materials, a climate which fluctuates from severe heat in summer to a rainy and cool winter, and a difference in life-style.

217

To build in Jerusalem, in that most beautiful city, is almost an act of arrogance. Only much love and respect for what is there may make it possible to do it justice. In tackling the project I found there were tangible, speakable things, such as designing the outdoor terraces, in which Israelis spend much of their time, for year-round use. As a generic solution to what is now accomplished by building little roofs and asbestos shutters round these balconies, we developed a dome-shaped sliding window which could rotate; it sits toward the inside of the building in summer while a domed shutter projects to shade the terrace. Window and shutter reverse positions in winter, the glass dome enclosing the terrace as a greenhouse, capturing the heat and the sun. The building's dominant feature would change from shadowed arches in summer to sparkling bubbles in winter. There was also the intangible, the spirit of Jerusalem. I wanted to build something that was wholly contemporary, an expression of life today, but that would be as if it had always been there – a kind of fugue with two instruments, a counterpoint on a remembered melody. Thus evolved the Habitat Israel building system: modular, concrete units, sand blasted to expose the yellow Jerusalem stone aggregate, room sections made out of fiberglass domes, and rotating windows, and shutters, all interlocking on the hills.

As I write, we have completed the working drawings and are about to begin building a prototype of a dozen dwellings. Soon, I expect, a full size factory will be constructed and go into full production. As the Jerusalem *Post* put it in a headline that moved me, "Habitat Comes Home."

The combination of assistance and self help proposed for the refugee town building program has potential application to other areas in the world. Since in construction about sixty per cent of the cost is for labor, it makes good sense to develop programs in which the prospective owners of the houses could construct them and be compensated for their labor by ownership. This is relatively simple to achieve in rural housing where materials can be supplied, but more complex in the urban context.

In the Fort Lincoln project, working with the George Fuller Construction Company, and Stressed Structures Inc., we proposed a formula for such a program. The project was to be in an area surrounded by several Washington ghettos. Many of the prospective tenants were unemployed and on welfare, officially classified as chronically unemployable. We suggested that the housing factory should give priority to employing those who would live in the project. A special training center would be established in the plant, training those who had not been involved in construction before and who had for many years been living on welfare. Such a program could be extended even further; built-in furnishings and cabinets and other elements, which presently are either included in the housing package at great cost or omitted, could be built by the tenants themselves. With workshops located in the community, materials supplied by the housing agency, and the necessary guidance, tenants could manufacture to their own needs and design. Landscaping could be done in the same way with plant materials supplied by the community.

Considering the industrialization problems of the developing countries, the potential of such a scheme becomes even greater. There we have a situation in which a very substantial proportion of the population is, in our terms, unemployed. (In the United States when we talk about employing the unemployed in a construction program, we must consider that welfare payments in the U.S. are higher than normal wages in the developing countries.)

Urbanization in a country such as India could come about with the construction of new towns. Housing factories would be established, families would be drawn to build the town and make it their permanent home. They could at first be paid minimal wages and their subsistence requirements. Later on they would individually or co-operatively own the entire physical plant they had constructed. Thus, the construction of new communities could take place with a substantially lower capital investment than under normal circumstances – as much as sixty per cent lower. In the dramatic case of refugees, who are living in temporary quarters anyhow and are being fed by welfare programs, their employment in a construction program would tap unemployed energies and they would enjoy the fruit of their own labor.

23   The city that could be

One day about two years ago I walked from my office to my house in Montreal, a distance of about thirty blocks. I met George Challies, a young architect who used to work in my office. I met a girl I knew at Expo and whom I hadn't seen for two years, and I met Bill Sofin, a Montreal druggist who is a friend. I met Harold Spence-Sales, who taught me planning at McGill. He told me that he was writing Central Mortgage that they were absolutely stupid the way they were running Habitat; they had a moral responsibility to Canada's reputation. One block farther on I met Arthur Erickson, the Vancouver architect, who had just flown in from Japan, was in Montreal for the day, and was then flying home. He told me all about Japan and the Canadian pavilion which he was designing for Expo 70 at Osaka.

That was just walking home from my office at 5:30. Had I not lived within walking distance, had I lived six miles from downtown, I would have got into my car and driven there and I would have met no one.

You may say, "So what? Does that matter when the cities are exploding beneath our feet? Is the quality of your city life relevant when compared with the very immediate issues of slums, of pollution, of congestion, of the things that we read about every day in the paper?"

I believe that our society can and will come to terms with the quantitative problems in the environment. I know that this is a big assumption and that this isn't what recent history indicates. But, the fact is that people are coming to understand the violence of pollution, the destruction of the equilibrium of nature. And they are slowly coming to understand that it will take a great deal of energy, of funds, a high percentage of our entire national income to deal with these problems, to clean the waters and the skies, to impose on industry the additional cost of controlling waste. (I don't think subsidized housing is likely to get such solid support because everyone suffers from pollution, but not everyone suffers from bad housing.) There is a wide gap between the earning

221

power of a substantial portion of the population and the kind of housing they require, and it is understood that whatever the means, whether by subsidies or redistribution of income, or by change of the tax structure, a great part of our national income will have to be diverted to the construction of decent housing and urban services for the entire population. This should in no way minimize the magnitude of the task or the means that must be devoted to dealing with it.

We are overwhelmed by the fact that we must build millions of dwellings, that we must stop pollution, that we must construct miles of expressways and mass transit, but we also assume that if we spend enough money, the results will be guaranteed. On one hand this obsession with the immediate problem encourages many in a policy-making position to adopt the "quick fix" attitude, to alleviate as fast as possible with the least possible means each of the problems mentioned above. On the other hand, those same people assume that if at one point sufficient funds are devoted to their needs, there will be no problem to getting the kind of city we want to live in. This is the most dangerous assumption of all. It is possible that with all the funds in the world devoted to reconstructing the city, the end results would be as disastrous as what we have today.

The city has always been shaped by cultural and personal values. The form of a city is an expression of what Jung called the "collective unconscious." It is necessary to clarify to ourselves what we want of our cities, how we want to live in them, the kind of cities we aspire to build.

I prefer San Francisco to Los Angeles, I prefer Montreal to Toronto, and I prefer New York to Philadelphia. Why? The kind of concentration that is achieved in them creates certain choices, an openness of society that is not possible in the lower-density environments. I want my children to be able to meet and play and communicate with many other children on their own, not only when they are driven somewhere. I want them to grow up in an environment that is not just a place where people sleep, but where people work too, and where people enjoy themselves, or as Goodman says in *Communitas*: "The city must be the integration of work, love and knowledge." I see the seeds of these possibilities in a city like San Francisco, I do not see them in a city like Los Angeles. You don't meet people passing them at sixty miles an hour on an expressway; you have to decide you want to see someone and make the effort of driving to see him. It is the difference between a city that makes possible random social association and one in which encounters are predetermined and therefore rigid. Los Angeles is of so low a density that it will never be able to provide public transportation, it is caught in a bind.

Solving our pollution problems, building more expressways, building good housing, urgent and essential as all this may be, will not give us a city that generates social interaction, that allows a child to grow up in an environment in which every aspect of life is experienced, that enriches the individual's experiences and expands his growth, nor will it give us an unstratified society. All these have to do with the basic structure of the city.

We rarely pause to state what *kind* of city we want. We usually state what we do not want. Critics respond to positive statements by calling them utopian thinking. They say that a positive statement cannot consider the many realities and forces that have to be coped with, all of which would compromise the ideal image.

But society today has the means, in terms of resources and productive capacity, to build whatever environment we choose, just as we obviously have the resources and the capacity to feed the whole world. We underestimate the real volume of potential food production we are capable of; just as we underestimate our capabilities in making our environment. Buckminster Fuller has been constantly reminding us what we could do in terms of productivity if we used our resources properly. Fuller has been saying, in the context of an extrapolitical reality, unique to our time, that environmental systems must be applicable to the total global population. To provide more for more with ever decreasing natural resources, we must rely on the potential of technology. I would add that fulfilling this "bare maximum" also creates the welcome burden of having to establish city structures that can give fulfillment to all.

I think people want space to live in, generous space. Individuals want private space. The family unit wants to be able to function with a fair amount of privacy. We want a house which has indoor spaces and outdoor spaces. We like the idea of a garden, I think, regardless of our cultural background. We like to be able to do whatever we want in our own dwelling, whether it is to have a party or listen to or play music, without being heard or hearing others. These things are independent of whether we live in a house, an apartment, a row house, or a cliff dwelling.

We want two extremes. We want the intensive meeting place, the urban environment, the place where everybody is together, and we want the secluded open space where we are alone in the country in nature. We need and want both. Suburbia is an expression of those desires – needing the city and wanting the country – but it provides neither. We also want great variety in our life, in what is available to us to choose from or to take part in. The average North American's ideal is to go shopping in New York, to have a choice of going to theaters, concerts, opera, museums, restaurants, discotheques, in London or New York – anything you can think of, available at any time, so concentrated that you can get to it with ease. And yet Manhattan is certainly not ideal environment. Because of the great concentration of people, it denies so many other things. The ideal environment would have the variety of Manhattan's amenities and the recreation space of the seacoast or the open spaces of New England as part of daily experience, close enough so that you could enjoy both every day; to live in a community of maybe thirty thousand people where you feel you can make decisions and participate in decision-making, but to share the life of twelve million people.

This is the contradictory desire in our utopia. We want to have our cake and eat it too. We want to live in a small community with which we can identify and yet we want all the facilities of a city of millions of people. We want to have very intense urban experiences and yet we want the open space right next to us.

The paradox of suburbia also grows from this conflict. In a certain sense, many of the virtues or amenities that people want are available in the single family house in the countryside. The isolated house in the country is ideal in one way and yet it's not ideal in another. It's ideal from the point of view of private needs in one's own house, but from the point of view of one's relationship to the community, it's not. The ideal environment is the integration of both.

For me it is a foregone conclusion that low-density dispersal cannot combine the advantages of the single isolated house with the numbers of people and opportunities that the urban environment provides. We can't handle the communication problems, and that means that people spend half their time travelling. This is not to say that this is a permanent conclusion. It may totally change in the next thirty or forty years, when technology gives us the means of flying as individuals.

Frank Lloyd Wright was very concerned with the individual's environment when he designed Broadacre City. You need, he stated, one acre per family – a homestead. Yet, if you need two or three or four million people to support the quality of life you want, at an acre per family, that means a kind of spread that we cannot handle physically in terms of communications, and I don't think we will be able to for a long time. Toronto or Montreal would need a thousand square miles of housing, and when you disperse families at that rate you have a compounding effect which creates a situation where forty per cent of the real estate is taken up with transportation facilities.

The fundamental question of optimum density must be answered and this is only possible in the context of a regional city. Metropolitan New York is approaching a population of fifteen million, and so is Keihin, the metropolitan area that encompasses Tokyo and Yokahama. We can say that most cities are evolving toward populations of that size. Even so, we will still desire open space within easy reach – I might say, even more will we desire open space.

What could an ideal city of fifteen million be like?

Assume that the city is no more than three miles wide, so that one can walk from anywhere in the city to the open space on either side of it in half an hour or less, or drive in just a few minutes. Now let us accept the concept of Frank Lloyd Wright's Broadacre City; each family on its own acre, with additional acreage for services. On these assumptions we will have a city three miles wide and four thousand miles long. Well, four thousand miles is not a workable entity. If we double the width of the city to six miles, then it's two thousand miles long, and it's still not a working organism.

If we increase the density to ten families per acre, which is double that of suburbia, we would get a city four hundred miles long. Four hundred miles is the kind of distance that could possibly be covered in a single hour's travelling, so we could have a single urban region at about twice current suburban densities. If we take another jump and consider a gross density of a hundred families per acre, a very high density, it would mean that our city would be forty miles long and three miles wide and have fifteen million people living together.

Obviously a city of that population and compactness could offer great variety, tremendous vitality, unique urban services. I have said that I look for a balance between community and privacy. So I must ask, if we build at ten times suburban density, must the dream Frank Lloyd Wright embodied in Broadacre inevitably be lost? I believe not. Many of the things, maybe all of the things Frank Lloyd Wright thought of in a Broadacre house are achievable in a denser environment. Not in the form in which we presently build them, but they are achievable.

When we think of Broadacre City, what immediately comes to mind is the possibility of privacy – that you have enough space to lead your own life. However privacy in the family sense is not the same as solitude. Suburbia, or better still super-suburbia with one family per acre, does give you space for your family to live privately, but if it spread for many square miles without any break in it, then the open country where you can really have solitude would not survive. A Broadacre City house would have to be a year-round place.

I think this was Wright's understanding of the rhythm of life, whereas I feel that we are moving toward a rhythm of life in which you alternate between the intense urban places and the open country, where great concentration and the open country are both ingredients of daily life. We are now experiencing wholesale migrations of people, like birds, to the warm climates in winter and vice versa. Fifty years from now new forms of transportation could change that completely, but we must not think of the far future, we must think of now, the immediate operation.

The commonest contemporary method for dealing with this issue is to build more and more high-speed expressways, and improve and automate them, enabling people to live at a great distance from the heart of the metropolis and still reach it quickly. But this has not worked, because you cannot bring half a million people on highways, automated or otherwise, into the city and store the vehicles, as Manhattan has already proven. What you could probably do is let them use private vehicles to a certain point, transfer them to mass transit where you have accumulated sufficient numbers, and then go on to the central city.

And what about the city core, the meeting place itself? If the city is purely a commercial-recreational center, without people living in it, then it's really a dead place too. It would be very busy during the day because people work there, but it would be dead at other times. But if people live there and work there and also come there for pleasure, then you have a much richer environment, a much more integrated life – a better place. It could mean that the place where three or four pedestrian pathways meet would become a museum or a gallery. A natural science museum could be a transportation terminal. We could let public libraries be situated anywhere along the streets. We could de-institutionalize and integrate these services.

The metropolitan city is a new scale city. Parts of it have existed in earlier cities but the problems were different because the numbers were different. Very few cities before this century exceeded one million people. Imperial Rome was one of the rare exceptions. If the qualities of life which obviously existed in the small town with its piazza and the shops on the piazza and houses over them and city hall and church are of value, and to be preserved, then the metropolis also needs a hierarchy. There should be places on the scale of a thousand families and on the scale of a million people and maybe there should be meeting places on the scale of ten million people. That hierarchy is very important. It's the lack of hierarchy that really makes our cities so unworkable. It's the fact that you are a part of ten million people often, but you are not part of five families or a hundred families or twenty thousand people, which are workable communities in which you can function with a quite different kind of participation and control over your environment than you can with ten million people.

In today's huge metropolises people have lost even the urban qualities they had in small towns before the beginnings of this century. If the man who lives in Brooklyn goes to Manhattan only maybe once in two months and to Atlantic City and the Adirondacks once a year, then the fact that he's living in an urban organism of twelve million people is quite meaningless. Let me put it differently. If we draw cities as plans on paper they appear to be something quite different from what they would be if we only drew a plan of the city as it is experienced by a single individual. Conventionally we draw New York, Manhattan, Brooklyn, the whole region, highways, rivers, and so on, extending over seventy miles. If we then make a list of all the things contained in the plan it will be rather impressive. But, if we draw New York as seen through the eyes of a man who works in the navy yards in Brooklyn and lives in Brooklyn, it would be a totally different thing, much less exciting, and in fact it might be quite limited.

I think the meaningful way of drawing city plans is what I call "one man's environment." This is the only way to assess what real mobility and variety of experience he has. If this man who lives in Brooklyn experiences Atlantic City and Manhattan and the Hudson Valley and the East River and Times Square as a daily routine, then the environment has really expanded to offer him much more than his ancestors had. As long as it doesn't, then he is a loser, which may even mean that the contemporary city has changed life for the worse. If we traced the path of the individual from his home to work and to his places of recreation and to the various places he would go in his daily life, we would have a drawing of what the city is to him, which in the final analysis is the only meaningful description. And if we traced similar paths for two million individuals, we would have two million city plans, and the sum total of these two million master plans would be the plan of the city. If in drawing these plans we discovered that there were many people in the city who were much limited in their experience as compared with others who enjoyed a greater range of activities, then that in itself would tell something about the nature of that particular city and its social and economic life. The master plan that you would draw for a man living in a Washington, D.C. ghetto would be quite different from the master plan that you would draw for a senior civil servant who lives in one of the suburbs in Virginia or Maryland and works in Washington. That in itself may indicate something about the structure of the city of Washington, including some of its problems.

All this pivots on the subject of mobility; people do want to physically fly. How wonderful it would be to take off anywhere you wanted into space, not tied down to the ground. You want to go home, you just walk out of the window and fly. If you want to go for a walk in the park, you fly there. The whole history of human mobility has been a development toward that moment. In the meantime the car is not a bad compromise. Any planner's talk that the car imprisons us and ought to be banned completely is utter nonsense, because the car has given us more personal mobility than we ever had before and we'll never give it up until it is replaced by something that gives us even more mobility.

Mobility is the central and most critical question, with the greatest influence on the form of cities. Increased mobility is the tool that will make it possible for us to have our cake and eat it too. Expressways have expanded the car's range, but we are finding one of two problems in our cities today. In cities such as New York or Montreal, where there is a concentration of urban activity, the car becomes a statistical impossibility. It is not possible for everyone to drive on the highways because there is not enough space for them. The car which has given us mobility in one context gives us no mobility at all in the concentrated environment. In desperation we resort to subways and taxis and buses, which partially alleviate the statistical problem by moving more people in less space but at the price of limiting freedom: you have to go by the timetable, you have to follow major routes, and you wait. The other trend, as in Los Angeles or Toronto, is that in the desire to keep the vehicles mobile the city has been continually dispersed. In avoiding the density or concentration that would eliminate the car the planners have so spread things around that an essential quality of urban life is lost. In Los Angeles the average person may spend two or three hours in his day just moving from one place to the other. Notwithstanding expressways and dispersal Los Angeles demonstrates that in rush hour the road system can't handle the traffic and yet the people are by now so dispersed that mass transportation is impossible, the density is too low to make it economically feasible.

What is the next development? I think the distance we can travel in an hour, which has traditionally limited the size of a city, is going to expand very substantially. The horse and buggy gave us a city with a radius of ten miles, and then the car made it thirty miles, and then we built expressways and made it fifty miles. The next step is going to be an enormous jump. The airplane hasn't affected the city at all, hasn't expanded the one-hour travel limit. The next step will be transportation on the ground at four or five hundred miles an hour. You can't have five-hundred-mile-an-hour trains going in all directions, and they can't be stopping every couple of miles, they don't work that way. By their nature, they will become a forming element for the city. You have to find a way in which a system like that can load and unload people without stopping, so that the system moving at five hundred miles an hour may slow to one hundred miles an hour while another system, which may be the equivalent of today's bus or subway, accelerates to a hundred miles an hour and people get on and off in motion. It would be like a system of gear wheels all turning at different speeds at the same time without ever coming to a stop, transportation systems maintaining very high average speeds by eliminating waiting time completely in the transfer from one system to another.

There must be a whole hierarchy of systems – the speed of an elevator, the speed of a pedestrian, the speed of a car, all the way to five hundred miles an hour, and all synchronized to exchange passengers in motion. These could be designed so that in the lower density range, people could use personal vehicles and then at the edge of the denser area, with some very easy transition, switch to a public system.

This idea of continuous systems in motion is just one possibility, but whatever the technical solution fast transit would have significant impact. It could create linear system with loops generating out of it, like a necklace. Toronto-Montreal or Toronto-Detroit would become one urban region – and we would create a situation in which ten or twenty million people are within a one-hour travel limit of each other and therefore within one metropolitan area, sharing all the facilities a population of that kind can support. There would still be points of greater and lesser importance. This regional city would not be homogeneous. There would be potential for growth along the necklace. It would be a necklace of communities, hundreds of communities each with a measure of identity but interdependent. It could almost be limitless. It could permit the integrating of agriculture and industry into a single environment, an optimum environment where the rural and urban become one, the concentrated and dense and the totally open space become a single environment, so that the Adirondacks or the Laurentians or the lake areas north of Toronto become part of the daily experience of the environment for the people in this regional city.

The linear pattern creates possibilities for growth that do not exist in the radial city. If we consider southern Ontario, the region around Toronto, linked by a linear spine, then existing centers, such as Kingston, Oshawa, Windsor, and Hamilton, become part of the necklace city. Toronto, though, would probably stop growing radially and growth would be re-channeled into new centers on the necklace somewhere between Windsor and Kingston.

This would completely liberate our thinking about the country's land resources. It would also deal with the artificial issue of new cities vs. satellite towns vs. the expansion of existing cities. The expanded city integrates all three. We could decide which areas we would open up for recreation by making the transport system give access to them, which areas ought to be forest reserves, which areas we want to preserve as open space, either for agriculture or for park land. It would give us an environment that constantly provided the contradictions we want – urbanity and the open country; great numbers for variety and small communities we can identify with; a great deal of personal mobility, notwithstanding the kind of concentration that makes mobility so difficult to achieve.

I am suggesting that the intensive growth of places like Toronto and Montreal could be deflected into new and less problematical areas. But at the same time this would actually expand the sphere of influence of these present great cities by increasing the potential population that lies within easy reach of their attractions. What New York has to offer is highly desirable, and it is understandable that so many want it. But with a new transportation system such as I describe they would not all have to live within spitting distance of the Empire State Building to have what they want. Cities the size of New York could usefully shrink while regional New York expands.

If I were president...

There is no mystery about "the crisis in the cities" in North America today. No miracle is going to solve it, except a hell of a lot more money. Our most prominent economists, such as John Kenneth Galbraith, have pointed out that the city today is a provider of services to a much greater extent than in the past. A much greater portion of the gross national product, raised from a broader tax base, will have to be diverted to the city.

Paradoxically, people have been spending progressively less of their income on housing in this century, though the cost of housing is now increasing even faster than real income, partly because of the inefficiency of the housing industry, and partly because interest rates have constantly increased, and every quarter one per cent increase means another sixteen dollars in monthly payment for middle-income housing.

People talk about low-cost housing and middle-income housing and luxury housing and the suggestion is that they are different things. I am often asked, "Is Habitat low-cost housing or middle-income housing?" and I say, "I don't know, it's just housing." The term "low-cost housing" is a fabrication intended to camouflage the fact that in the past thirty years it has been public policy to provide middle-income housing to low-income families at subsidized rent. Low-income housing has never cost less to build than middle-income housing and in some cases it has cost more. In fact, luxury housing is not more expensive today per square foot than middle-income housing. There may be a difference of five or ten per cent. The major difference is in land costs because of location, and the kind of services that are provided. You pay for the address and you pay for the doorman. Their rooms may be bigger but the cost of construction per square foot is not appreciably greater. You could say that the housing market is a single market, and tackling the housing problem technically is tackling the whole range of incomes. If you can build cheaper housing which is good for the low-income family, it's going to be used by the middle-income and high-income families too. The standards of Habitat in terms of room size and arrangements and the organization of the house were very conventional Canadian housing. There is nothing revolutionary about the inside of the houses in Habitat.

To be able to Plan with a capital P, one has to have – the public has to have – a measure of concentrated power. The individual in North America feels very much threatened by centralized power. The whole political tradition of North America is that centralized power, bureaucracy, is eventually a threat to individual freedom of action and choice.

To me the Number One political issue of our time is that on one hand we must have planning, which I believe to be essential to the functioning of the city complex, and on the other hand we must liberate the individual from the bureaucratic oppression that commonly results from central planning.

Consider the ghetto slum; we are all impressed, depressed, and concerned about it. The ghetto is not an isolated problem, its roots are in basic social and political structure. Obviously, the ghetto slum relates to the distribution of income, to patterns of migration, to problems of race. Each of these problems must be confronted if the ghetto is to cease to be. But, in terms of the immediate action, the common attitude is that ghetto slum housing is bad, it must therefore be replaced; if we have large-scale renewal we will correct the ill. To put it in other words, we need "more funding"; more funding will solve the problem; more funding is a kind of charity; if we will be charitable enough we will take care of the ghetto.

But, even if we do, for a moment, divorce ourselves from the more fundamental questions of income distribution and limit ourselves to the problems directly related to urban planning, more funding for reconstruction of the ghetto is not sufficient. It is in a sense a diversionary tactic that camouflages the fundamental city characteristics that create ghettos. The ghetto and the slum are symptoms of a deep structural malady. They are impressive because they are the extreme symptom of a much broader problem. Our energy at this point should be directed to questioning what has gone wrong in our urban legislative and urban economic systems.

If the ghetto is a symptom of a malady and the malady has to do with our urban structure, then it stands to reason that the disease is affecting the total city. If the ghetto has a housing problem, it is also true that we have a total housing problem. The ghetto is the most dramatic and obvious expression of it. If the ghetto is immobile and has a transportation problem, it is also true that we have a total transportation problem. We have a total conservation problem. We have a total pollution problem. The ghetto is an eruption of boils, only indicating a spread of disease throughout the body.

Five years ago twenty per cent of all Americans couldn't afford to buy houses unless they were assisted by subsidy. With the costs of construction and the interest rate going up it will soon be fifty or sixty per cent, and maybe in twenty years, if we go on in the way we are going, nobody will be able to afford a house.

The causes range from the general to the specific. North American legislation concerning the environment was evolved in a rural society in which the dependency of the individual on the community was minimal. You could build your barn of any material because if it burned down it wouldn't affect the neighbors. You could toot your car horn or play the violin all day and nobody else would hear you, whereas in the city when you toot your horn it bothers other people, so there is a law against horn tooting. You're told what construction materials to use in the city because if your house burns down it may burn down your neighbor's house too. You can do whatever you wish with the outhouse when you have a hundred acres, but you can't ignore the smell from somebody's sewage system when he's living two feet away from you.

Continuous urbanization, however, has not been accompanied by reform of the law. The degree of the individual's dependency on the community increases directly with urbanization, but our legal system has not changed. In a general way, this is reflected in the electoral system. The political voice of the urban inhabitant of Canada and the United States is not equal to the rural citizen's. Redistribution is slow and never reflects the rate of urbanization, so that the urban citizen is always unequally represented in his government.

This legislative backlog obviously helped to create the ghetto. In a typical U.S. city, numerous jurisdictions of governments exist, unrelated to the reality of the total region. The metropolitan city is broken up into many municipal jurisdictions, each an entity in itself which has no relationship whatsoever to how the region really functions as a city. Each municipality is selfishly concerned with its own interests, that's only natural, so that it is impossible to consider some aspects of the total regional city.

What we must have is a planning authority that expresses what the regional city is. If "Toronto" really stretches from Hamilton to Oshawa and functions as a single city then there must be one governmental authority that's responsible for dealing with it. The same for the Atlantic seaboard agglomeration, Boston-Washington, or the other megalopolises that are evolving in various places. The immediate reaction is: "Well, people don't want a government that's dealing with twenty million people, they want to be part of a nice little community of twenty or thirty thousand people where they can take part in community life and feel they have some influence on it." I believe this desire to be a genuine one that we have to respect. It suggests to me that what we must develop is a new federal structure for urban government, so that there are various small municipal authorities each dealing with things that are purely local, such as community facilities and education, and a federated authority that deals with those things that affect the total region, such as transportation, land use, and conservation.

Now the ghetto arises, among other things, from the fact that very little tax money is available in a particular area and therefore very few and poor services are provided. Under a federal city structure of local government a more even distribution of services would be possible. I believe that the tax base in the cities is inadequate when compared with the tax base of the federal and provincial governments. The services that cities are called upon to provide are constantly increasing with urbanization. Increasingly the problems of the cities are the major problems of the country.

At three hundred million dollars, the annual budget of the City of Montreal is larger than the budgets of six provinces – the four Atlantic provinces, Manitoba, and Saskatchewan. And at six billion dollars, New York City's budget is larger than the budget of any state in the union, and larger than the budgets of all the Canadian provinces together.

But legislative reform must go further. Our legislative tradition is that you do what you want with land that you own, and as we have urbanized we have stubbornly continued to pay lip service to that concept. Yet, we have progressively restricted the freedom of the individual to use the urban land he owns – we have had to – to the point now where the individual owning land in an urban area is extremely limited in his use of it, he's restricted by zoning and planning authority and so forth. So, on one hand, we do restrict individuals, on the other hand we want to stick to private ownership of land. In the frontier tradition factories spouted out smoke into the air and acids into the river, and no one told them not to do so. Today we're reaching the point where our very survival as a species is threatened by pollution.

We must face the fact that the concept of private ownership of land in the urban context is obsolete. As we move into more concentrated developments, the use of land itself becomes secondary to the use of space. Air rights may be more significant than surface rights. Furthermore, it is not possible to plan a city or to guide growth by planning without prescribing land use, and if we are to prescribe land use I think the public should own the land. That does not mean that public authorities should build everything or that they should hold onto all land, but it may mean that land is leased on a fifty or hundred year basis to be used in conformity with the overall plan. This gives the public the chance to re-assess the situation every fifty or a hundred years without going through the impossible process of re-purchasing land from individuals in order to exercise a decision. Yet, we do this in urban renewal: we buy land, we demolish, we write its cost down, but then, instead of leasing it after prescribing the kind of development that should take place on it, we sell it back to developers who put up some miserable building on it – and we will have the same problem twenty years later. We will have to buy it back, demolish, and go through the whole process again. Public land ownership is thought of as a threat, Big Brother up there making all the decisions. Yet, in our society central planning is done by the elected representatives of the people. If we have any faith in the democratic process we should not worry about it.

234

One of the best examples we have of centralized planning is the telephone system. A group of companies, mostly private, have on their own initiative used central planning to make the whole telephone network on this continent – and now spreading over the whole world – into a single integrated system. It would not have been possible any other way. Does this limit us or restrict our freedom in any way? It's a fantastic thing. Every time I dial direct I get impressed by it all over again. Just imagine if the same was true of our transportation system! Yet, if we put our minds to it, we could deal with transportation as a single integrated system. If we did that, no one would feel deprived by it – and yet it is essential to such a system that someone have authority on a national scale to draw up a national transportation plan and bring together those involved with every form of transportation and in a sense subjugate them to a central plan. If one telephone company decided to opt out it would immediately put itself out of the total national network. It would be committing suicide. The same ought to be true of the transportation network.

There is a good deal of resistance to any kind of legislation that gives the public the authority to prescribe land use, but is that so very different from transportation planning – or telephone planning? Maybe a good way of putting it in perspective is to recall other legislative programs that have been introduced in the last twenty years where the public good has transcended the right of the individual to free action in the business world. For example, the food and drug act prescribes what the individual may sell as food and what is manufactured and sold as drugs because it's considered essential that the public be protected. We've come to accept such legislation. The idea that anybody should be able to sell food that could damage people would terrify us. It seems to me that the use of land is very similar. As people are living in a more concentrated way, land use becomes a matter of survival.

Even minor legislation, such as the income tax structure, can affect the environment. The city is made up primarily of two types of buildings, commercial-institutional and residential. Commercial buildings are put up by corporations for whom the cost of construction is a business expense. That means that if a company has a gross profit of one million dollars and has spent two hundred thousand dollars on construction, it will pay tax on only eight hundred thousand dollars. If the corporation is in the fifty per cent tax bracket, the public has indirectly contributed fifty per cent of the cost of the building – or it might be better to say, had the expense not been a tax deductible item that much more tax would have been paid. By contrast all residential construction is paid for out of income after taxes. As a result those involved in the construction of commercial building can spend more money per square foot than those in housing. The average cost of commercial building is thirty dollars a square foot and the average cost of residential is fifteen dollars, so the ratio of two to one, I think, is expressive of the tax structure.

Realizing that tax structure and other economic aspects of legislation have such a fantastic impact on the environment, we could reverse the process. We could see what kind of tax structure could be introduced to improve the environment. One might reach the conclusion, for example, that individuals ought to be able to build their houses from income before tax, thus giving them an incentive to put more into their environment. If people knew that when they filled out their income tax forms they could put the construction of their house or rent as an expense before paying taxes, it would immediately affect the way they spend money; just as businessmen spend all kinds of money on entertainment and promotion. The whole price structure of the more expensive restaurants is based on the fact that their charges are handled as a business expense before tax.

There is no single structure for financing construction. Instead we have several separate and independent structures. Insurance companies and banks make money available for construction at market rates of interest, the government guarantees mortgages under the National Housing Act, money is made available below market rates – three per cent in such programs as 221(d) (3) in the United States – and there is public housing which is not financed at all but paid for in cash by the government, the rents then being subsidized directly. The fact that we have all these independent systems makes it inevitable that we have segregation of income groups. It also means that each project utilizing a particular financing system must be separate from the others. We have developed no formulas for using all these financing systems within one project. It has automatically meant that people with incomes between four and five thousand dollars live in one place, those who are below four thousand live in another place, those earning above five and up to seven thousand live in another.

The Fort Lincoln project in Washington called for one hundred and twenty housing units, half of which were to be public housing with subsidized rents, the other half 221 (d) (3) housing at subsidized interest rates. There was no difference whatsoever between the specifications for the two groups and no difference in their costs yet the authorities insisted that the two parts be separated by a property line. Thus, on a project established to explore new approaches to housing, we were told to separate the low income from the moderate income families. HUD insisted on having the project split in two, because "It's too complicated to administer it any other way."

Our financing patterns have created segregation, and public housing makes it worse, because its inhabitants are subsidized and therefore not consumers in the usual sense. The problem is to find a way of giving a subsidy that still allows the recipient to be a selective consumer in the open market. One solution is for each family to get a coupon equal in value to the subsidy public-housing families get anyhow. They could then spend this coupon on housing anywhere they chose; but they would have to add to the coupon at least the amount of money they would have paid out in rent in the public housing project. This method would avoid the institutionalization of low income housing. In such a system we would also have to remove from the market whatever we considered to be uninhabitable or sub-standard. Then we could leave people to make their own choice.

I'm sure there are many other formulas, but the basic aim is to finance housing in such a way that we do not, by the necessity of the financing pattern, create segregated ghettos and that we do create the opportunity for different types of housing and people of different income levels to mix within a single community.

What I'm basically saying is that a particular economic or tax structure can have more impact on the environment than ten master plans and all the ideology in the world.

Just as there are big legislative reforms that can help the city, there are also small legislative tricks that could help. For example, the minimum parcel of land that could be developed in built-up areas of the city should be fifteen or twenty acres, and the minimum parcel in undeveloped parts of the city should be a hundred or two hundred acres. This would automatically eliminate the haphazard disintegration of urban areas. It would create the circumstances where comprehensive planning could take place. Not that size guarantees results. Stuyvesant Town in New York and other similar projects show how tragic large developments can be. But at least such a law would make a good development possible. Today it is totally impossible for developers, architects, and planners to solve the basic problems as long as they have to work on an area that is owned by hundreds of people and slowly disintegrating and being rebuilt in fragments.

Moral of this story: You can make all the plans you want but in the end it's legislation and tax structure and the subtleties of the law that shape the environment.

If I were to run for office in the Federal Parliament in Canada or for the U.S. Senate or for that matter President of the U.S., I would adopt the following environmental platform as a matter of top priority to be implemented in the first four years.

An *Environmental Bill of Rights* outlining the basic housing and community requirements of every citizen. This bill would be enacted into law and would be subject to review and revision every four years:

1   Subsidies for families and individuals who could not purchase such housing with twenty-five per cent of their income. These subsidies would continue until income, purchasing power, and housing costs converged.

2   A survey of the number of people in the country who live in housing below the standards set by the Bill of Rights.

3   Funds for a massive construction program to fill the gap. It would have top priority in the national budget.

4   An amendment to the income tax act to allow taxpayers to treat money spent for housing, up to a stated maximum, as a non-taxable expense, and to deduct it from income before the payment of taxes.

5   Construction of three metropolitan regions and ten prototype communities of twenty-five thousand people each, carried out under administrative procedures similar to those of the NASA space program, with research and development funds, a prototype stage, and full community construction. The inhabitants of the community would be encouraged to participate in the planning.

6   A national transportation master plan to include every means of transportation, personal and public, similar to the telecommunications and telephone system master plans. A Federal body for co-ordinating all systems would be established.

7   A five-year program to end all forms of pollution. During the transitional period, massive federal aid would cushion the impact on industry.

8   A massive land purchasing program to preserve a minimum of one half of all land in each defined metropolitan region (excluding roads and highways) as public open space and land reserves for future development. The Federal government would allocate funds to the states, and the states and municipalities would use the program as a tool for planning and guiding growth.

9   Integration of the various Federal housing programs to end the enforced economic segregation of housing. In all projects above a certain size aided by Federal financing, a mixture of housing intended for various income groups would be mandatory.

10 A master plan for urban dispersal, designating locations suitable for the development of new metropolitan regions. A sliding scale of concessions on individual and corporate income tax would apply in these new metropolises (full exemption in Year 1. . . no exemption in Year 20). Land in the new metropolitan cities would be publicly owned by the state and municipal governments and leased for development.

11 To cover the large cost of all these projects, the percentage of the Gross National Product devoted to the environment would be doubled.

If I were running for provincial or state office or as mayor of a major city, I would adopt this program:

a   All metropolitan regions to be reorganized into city-states each having a federal structure. Regional governments would be responsible for those aspects of the administration and planning of the region that could not be undertaken at the community level. Local sub-municipalities would be guaranteed certain rights and responsibilities within the federal city-state structure.

b   Transportation system and land use planning, land banks, and the purchasing of public land for open space to be responsibilities of the city-states.

c   A substantial portion of municipal taxes to be equalized on a per-capita basis throughout the region.

d   The minimum level of services provided by each sub-municipality to be determined for the whole region. If any sub-municipality could not afford to provide services at that level, the city-state government would give assistance.

e   All mass transportation in metropolitan region to be provided as a free service paid for through general taxation, as roads, street lighting, and garbage disposal are.

f   Through negotiation with the Federal government, an agreement to increase the revenue of state and municipal governments for expenditure on physical plant. If necessary, regional and municipal income taxes would be introduced.

g   In existing urbanized areas, a crash program to consolidate land use. Legislation and increased taxes would be used to discourage vacant land and open parking lots. Minimum sizes would be set for urban developments to provide sufficient magnitude for comprehensive development: in a central business district, fifteen acres would be the minimum development, in the less dense areas of the periphery one hundred acres would be the minimum. Municipal legislation to facilitate the assembling of land for development would be included in this program.

h   Strict enforcement of the minimum standards of the Environmental Bill of Rights in new and existing construction. Special assistance would be given for renovating existing construction to conform to these standards. Where renovation could not meet such standards, existing construction would be replaced.

i   A state or multi-state transport commission responsible for synchronizing all forms of transportation. Where necessary, existing systems would be purchased and integrated into the system.

j   A public or semi-public corporation to provide self-driven taxis. These personal vehicles would be widely available and users would pay for them on a time-and-distance basis. They would be low-cost, low-maintenance vehicles, and their use would greatly reduce the number of vehicles needed to provide the same service, and the number of parking spaces, without reducing personal mobility.

k   Extension of the concept of public right-of-way to multi-storey developments where feasible. As it does on public streets, this public right would also include public responsibility for policing, service, and maintenance.

The question is, with such a platform, would I be elected?

Epilogue: A magic machine

Back in 1960 I was wondering what to call my thesis. I finally gave it the title, "A Three-Dimensional Modular Building System". That proved to be an important decision. I didn't think of it as a building. By talking of building systems I implied a departure from the concept of "The Building" as I understood it as a student.

I think it is important to keep emphasizing that there are two issues, not just one: the technical problem and the environmental problem. My intention at Habitat was to organize the building into small repetitive components that lent themselves to industrialization and then to unite them by a formal language of permutations and combinations, rhythms and variations, that would provide the sense of place people need and allow them to retain and develop their sense of identity.

I would say again, that ideally each house should be different from every other house, as each person is different from every other person, and that communities should differ from each other as much as their inhabitants do. The Habitat space cell was only a crude start on the development of this ideal.

Then there is another scale of variations, what the individual can handle once he gets a house: Can he move the walls? Can he change the floor? Can he adapt the space to put books where he wants them? Can he, in short, adapt the house to his habits? The problem is to build adaptability into a house that is mass-produced out of modular components and has standard plumbing and electrical circuits and standard structural components.

Now those people living in Habitat are, to put it simply, happy. But at another level, I feel a shortcoming of Habitat is that even though there are twenty house-types with a variety of internal arrangements the spatial characteristics of the box are so strong that they feel very similar. I have subsequently explored the possibility of greater variation. I designed a system that was basically a cube measuring twenty-one feet on each side, subdivided into nine cubes each measuring seven feet on each side, and assumed that it would be technically possible for the tenant to place walls, floors and ceilings on any grid line in the box. He could have a three-storey house with seven-foot ceilings or a one-storey house with a twenty-one-foot ceiling, he could have the walls anywhere he wanted, he could rearrange it at any time. There are several million different permutations possible with this system – and yet with all that variety there is no real mathematical differentiation. Each permutation feels the same. All those variations are essentially rectangular and are dominated by the specific rectangular nature of the space matrix. There is a difference between variety in the mathematical sense and variety in the psychic sense.

I set out on another exercise, coming at the problem from the other end. Could you design a system made up of a five or six component assembly that combines its elements to form different houses whose spatial characteristics will be so varied that the man who lives in one will feel that it is totally different from his neighbor's, so different that he will consider it as different in nature, of a different geometric order? I developed a system based on a cube and five additional components, a semi-circle, a hemisphere, a prism, a semi-prism, and a half cube, and put them together, each of the sub-components attaching to the cube. It was obvious that a whole family of different forms could be generated out of this simple repetitive system. If one took that a step further and said that the tenant could change or rearrange these sub-components at any time then it was theoretically possible to devise a system of infinite possibilities. And that means that you can have mass production, you can have repetition, and still you can give the individual great control over his own environment.

Working on the San Francisco Students' Union I became aware of the other dimension of the word *system.* Here was a building with many complex spaces of different sizes and different requirements and nevertheless you could find some common denominator which I called "space-maker." It wasn't just technology that made me want to find a common denominator. It was that the space-maker could be put together by the students and the building they would make, while not exactly the same as mine, would have been the same environment. The problem was generalized. I did not permit it to be specific, I tried to find the essence of the general, a common denominator that I later came to realize had the generic essence. I could let this space-maker loose and it could design itself according to the laws or rules I had given it, its own laws of arrangement. If the space-maker is a musical note, then the building system is a repetitive theme and the building is a fugue.

The San Francisco Union was not a composed building in the traditional sense. There was a form-making process in establishing the system and then there was another process in putting it together, but at no time did I compose in the sense that I thought it would look better this way or that way, at no time did I draw an elevation and think what proportion would look nice. This is also true of Habitat. I didn't design the space under the houses in the plaza. No one could compose such a complex space. It would be like trying to compose the kind of environment you experience when you're under a tree in sunlight. The branches and leaves come together in certain ways, the sun shines through morning clouds, the tree moves in the wind, the result is unique at each moment.

I can illustrate this point by comparing it to a building I love – Le Corbusier's courthouse in Chandigarh. It has the soul of a courthouse, it is shaped by the movement of people and it has a sense of place. But it is a composed building, a finite solution to a specific problem at one given point in time. Le Corbusier fixed it as a specific structure – the proportions, the grille, the patterns, the ramps – composing it step by step from its various elements. You could not change the building, you could not add to it. Only Le Corbusier could put it down, only he could modify it to make another courthouse.

The courthouse is an individual specific building. It's fixed, finite. In San Francisco, while I was trying to capture and understand the spirit of a students' union and give it physical form, I tried to arrive at it by breaking it down, going a step further back. The students' union has offices, dining halls, libraries, and so on, but in that respect the courthouse is exactly the same. It has offices for clerks, waiting rooms, courtrooms, laboratories. There's a difference in the spirit of students' social gatherings and of a place of law, but not in their basic natures, both of which the system must acknowledge. Instead of finite solutions we must try to find the genetic code of a particular environment. The genetic code produces an infinite number of adaptations, each in itself not finite – not buildings with beginnings and ends, but continuums capable of growth and change.

This is exactly what happened in the vernacular village. There is a certain similarity between the San Francisco union building and the village that a group of peasants building their houses with an evolved formal vocabulary might create. That's where I feel my work is vernacular and not an extension of the Renaissance tradition in architecture. It's not a solution for all things. In each case I search for a solution that is organically valid for that particular problem. It's very specific, in fact. If I were given the problem of designing a city for Frobisher Bay, I would evolve a system solution that was specific to the spirit of Frobisher Bay, the cold north, a very specific problem. I am quite sure that I would draw on the geometric experience of my previous work, just as I am able to find common geometric experiences between a housing problem in Puerto Rico and a social building in San Francisco. But each particular problem generates a particular adaptation.

Trying to find an architectural DNA molecule – or, as a friend suggested, abandoning the *act of creation* and seeking to make the *means of creating* – is an ambitious act. But, I am sure that if solutions are worked out by architects in this way, if each is true to the laws of human nature and environment, the results must have unity. This is where my hope lies for a true contemporary vernacular, which is the diametric opposite of a world where style and fashion are the dictating motivations. That is so arbitrary, so irrational, that no vernacular can result from it, only chaos.

Each architect would use, adapt, and add to the totality of environment. I have faith that, thus, many men's efforts and solutions could fit into the macro-matrix of the whole environment in harmony. Each is governed by enough of the same laws of nature and of the physical environment of man that they should have unity. No man's expression can supersede the laws of human nature and environment.

Our problem is always to combine order and freedom: freedom without chaos and order without sterility. Heretofore we have thought of building in terms of the technology of today – the stamping machine, repetition. But the technology of building will become all-capable, like a computer punch card with millions of possibilities extended in four dimensions or fluids capable of limitless forming. Ultimately, I would like to design a magic housing machine to do just that. Conceive of a huge pipe behind which is a reservoir of magic plastic. A range of air-pressure nozzles around the opening, control this material as it is forced through the edges of the pipe. By varying the air pressure at each nozzle one could theoretically extrude any conceivable shape, complex free forms, mathematically non-defined forms. People could go and push the buttons to design their own dwellings. One restriction built into the machine would be that it would have to make sure that all its extrusions interlocked to form one building by insuring that all designs included certain fixed points of contact.

This is a very exciting idea, indeed, because it suggests that in the ultimate evolution of technology in the building process, we may find that the highest form of organization means the least standardization, that technology can make industry as flexible as nature.

I haven't yet been able to translate this into a buildable solution any more than I have technically solved the six-component assembly. But I am convinced that in Habitat there is the seed that will eventually grow to the point where the individual has much greater ability to shape and change his living space so as to produce something that corresponds much more closely to his feelings of what his whole environment should be. And that is the idea of the vernacular, which is made by men for themselves – and the architect is their instrument.